UHURU'S FIRE

# UHURU'S FIRE

African literature East to South

ADRIAN ROSCOE

CAMBRIDGE UNIVERSITY PRESS

CAMBRIDGE

LONDON · NEW YORK · MELBOURNE

Published by the Syndics of the Cambridge University Press
The Pitt Building, Trumpington Street, Cambridge CB2 1RP
Bentley House, 200 Euston Road, London NW1 2DB
32 East 57th Street, New York, NY 10022, USA
296 Beaconsfield Parade, Middle Park, Melbourne 3206, Australia

First published 1977

Printed in Great Britain at the
University Press, Cambridge

*Library of Congress Cataloguing in Publication Data*
Roscoe, Adrian A
Uhuru's fire.
Includes bibliographical references.
1. African literature (English) – History and
criticism. I. Title.
PR9340.R6    820'.9    76–3038
ISBN 0-521-21295-2 hard covers
ISBN 0-521-29089-9 paperback

# Contents

FOR GERT,
JULIAN, WILMA,
CLAIRE, AND
JENNY

# Preface

Discussing anglophone writing from East, Central, and Southern Africa, this book is a companion to an earlier volume, *Mother is Gold*, which surveyed the literary scene in West Africa. I have tried to produce a critical introduction of interest to both the general reader and the specialist student – the man in the street, in Boston or Kampala, who has heard vaguely that the new African writing is fresh and dynamic, and the college student who wants detailed comment on particular works and also an overview which journal fragments cannot provide. I have tried, therefore, to keep in mind the need to present a broad scene clearly and to give that scene's landmarks adequate scrutiny. Thus, a reader should know that a debate is raging over the whole drift and posture of modern African verse, and he should also know the positions of particular writers within it.

Because literature does not emerge from a vacuum, it is important to know what shaping influences, what events and circumstances, have helped it to grow. And since Africa's Universities are unrivalled centres of literary debate and experiment, I have described, in a brief excursion into cultural history, events at the University of Nairobi in the 1960s when radical heart surgery was performed on the Literature syllabus, changing it from British to African. Designed to achieve an artistic version of political independence, this exercise held profound implications not simply for East African writing – its quantity, content, and the influences at work on it – but also for patterns of development elsewhere. Kenya's lead has been followed by Malawi and Uganda. Word spreads to Lesotho and Zambia. Rhodesia hesitates, but plans for the future. The change has particularly accelerated for African Literature the creation of its own inner dynamic, its own network of internal interchange and influence. In East, Central, and Southern Africa as the voices of Wordsworth and Tennyson grow dim, those of Okigbo and Soyinka grow loud.

*Preface*

In all literary discussion, questions of language are crucial. This is especially true in Africa, not simply because of the second-language problem but because national language policies can shift rapidly (witness the current vacillation in Kenya over Swahili) and put the very future of English-language writing at risk. There is, too, the steady revival of the vernaculars, and the number of authors choosing to express themselves in their mother tongue increases daily. Most importantly, the language question leads into the area of oral literature, without which no understanding of modern African writing can be complete. As Graham Hough puts it, the critic's task is:

> first to maintain the literature of the past as part of present experience; and secondly to see the literature of the present as part of the historic process. No critic of present literature can afford to be unaware of the past. No critic of past literature can afford to be unaware of the present. To write of present literature without awareness of the past is to be merely a journalist; to write of past literature without awareness of the present is to be merely an academic critic.

Occasionally, then, in addition to discussing language and the oral heritage, this book glances at the underlying effects of the oral past on the modern writer, whether as folk material worked into the stories of Grace Ogot, Kenyan rumour filtering south to be woven into a Malawian short story, or local legend as the substance for plays such as Steve Chimombo's *The Rainmaker*.

A long section on the East African Song School is included because the work of Okot p'Bitek and his disciples represents the most interesting poetic experiment yet seen on either side of the continent. Furthermore, Okot's two long poems, *Song of Lawino* and *Song of Ocol*, provide between them the most sharply crystallised account of the battle over tradition and modernity that any African artist has yet produced.

The need for compression means that a number of writers get no coverage at all. These include novelists like Seruma, Bukenya, Ruhumbika, Asalache, Mulaisho, and Mwangi, and short story writers such as Kahiga and Mulikita. A major figure like South Africa's Peter Abrahams makes way for Alex La Guma, because the latter's enormous talent has so far received scant recognition. Finally, compared with the space allotted to other literary forms, drama has received much thinner treatment than ideally I would have liked to give it.

*Uhuru's Fire* is a title meant to convey both the fierce energies of the struggle for independence and the pains consequent upon its attainment. Bright dawn hope and deep harrowing disillusion both inform the texts discussed in the following pages.

ADRIAN ROSCOE

*Zomba, Malawi*
*1976*

# Acknowledgements

While this book's appearance owes nothing to either philanthropic foundation or University research committee (they provided not a pencil or paper clip), it does owe a good deal to the encouragement of my editor, Adrian du Plessis, who first invited me to attempt the project, and also to the work and influence of many individuals – students and colleagues – with whom I have worked at the Universities of Nairobi and Malawi. They include Jared Angira, Angus Calder, Richard Gacheche, James Gecau, Tom Gorman, Andrew Gurr, Arthur Kemoli, Taban Lo Liyong, David Mulwa, Onyango Ogutu, Ngugi wa Thiong'o, and Chris Wanjala, all of Nairobi; and, from Malawi, Innocent Banda, Steve Chimombo, James and Patience Gibbs, Chris Kamlongera, David Kerr, Ken Lipenga, Jack Mapanje, Sam Mchombo, Felix Mnthali, Joe Mosiwa, Patrick O'Malley, James Stewart, Enoch Timpunza, Mupa Shumba, and Paul Zeleza. Others who have helped in one way or another are Hamachi Ajisa, Margaret Bown, Bernie Butt, Bert Damico, Julia Hunter, Ken Mew, and Nelson Mlomba. My wife's patience has sustained my efforts during difficult stretches and her firm belief that literary criticism is always an exercise in futility has kept my feet, I think, firmly on the ground. The following authors and publishers are thanked for permission to quote from copyright material: East African Publishing House for work by Jared Angira, Sam Mbure, O'kot p'Bitek, Joseph Buruga, Okello Oculi, Leonard Kibera, Taban Lo Liyong, Onyango Ogutu, R. C. Ntiru and Albert Ojuka; André Deutsch Ltd for *Exile* by Mazisi Kunene; Penguin Books Ltd for lines from 'Then I'll believe' and 'I heard the old song' by B. W. Vilakazi from *The Penguin Book of South African Verse*; Heinemann Educational Books Ltd for quotations from *Franz Fanon's Uneven Ribs* by Taban Lo Liyong, *A Simple Lust* by Dennis Brutus and *Silent Voices* by Jared Angira.

# 1

# Language problems:
# English and the vernaculars

It is well known that the wealth of language Africa has inherited from the past hangs on the continent like a mill-stone, obstructing basic communication, exasperating central governments, confusing education systems, and making the overall task of development hopelessly tough and expensive. Assurances from linguists that the African tower of babel contains really far fewer languages than was thought, that many vernaculars are not fully languages in their own right but dialects or offshoots of a larger branch, help little. At the Ibadan Conference of 1961, Neville Denny argued that there were approximately 25 languages spoken in the Central African Federation (now Malawi, Zambia, and Rhodesia), and roughly 150 in East Africa, with over 100 of these in Tanzania alone. Many are the property of small groups and face the problems of minority languages everywhere. Is it worth researching them? With creeping centralisation and the passion for national rather than local thinking, who will encourage their reduction to writing? More pressing problems demand a Government's time, money, and energy. Who will foster creative writing in languages with so small a potential reading public?[1]

While African writing in English, French, and Portuguese swiftly increases, questions of vernacular writing and *linguae francae* still loom in the background. At one level the argument is simple and commands unanimity: African aspirations, ideally, should be expressed in African languages. How can national hopes, with their special nuances rising from traditional societies and their values inherited from a non-European ethic, resonate in people's hearts via a language which is firstly alien, the product of a foreign way of life and world view, and secondly spoken by only a small minority?

One might argue the need to build solid monuments to the future by ignoring the constrictions of the present. Give English more time

1

in the schools, more time on radio and television, let the British Council do its job with newer tools and more professional workers, and within the present century peasants and nomads from Rudolf to Cape Town will have the language singing through their veins. But patience of this kind, once so familiar in Africa, is a rare quality among modern states. The feeling that our planet spins faster than it did thirty years ago is felt along the Zambezi and in the plains of Marsabit almost as sharply as it is in Ohio or Moscow.

The second stage of the problem, the choice of a solution, commands far less agreement. Each language has its spokesmen who know, feel, and can prove, the superior qualities of their particular vernacular, can point to its flexibility, its richness in proverb, its simplicity for others, texts which have already honoured it, and the speed with which it is spreading among neighbouring groups. Newspaper columns in East, West, and Central Africa have long carried the rhetoric of language apostles; and the charms of small languages like Lugwe are as likely to be canvassed as those of major tongues like Hausa, Yoruba, or Chichewa. But power now lies with central governments, and given the sensitive nature of language issues, even in a world of increasing centralisation, only a foolish statesman would dare impose one language on a nation without the clear support of the majority.

Hence, the attractions of English, French, or Portuguese remain, whether for politician, scholar, businessman, industrialist, or writer. But patterns are changing, and triumphalist assertions about English's strength in, say, West Africa cannot be repeated for countries to the East, for in these parts there is a groundswell of support for the adoption of a regional alternative to English as a *lingua franca*: Swahili.

Swahili has penetrated deep enough into East and even Central Africa for it to appear as a genuine alternative to English. Rising along the coast of Kenya and Tanzania, with its springs in Zanzibar and the Islands, Swahili has spread inland through Kenya and Uganda, across Tanzania, into Zaire, Mozambique, and even deep into Malawi, where it can be heard among the Muslim communities of lakeshore towns like Karonga, Mangochi, Nkhota-khota, and Nkata Bay. According to Professor W. H. Whiteley, Swahili is now poised to emerge as Africa's most dynamic modern language.[2]

Whiteley's confidence is shared by Ali Mazrui, who argues that while Swahili is still primarily associated with the coastal strip of East Africa (where Arabic has long influenced its vocabulary though not its struc-

2

ture), it has dramatically penetrated inland areas and, crucially, has crossed ethnic boundaries; for while it is opposed politically by the Nilotic Luo as being a Bantu language, it is in fact spoken widely by the Luo themselves, and a knowledge of Swahili is universal among their leaders, whether in business, politics, or scholarship. Jared Angira, one of the finest Luo poets, already uses Swahili as well as English. Swahili is taught in Kenyan schools, and though what is spoken in Nairobi's bazaars is what coastal people see as a corruption, 'the chances are', says Mazrui, 'that Swahili will eventually complete its conquest of Kenya'.[3]

In Uganda, outside the special area of Buganda where Bagandan pride has traditionally cultivated both English and Luganda to fight off the challenge of other tongues, Swahili is also making long inroads. Its very potency, Mazrui argues, was the reason for its removal from Uganda schools since it was feared as a potential rival for Luganda as a *lingua franca*. It enjoys, further, he claims, an important status within the army and police, the trade union movement, and the professional ranks of the Uganda sectors of the East African Common Services. What Mazrui claimed for Kenya he repeats for Uganda. Swahili, he says, is 'on its way to conquering all Uganda towns and cities'.

Tanzania's situation is different. Swahili here is already more widespread than in Kenya or Uganda and there is government concern to farm the language's political strengths among a people determined to build a new society on old African foundations. Nyerere sees Swahili as a medium of national rather than tribal aspirations. Statesman, scholar, and poet, he was quick to see the point at which politics, language, and literature meet; and the choice of the Swahili word *ujamaa* to name the kind of socialism Tanzania wanted to pursue was no mere gesture to a fleeting nationalism. The English word 'socialist', alread current in the Swahili form *kisoshalisti*, simply did not express the idea, whereas *ujamaa*, of local birth, caught its essence exactly. Nyerere explains:

> The word *ujamaa* was chosen for special reasons. First, it is an African word and thus emphasises the African-ness of the policies we intend to follow. Second, its literal meaning is 'familyhood', so that it brings to the mind of our people the idea of mutual involvement in the family as we know it...By the use of the word *ujamaa*, therefore, we state that for us socialism involves

3

> building on the foundations of our past, and also to our own
> design. We are not importing a foreign ideology into Tanzania
> and trying to smother our distinct social patterns with it.[4]

Swahili's adoption as a national language alongside English has
important implications for social cohesion. The subtle involvement of
language with class privilege, division, and exploitation, is a story
socio-linguists are only beginning to relate. Britain introduced into her
colonies a language born of a class-ridden society, bearing in its sounds
and structure a history of social discrimination, oligarchic gamesman-
ship, and blatant inhumanity. The pernicious effects of English on the
broadly egalitarian societies of traditional Africa are not hard to
unearth. In the new order, English was seen as the golden means of
breaking out of the old peasant pattern into the money economy and
white-collar comfort of the coloniser. A knowledge of English was one
guaranteed way in which a breakthrough could be achieved.

What seems clear about Swahili, however, especially in Tanzania,
is its classlessness, its status as a people's language, its lack of
identification with Mandarin groups and elitist castes. This is important, for it means that where once only a small pool of English-speakers
was available for posts in government and administration (and these
not necessarily representing the nation's best minds and abilities), an
imaginative language policy now allows Tanzania to recruit widely
among its people. It is significant, as Mazrui points out, that the late
First Vice-President, Abeid Karume, had no command of English at
all, and that there are many key figures in Nyerere's government whose
English is by no means fluent.

The literary implications are obvious: if a writer sees that there is
a growing audience for works in his own language and finds publishers
prepared to produce books for this market, he is likely to find the
attractions of English as his chosen medium suddenly weaker. This
has now begun to happen, with several young East African writers
already producing work in both Swahili and English. Furthermore,
the number of writers who want to work only in the local language
has increased sharply since the status of Swahili was officially recognised by the post-colonial language policies of all three East African
territories. The position of English is no longer as secure as it was.

*English versus vernaculars*

This is not the place for a detailed examination of the impact of English in East, Central, and Southern Africa. The subject is complex and under examination by professional linguists. A few points must suffice. First, there is the obvious fact that English gave local people both a window onto a wider world and a new tool with which to interpret their own experience. Politically, it allowed African leaders to address pleas for freedom to the world at large and also to the diverse ranks of their own people. Similar advantages also became apparent to aspiring scholars and writers. In a sense, then, English could be seen as an instrument of cohesion and unity, a means of cultural and intellectual liberation, of new-found self-expression. On the other hand, its potential for social divisiveness was enormous. Not only did clan harmony suffer, with the young carrying their new language skills to the towns, often to reverence their families no more; traditional society suffered a double blow, for social disintegration was coupled with an eroded respect for tribal culture in all its facets, and especially its vernaculars. Languages which had done service from time immemorial, bearing the people's sorrows and triumphs, their laments and entertainments, mundane transactions and great flights of imagination – these suddenly were devalued, scorned as the mumblings of backwardness, the badge of the outdated, the prison-pens of conservatism. Without asking if vernacular flexibility might accommodate the new ideas brought by the stranger, a rapid importation of English words began, providing clear evidence for the weakening effect which English had on local languages. The experience of Uganda in this regard is a case in point. M. B. Nsimbi, a Luganda-speaker, writes:

> In the matter of languages, foreign languages, particularly English, became languages of prestige and snobbery. Ability to speak and write English became a status symbol. In the eyes of the common native of Uganda, education meant the acquiring of a knowledge of English. While this was happening the local languages were being relegated to inferior positions in the eyes of the people and in schools. As more and more English was taught in schools the vernaculars began to disappear from the school timetables, particularly in the high schools...The most damaging insult the local languages ever received was to be called 'primitive'.[5]

## English and the vernaculars

In the same piece Nsimbi asserts that the importation of English words into Luganda was an unnecessary exercise undertaken by those Baganda with a western education. The word 'late', he says, replaced the perfectly good term *kikeerezi*, and 'busy' was brought in to oust *okutawaana*. The effect on Luganda is one example among many in East Africa. In Central Africa the Chichewa speakers of Malawi use *touni* and *dilesi* for 'town' and 'dress' when perfectly useful vernacular words are available, while among the Yao *bokosi* is used for 'box' when the local word *lijamanda* would be entirely adequate.

Faced with this development, linguistic free-traders shrug their shoulders and declare that such is the law of life. Where language is concerned, whatever *is*, is right. While the appeal of such openness is plain when set beside a death-bearing purism, it is clear that certain kinds of language policy, spelled out or implied, can undermine human community and strike at the roots of a people's pride. In a related example, Dr B. Pachai has argued that the hated *thangata* labour system in Nyasaland survived 50 years because early legislation to change it was never rendered in the vernaculars, thus keeping locals ignorant of their rights. If a Samburu warrior with a Sheffield-made spear is a victim of economic lawlessness, his brother who despises his own language because he feels it is primitive is surely no less a victim of linguistic crime.

### Vernacular literature

As local languages regain their pride, and their respect in the eyes of the world, there is a growing tendency to use them for written literature. Initially, as in West Africa, the bulk of vernacular writing in East, Central, and Southern Africa was mission-sponsored. The Church Missionary Society, The London Mission Society, The Church of Central Africa, The British and Foreign Bible Society, the Catholic Church – each shared a common interest in the promotion of local writing. Though foresight was not always matched by action, evangelists realised early on that their African flock should be given the Christian message in the vernaculars without delay. It might be argued from the preliterate nature of African societies that they were backing the wrong horse and that a drive for vernacular fluency among mission officers might have proved more effective. But the impetus for the beginning of vernacular writing was there and the Bible especially was rapidly, and often badly, translated.

6

The scandal of a divided Christianity proved an obstacle, and theological chaos was compounded by that marvellous aural diversity whereby two men can never perfectly agree on what they have heard. Orthographic problems in reducing vernaculars to Roman script were legion and probably increased by British ineptitude at languages. Okot p'Bitek, a man with a poet's ear, complains of 'the Bible and the Prayer Books and the *Pilgrim's Progress* that have been so hopelessly mistranslated into the vernacular' and M. B. Nsimbi states that until recently it was possible in Uganda to pick up a text and say whether it came from either the Catholics or the Church of Uganda, so distinct were their systems of transcription and orthography.

There was and is a case here for government subsidies; but which government, given its doubtful acceptance of vernacular literature as a priority matter, can subsidise writing in *all* the language spoken within its boundaries? And if selective subsidies are canvassed, by what process of choice could political chaos be avoided? In an essay on the future of vernacular literature in Uganda, Nsimbi sketches the problem in painful detail.

Basing his figures on the census of 1959, he describes a nation of 6½ million speaking at least 26 languages, many of these the tongue of only a handful of people. These include Runyankore, Runyoro, Rutooro, Rukonjo, Rwamba, Luganda, Lusoga, Lunyole, Lusamia, Lugwe, Lugwere, Lumasaba, Ateso, Akaramojong, Kakwe, Sabiny, Acholi, Labwor, Kumam, Lango, Dhopadhola, Alur, Madi, and Lugbara. Accepting that many are related, Nsimbi reduces them to six groups. Into three distinct Bantu groups he places all those tongues with names beginning with an *R* or *Lu*. A fourth group is Para-Nilotic and consists of Ateso, Karamojong, Kakwa, and Sabiny. A fifth group is more truly Nilotic and covers Acholi, Dhopadhola, Lango, Kumam, Labwor, and Alur. The sixth group he calls Sudanic and consists of Lugbara and Madi. Thirty years ago the Uganda government decided that a language would be chosen from each group and developed as a literary medium, popular acceptance being guaranteed because in each case the chosen tongue could be seen as representative. Agreement, however, was impossible. The first two Bantu groups split and were followed by conflict in group four between Ateso and Karamojong.

Given such problems, the wonder is that, outside devotional literature from mission presses, any vernacular writing should have appeared at all; yet East, Central, and Southern Africa have all produced

7

a fair amount of work. Swahili poets from the coastal towns of East Africa show that a school of written verse thrived there as long ago as the eighteenth century, and circumstantial evidence points to a tradition even older than that. Islamic in flavour, this writing has all the formality and conventional prosody characteristic of Muslim verse. According to Whiteley, the Swahili tradition had moved south from Zanzibar to Mombasa by the nineteenth century, when bards like Mukaya bin Haji were making the city famous for nationalist poetry, used in constant feuds between the various settlements, and for new shorter verse forms carrying strongly secular material. In Pemba, 'a vigorous tradition flourished until well into the present century, with some professional guilds of poets, each with its own pupils'. In accordance with a universal pattern which scholars cannot explain, good prose developed later than verse, and there is only a meagre supply of Swahili material from earlier than the mid-nineteenth century.

With the recent spread of vernacular newspapers, and the insistence on vernacular teaching in the schools, there has grown a steady demand for materials written in Swahili. Scholars complain that there is still too little writing available for study beyond the primary level, the old texts of Lamu, Mombasa, and Pemba being too archaic or too worldly for use in the classroom. Exceptions, however, are Martin Kayamba's *Tulivyoona na Tulivonfanya Uingereza* (London, 1932), James Mbotela's *Uhuru wa Watumwa*, the stories and biographies of Shaaban Robert, Mohammed Said Abdulla's *Mzimu wa Watu wa Kale* (Nairobi, 1960) and *Kisima cha Gihingi* (Nairobi, 1965). Also, EAPH has now published Swahili editions of Chinua Achebe's *No Longer at Ease* and *Things Fall Apart*, and Orwell's *Animal Farm*. With newspapers and vernacular journals offering an outlet for poets, the position of verse is healthy enough. Poets making a reputation in English are also working in Swahili and collections such as *Just a Moment God* (edited by Robert Green, East African Literature Bureau, 1970) and M. Mnyanpala's *Mashairi ya hekima na Malumbano* are useful additions to the scene.

Swahili apart, East Africa has seen a small but growing amount of work done in Gikuyu, Gikamba, Luo, and Acholi, encouraged by publishing houses prepared to stand the cost of their convictions. The East African Publishing House and the Equatorial Press are two examples, while the East African Literature Bureau, an arm of the East African Community, has been a champion of vernacular writing since its inception. Mohammed Said Abdullah was first published here; so too a collection of the earliest Swahili prose texts, *Habari Za Wakilindi* (1960). But if progress is slow with most vernaculars, the advance of Swahili publishing is spectacular, for EAPH already finds that approximately half its entire output is now given over to this language.

The steady move towards vernacular writing is a natural part of the post-colonial drive for a freedom genuinely African in essence. It will be interesting to see, however, if Africa repeats the experience of Europe where, after a long apprenticeship to Latin as an international language, writing developed in the vernaculars and literary Latin became a dead letter. Should history repeat itself, it means that we are watching a rich growth of African work in the European languages already doomed to wither as vernaculars mature in their role as literary media. Vernacular developments deserve a more detailed study than is possible in a book of this kind; but already, despite the obstacles and cries of despair, there are signs that English writing in Africa has some formidable rivals growing under the sun.

Vernacular writing can be seen as the outgrowth of an oral literature which has begun to die before the world knows much about it. The last decade has seen a growing concern to encourage scholars to examine the oral legacy, and a widening range of studies and translations is one result. A useful approach, pioneered by Whiteley, Lienhardt, and Evans-Pritchard in their Oxford Library of African Literature, is to offer in each volume a critical edition of an oral text complete with essays, footnotes, and parallel versions in English and the vernacular. The results are admirable and the Oxford Series texts on the literature of the Tswana, Ankole, Hausa, Yoruba, and Somali have all displayed a high degree of textual finesse and scholarship. The range of oral literature now available to modern readers is enough to suggest that, by comparison, the literature extant in English or French, while strong in its own right, resembles little more than a coral outcrop on an ocean floor.

The range and importance of this area of literature (or 'orature' as the Ugandan scholar Pio Zirimu insists on calling it), was summarised by Whiteley and his colleagues in a preface to the Oxford Library Series:

> We approach Africa now as general editors of this library of her literature...with a sense of exhilaration and of urgency: exhilaration because so much unexplored country can be dis-

9

cerned ahead, urgency because in our own short time many compositions recorded only in human memory are being every-where lost... But our intention is not to be misunderstood as the conservation, merely, of archaic conventions or of passing forms of social experience. On the contrary, we think it harmful to African literary studies to divide the past from the present.[6]

The urgency these scholars feel is reflected in the recent findings of Dr Matthew Schoffeleers, working on oral literature in Central Malawi. Mounting an effective project among small isolated groups, Schoffeleers has discovered evidence of a massive falling away in knowledge of oral tradition among the younger age-sets of given families – a result, no doubt, of literacy, schooling, films, and the transistor radio. Yet the oral traditions are still alive. Okot p'Bitek, a spokesman on oral matters, offers these reflections:

In the evening, we have sat on our big sofa and put our legs on the tea table, and said, 'There is very little vernacular literature', and have pulled out a volume of Achebe or Wole Soyinka or *Transition*. Meanwhile all over the countryside, the outdoor fires have been lit, and the folk tales are being performed. And the moonlight dance drums are throbbing in the distance, and the beautiful love songs come floating through the air. Boy is meeting girl, and the witty and lively love debate is raging...The vast majority of our people in the countryside have a full-blooded literary culture, so deep, so vivid and alive that for the moment the very little written stuff appears almost irrelevant.[7]

Yet it reflects falsely on the nature of the oral heritage to come at it with needle, formaldehyde, and scissors, to cut up and separate out its component parts, for to the villager it is seen as one broad form of word-use, an art which covers the whole of life and is, in its essence, purpose, and forms, a living part of the human scene from birth to burial. Verse shades into prose, prose into verse, songs are poems, poems are songs, and much can be danced and sung in the way that Western literature was danced and sung when it had a fuller, more popular life than it has today. Whiteley uses the distinction between 'What is spoken and what is sung' as his main criteria for setting off prose from verse. But he acknowledges a real difficulty here and suggests that 'it is perhaps preferable that one should regard the prose/verse distinction in terms of points on a single scale of 'pattern-ing', with metrical verse at one end and everyday speech towards the other'. The Dar es Salaam conference of 1974 stressed the lack of an adequate theory of criticism and analysis to deal with oral literature and urged the need for a wholly new methodology. Convened by UNESCO to obtain expert advice on a proposed Regional Office in Eastern Africa for the study of traditional literature and the promotion of African languages, the conference explored, among other topics, the relationship between language, literature, and culture, the need for national research centres, and new ways of studying oral literature. In a conference report, Schoffeleers writes: 'There was a great need for analytical theory. Finnegan's pioneering study was recommended but University departments were urged to go beyond it and develop theories specifically based on African data...'[8]

Examining the oral heritage frequently involves encounters with material rarely covered by conventional literary scholarship. One example is prayer, surely among our primal literary forms, a species of poetry older than story and song. Yet man's primal communication with the source of his being is usually defined merely as the raising up of the mind and heart to God, an unsatisfactory definition because it describes an act of meditation, a spiritual song-without-words, rather than prayer as we know it. Nor does it suggest that prayer, like poetry, is an outlet for emotion, for heightened and formal statement, for verbal utterance that reflects landscape, custom, and values as richly as later poetic forms. Prayer is lyric poetry in its highest form.

Given a situation in which humble man praises and beseeches his Creator, it is natural that basic prayer form is almost universally standard. Take two examples from Africa. The first is from ancient Egypt, a prayer to the God Thot:

> The tall palm tree sixty feet high
> heavy with fruit:
> the fruit contains kernels,
> the kernels water.
> You who bring water to the remotest place
> come and save me because I am humble.
> O Thot, you are a sweet well
> for him who starves in the desert.
> A well that remains closed to the talkative
> but opens up to the silent.
> When the silent man approaches the well reveals itself;
> When the noisy man comes you remain hidden.[9]

11

The second is from the Galla, who live near the Horn of Africa and whose way of life shows through sharply in the details of the prayer:

> Listen to us aged God
> listen to us ancient God
> who has ears!
> Look at us aged God
> look at us ancient God
> who has eyes!
> Receive us aged God
> receive us ancient God
> who has hands!
> If you love beautiful horses take them!
> If you love beautiful women take them!
> If you love beautiful slaves take them!
> Listen to us O God,
> O God listen to us.[10]

These two examples show how prayer deals in those special skills which man employs to make his verbal utterance more vivid, memorable, and beautiful, for only the best is good enough for God. Designed in part for success in cosmic bartering, prayer reaches for imagery and symbol, harmony and coherence, and a discreet handling of logistics. In the process there is inevitably a reflection of a society's life and culture. Hence in the prayer to Thot, the water-and-well figure used for God suggests the work of a desert people for whom water is the most potent manifestation of the deity. In the second prayer, the horses, women, and slaves of the Galla reveal clearly enough their earthly tastes and life-style. On prayer structures, Professor Francis Berry has argued that common features arise from man's basic position facing the deity. These include:

> An invocation of the God or power addressed; a listing of the God's superior or divine attributes (with the intention that He, She or It should be propitiated or flattered by the recital, and reminded of His, Her or Its capacity to grant a petition); a confession by the suppliant of his inadequacy and failure unless he is divinely aided; and a Petition.[11]

These features need not appear in the order Berry mentions them, and the petition, witness the Galla poem, might not be specified in any detailed way within the prayer itself. In the examples above, the

12

invocation or naming of the God Thot comes only at line seven, although there is a call to him in line five; and in the Galla prayer, the request, falling with emphasis and diplomacy at the end of the poem, is merely that God should bend an ear and listen. The other features recounted by Berry are evident or implied in both poems: a counterpointing insistence on the deity's supremacy, a confession of man's weakness, and an assumption throughout that the deity can right all things, if only he can be persuaded to listen.

The following prayer is from the Masarwa of Botswana, usually described, in a choice piece of linguistic thuggery, as Bushmen. Along with the El Molo of Lake Rudolf, the Masarwa have been among Africa's most hapless people, and this prayer to the Moon reveals much about their melancholy:

> Take my face and give me yours!
> Take my face, my unhappy face.
> Give me your face,
> with which you return
> when you have died,
> when you vanish from sight.
> You lie down and return –
> Let me resemble you, because you have joy,
> you return evermore alive,
> after you vanished from sight.
> Did you not promise us once
> that we too should return
> and be happy again after death?[12]

The Luo of Kenya have a complex conception of God, though their acknowledgement of a Supreme Deity remote and rarely accessible is not unusual. Multiple names describe facets of His being and conduct. One, Nyakalaga, suggests that He is seen streaming through all things, flowing over creation like the wind, bathing all with his care no matter what their station or place. The example that follows shows a Luo prayer structurally similar to standard patterns:

> O Nyakalaga, you the ancient one,
> O Nyakalaga, our father,
> Stream well for us,
> Flow well through all our families
> Make our children numerous as the sand

13

> Make our hearts clean like cowries
> You the mighty one
> Confound our enemies
> Keep our fields fruitful
> Our wives faithful
> Keep dissension away from our homesteads
> O Nyakalaga, join us for our feasts,
> Take this offering and drink it with us![13]

Another common form, the praise song, lived most luxuriantly in pre-colonial times, but is still vigorous enough to celebrate the heroes of Independence. Praises can be sung to anyone or anything, man or beast, but those recounting the might of chiefs and warriors are cast in a special heroic mould, with much stylisation, word play, and complexity. Of the Southern African Tswana, for example, Dr. I. Shapera writes that their praise poems, cherished as much for historic content as for moral support, are regarded as the 'highest products of their literary art'. Schapera's analysis, in *Praise Poems of Tswana Chiefs*, is a valuable account of how oral poets in one African society practise their art and a useful service for scholars examining modern written verse, especially as it might build on a system of poetics familiar to the consciousness of the new poet and his people.[14]

Schapera reveals among the Tswana a tradition of careful craftsmanship, guarded and cherished as holy writ, recited in specific formalised ways, and exploring a range of oral-formulaic devices widely found in preliterate traditions. There is a definite organised rhythm, a love of simile and metaphor (the chief is always drawn as bull, elephant, rhino, or buffalo), a standard line about three words long, and breaks in the line-flow to divide the verse into manageable units for delivery. In the following lines there is parallelism, a device taken over by many a modern poet and used with special skill in the verse of Okara:

> *Letlhôla bommaêno gobeolwa,*
> *Letlhôla bommanêo golala balla*

> (you foredoom your mothers to mourn,
> you foredoom your mothers to weep all night)

> *Moleti amatlotla,*
> *molebêlêdi wamarope abatho,*
> *modisa wasope lagammaagwê.*

14

(Watchman of derelict homes,
caretaker of people's ruins,
guardian of his mother's deserted house).

Chiasmus is also used, as in the following:

*Batho bakilê batsenwa kelegorwe*
*Kenôga etala, tlhômaganya-batho*

(people were once attacked by a tree snake,
by a green snake, dogger of people)

and the device of linking, again widespread in modern written verse
from West, East, and Central Africa, is also common:

*Oêmê fôo ketlê kegolaêlê,*
*Kegolaêlê, kegonêyê dikgang*

(halt there, that I may command you,
may command you and give you a message)

*gotwe Rramono okobilê Maburu,*
*okobilê Maburu kafakayê*

(it's said Ramono drove away the Boers,
drove away the Boers at Kaye)

The flaunting language of Tswana praises echoes in the poem of
Pilane, who died about 1848:

I am Pilane the war-monger,
the scratcher, companion of Motswasejane
[...]
Pilane is a rock of ironstone,
he is a slippery rock, Pilane;
those who touch him will lose their fingers;
Mabine touched him and lost his fingers.

Among the pastoralist Bahima, who live in the Ugandan kingdom
of Ankole, there is a similar heroic tradition. Here, however, since the
individual Muhima must compose his own verses, the stress is less on
professional practice than on spontaneous composition. There is not
the same concern for an inherited body of literature as there is among
the Tswana; and verses here enjoy but a fleeting life, born but to die
on the breezes of the Ankole grasslands. Yet Ankole poetics are

15

codified and so too is the art of delivery. In his introductory essay to *The Heroic Recitations of the Ankole*, Dr H. Norris states that each line is firmly metrical, comprising the same number of words as a paired second line, and with each line shaped as a grammatical unit ending with a pause.[15] The reciter delivers the two-line stanza rapidly without pause, and then snaps his fingers, a signal for his companions to rush in with a chorus of '*Eeee*'.

Among the Bahima, however, such poems are as likely to be paeons for cattle as for a warrior or chief. The reciter, or *omwevugi*, faces his audience with a few friends and begins a sort of drama as, narrator and actor, he moves swiftly through his lines, delivering them with as much speed and histrionic brio as he can manage. He holds a spear, vertically or horizontally, and jabs with it from time to time to emphasise a point.

One feature of the tight stylisation of Bahima recitations is the extent to which each line is dominated by an elaborate praise name, ingeniously embellished in the manner of a kenning and leaving little room for the poet to extend himself imaginatively. This can be seen in the following extract from a poem in praise of cattle. It is part of a long narrative piece of a gently affectionate style taking us with the cattle across the East African countryside to learn about the minutiae of their behaviour. It is a measure of the intimate relationship that can exist between herdsmen and their beasts:

> At Katunguru near Rurangizi, She Who Teases lay back her horns and so did She Who Approaches The Fighters;

> At Kahama near Kambarango, we deceived The One Who Drives Back The Others with the calf of The One Whose Horns Are Well Spread pretending it were hers.

And so the poem proceeds. We watch the cattle walk proudly after they have killed an enemy, giving birth to calves, playing with antelopes, showing off the tips of their horns, dancing in the rain, showing patience in the face of death, amazing strangers who ask after their lineage, leading their herdsman into desert areas, fighting among themselves over a dispute not detailed, and running happily at the sight of home. The poem even possesses a circular, episodic plot, the cattle moving across the countryside and then eventually returning home.

Children's songs and love songs are yet further areas where research remains to be done, though scholars like Beier, Knappert, and

Finnegan have made a good start. Songs to separate the sexes at play, songs to sing with finger games, songs for stories and riddles, the reservoir of children's poetry is vast, its contents self-renewing, the tradition alive and flourishing. Two brief examples must suffice, both from Malawi. The first records how Europeans appear to the eyes of an African child – a common enough theme of verse throughout the continent. Where often the European's delicate skin reminds the singer of a baby, here it is his behaviour that stirs comment, especially his passion for slaughter:

> Europeans are little children.
> At the river bank they shot an elephant.
> Its blood became a canoe, and it sank;
> and it sank oars and all.
> I collected wild sorghum for Miss Mary.[16]

This childish mixture of narrative and reflection, fact and fantasy, has flown lightly off the butterfly mind of the singer. Its poignancy, which is the special poignancy of both first and second childhood, consists partly in the innocent spontaneity of its unrelated statements and partly in the way the humane impulse to collect wild sorghum for Miss Mary reflects on the senseless slaughter of the elephant. A second piece, also collected under the children's section of Ulli Beier's *African Poetry*, has a more mature ring:

> Mother Mother shave me
> let us go and see the bird
> with the bright red beak.
> Let's go to the bush Mother
> to the small bush.
> Let's brush off our hair
> each other's hair.
> Let us leave a guide-bone
> for the goats that graze
> that graze in my little field.
> The little field I cultivate
> I cultivate with a hoe
> I bought in the European's home
> the home where moss grows.
> We shall bring forth a child
> and we shall name him
> and we shall name him darkness.[17]

17

Beier's editorial note reads: 'This is the type of improvised song which children often sing when they put everything that comes to their mind to a tune. The poem has no logical sequence and no story. Its mood is carefree and lighthearted.' This is probably wide of the mark. While the middle section is hard to explain, especially the reference to guide bones for the goats that graze in the girl's field, both beginning and end sound like an epithalamion, an interpretation suggested recently by Fr Patrick O'Malley. The expectation of the singer appears to be the conception and birth of a child. But whatever its meaning, the poem's obscurity points to the urgent need for local African scholarship to resolve such problems.

Given the interpenetration of the physical and celestial worlds in traditional cosmologies, death has been a potent catalyst for literary creation. Recent African scholarship has destroyed the fallacy that African societies share a common attitude to dying and diversity is revealed where supposition suggested uniformity. There is no standard view of death and no agreed explanation for its coming; and as for the other world, if some see it in the sky, others see it lying over a river, under the earth, or even in the village where the deceased once lived. Professor John Mbiti is foremost among African scholars in this field, and his *African Religions and Philosophy* is already a source-book for both students and the general reader. The expressions he quotes for the act of dying, themselves evidence of how varied attitudes are, are often metaphors carrying a sharply poignant image. From the Bagosa of Uganda he culls the following: 'Our friend was told by death to tie up his load and go'; 'he is dry as if from yesterday'; 'life was snatched into two like a brittle stick'; 'it is fair, he has died, he has eaten enough' (of an elderly person dying a natural death without interference of external agents like witchcraft, poisoning, or sorcery). Among the Abaluyia of Kenya expressions include 'stepping into the sheet', 'going home', and, for a hated person, 'looking for an exit'. From his own Akamba people Professor Mbiti quotes: 'to follow the company of one's 'grandfathers'; 'to go home'; 'to stop snoring'; 'to be fetched or summoned'; 'to empty out the soul'; 'to sleep for ever and ever'; 'to reject the people'; 'to reject food'; 'to become God's property'. Among Nilotic people like the Acholi, Luo, Nuer, and Dinka are expressions such as 'to be blown away by the wind' and 'to disappear on the breeze', while among Malawi's Yao we find *Jayiche mbungo ja nya isulile,* 'the wind came and he was carried away', and *Wa katage mteka niwagwilile,* 'he was cutting wood and the tree fell on him'. Perhaps plainest of all is the Chitumbuka *Wali kuluka:* 'he is gone'.[18]

The Funeral poems of the Akan of Ghana and the Yoruba of Nigeria are well known. People elsewhere on the continent with rich traditions have yet to enjoy the midwiving attention of the scholars. The Nilotes are one example, though they have been fortunate in producing the redoubtable Okot p'Bitek, a modern poet whose success stems in part from his passionate care for his people's traditions. In the following translation from the vernacular, clansmen gather at a house where death has come, and take up spears and shields in a proud defiance of death, singing:

> Fire rages at Layima
> Fire rages in the valley of River Cumu
> Everything is utterly utterly destroyed
> If I could reach Death's mother's homestead!
> My daughter
> I would make a long grass torch
> If I could reach Death's mother's homestead
> I would destroy everything utterly utterly
> Fire rages in the Valley of River Cumu![19]

In gloomier mood is this piece from the Hottentots of South Africa:

> The gates of the underworld are closed.
> Closed are the gates.
>
> The spirits of the dead are thronging together
> like swarming mosquitoes in the evening,
> like swarming mosquitoes.
>
> Like swarms of mosquitoes dancing in the evening,
> When the night has turned black, entirely black,
> when the sun has sunk, has sunk below,
> when the night has turned black
> the mosquitoes are swarming
> like whirling leaves
> dead leaves in the wind.[20]

This is unusual, not, as Beier argues, because it is fraught with gloom and hopelessness, but because an apparently traditional poem, conceived in familiar oral-formulaic devices, closes with God coming to judge his children, a rare notion in traditional African theology. This is perhaps an example of syncretism, a poem accommodating Christian concepts alongside orthodox traditional material.

19

A poignant dirge from the Yao destroys any idea that death is uniformly welcomed in Africa. Conjuring a frightening loneliness, it pillories death as the destroyer of community, friendship, blood-ties, and family togetherness – all that makes life bearable for social man:

> *Nalifi ni Baba ni Mama*
>   *Wosope wawile;*
> *Chemwali a chimwene*
>   *Wawile;*
> *A nganga a mbuje*
>   *Wawile;*
> *Sambano sigele jika*
>   *Osope wa wile.*

> (I was born of my father and mother
>   Both have died;
> I was born with my brothers and sisters
>   All have died;
> There were grandfather and grandmother
>   Both have died;
> Now I am alone
>   All have died.)[21]

Meanwhile, the tales, legends, and myths, the object of much scholarly attention, are being recorded, translated, and published at a frantic rate. Throughout East, Central, and Southern Africa work is under way on a salvage operation to bring ashore the bulk of Old Africa's folklore before the seas of modernity wash over it completely. It is a sign that colonial scars have yet to heal that there should be any need to emphasise the importance of oral tales. Yet the need is acute, as any educational worker in Africa will agree. African students, by and large, simply do not appear to value their past. Indeed, an ironic moment of history has arrived when, on the one hand, African youth pursues a gadarene flight from a myth-dominated, spiritually rich past into a westernised modernity, and, on the other, cohorts of western youth rush in the opposite direction, seeking a world of poetry and myth, anxious to quicken the shrivelled seeds of their spirituality, determined to reforge broken links with the soil, and shouting abuse at the sterilities and empty cans of industrial civilisation. While African youth reads Galbraith and dreams of air tickets to the centres of Europe and America, western youth pores over the latest text on witchcraft, learns the art of making dugouts, and hitch-hikes through Africa with a rucksack stuffed with *Tales of the Swahili, The Origin of Life and Death, Not Even God is Ripe Enough,* and *Legends of the Congo.*

There is a danger, however, that even when due significance is given to oral tales, they will be given the significance only of interesting relics, shards from a shattered past that antiquarians find quaint and uselessly fascinating; pieces to dream on because they conjure nostalgic images of a former life. This, surely, is not enough, for what needs to be emphasised is that if a modern African society wants to understand the essence of itself, appreciate its special history and attitudes, then the oral heritage provides the only useful source of information. Statesmen, for their part, know well enough that there is no better way of leaving Africa open to the continued influx of alien solutions for local problems than to toss a care for the past into history's dustbin.

Students despise the oral tales because, they say, confusing truth with fact, they are not grounded in reality; they cannot be true, and have nothing to say to the modern world. How can a mere tale of Hare and Tortoise possibly engage minds fresh from an encounter with Marx or Rostow? This is a particularly sad charge, partly because it misunderstands the nature of literature, and partly because it is an insult flung in the teeth of the ancestors. It says, in effect, that traditional people, eking out spartan lives on a capricious soil (drought and famine are commonplace in the tales), were foolish enough to create art that didn't speak to real problems. Yet even a cursory glance at oral tradition shows that it is as rooted in the practicalities of African life as the baobab tree is rooted in the soil. With precious little time for art that is monumentally useless, oral compositions have sprung up to answer deep human needs, whether these concern the physical organisation of the people, behavioural codes dictated by the need for group survival, or the need for knowledge about the nature of man, his world, and his purpose. Oral literature, indeed, is nothing less than a record of how a given society has faced and solved the problem of survival into the modern age. What rises vividly from the stories is a truth (often lost in the smoke of industrial societies) that codes of morals and systems of values arise from, and speak to, real human situations and are not the mere dreams of sages and divines. A code condemning greed arises because this is a pernicious form of individualism menacing not only the rights of others but, ultimately, the very survival of the group. Lying, laziness, theft, murder are pilloried because they rot those bonds that hold men together and give them the security necessary for happiness and growth. And if such urgent matters require a myth, a fable, or a proverb to carry them, if a hyena must symbolise greed and a hare the criminally clever, who can object to that? Societies throughout the world have shared this convention.

As for the charge of simplicity, that the tales provide insufficient exercise for the modern mind, one can only insist that they often deal with highly complex moral situations which the modern reader skips over too lightly. The opening tale of Beier and Gbadamosi's collection *Not Even God is Ripe Enough* is a useful example. It begins: 'A long time ago there was a hunter who was a great lover of animals. He kept goats, sheep,chickens, turkeys and ducks. He loved his animals in the bush, and so gradually the love of animals turned him from a hunter into a farmer.'[22] The paradox and major statement about man's development here could detain us for another ten pages, and the complicated issues raised by the rest of the story for another twenty. Yet the modern student, perhaps because of a taught animosity, is apt to skim over this without pause for reflection. Knotty ethical problems, individual rights against those of society, the problem of virtue sometimes leading to disaster, the occasional triumph of evil, the role of women – these all have their place.

Sceptics on the modern relevance of oral tradition might examine the researches of the Canadian scholar Albert Damico, who has firmly tied the question of oral literature to Africa's liberation struggles. An essay of his in the *Pan-African Journal* suggests that the will to dislodge the colonial presence has often been related to the possession of a body of myths about land tenure.[23] He cites the classic case of the Kenyan struggle which was fired, fuelled, and sustained because the Agikuyu possessed and cherished a body of myths which said that their land was God-given, sacred, and theirs for eternity no matter how powerful the forces that might, from time to time, try to steal it. Myth and freedom. Legend and Uhuru. These are not fanciful combinations. And the work of Ngugi supports Damico's thesis, for in his pages oral tradition and modern protest meet when peasants, singing freedom songs and buoyed up with the spirit of their past, fall before colonial guns in the streets of Nairobi with the sacred soil of Gikuyuland clutched in their fists.

To appreciate how central the story-telling tradition is to a typical African society one might examine the conventions of the Kenya Luo.[24]

Traditionally, Luo stories were told in *siwindhe* or the house of a widowed grandmother, a circular building with a thatched cone-shaped roof, its walls often decorated with animal paintings and the floor patterned in geometric lines cut with *ogaka*, a plant resembling sisal. Here in *siwindhe*, in the home of a woman who could talk freely about all subjects, Luo boys and girls gathered together to be taught the ways and thinking of their people. *Siwindhe* might well be called the 'Luo Institute for Cultural and Social Preparation' and its basic medium of instruction was the story. For boys who had reached eleven and undergone the dental operation called *nak*, which involved the extraction of six lower teeth, sleeping in *siwindhe* was compulsory. Absentees were upbraided with the insult, 'Plucker of women's ticks' or 'Hunchback, sleeper in his mama's house' – this last a most abusive term among so patrilocal a nation as the Luo. So crucial was the *siwindhe*-and-story tradition to a Luo's formation that there arose a favourite saying for those who behaved stupidly: *Ining' ka manene ok onindo e siwindhe.* 'You are uneducated, like one who never slept in siwindhe.'

The Luo placed a taboo on daylight story-telling, threatening their young people that a broken rule would stunt their growth. Hence the *Tinda* or Amen at a story's close was normally followed by a relieved gasp of faith: 'I should grow tall now, tall as the trees at my uncle's'. A typical night in *Siwindhe* would begin with the door firmly locked and the mats and bedding spread on the floor. With the young people settled, grandma, revered for her age and experience, would formally declare, 'Now let the house be quiet', as though officially breaching the border between day and night. Like rough waters suddenly calmed, the assembly would relax into silence and begin the riddles, those essential pointers to an apparent disorderliness in life that the tales will try to explain. When all had recited a tale, the evening's events were brought to a close with the following formula:

*Sigana go tielo*
*Sigana go dhoot*
*Sigana go tielo*
*Sigana go widhi*

(Tale end at the bedroom
Tale end at the door
Tale end at the bedroom
Tale end at the ledge.)

23

As for the stories themselves, they are of course a storehouse of Luo values and thought. A particular emphasis among the Luo is concern about correct attitudes to weaker members of the community. One of their most memorable tales concerns one Opondo, whose wife constantly produces monitor lizards instead of humans. After repeatedly flinging these offspring into the bush to die, Opondo finally keeps one, only to discover that when the lizard bathes in the river it strips off its scaly skin to reveal a perfectly healthy child who ultimately brings the couple peace and happiness. This is a plea for the tolerance of children born with physical defects, who might, like Opondo's lizard, turn out to be happy creatures contributing much to family harmony. The story can be seen therefore as both a statement of the Luo attitude towards deformed children and a rationalisation of it.

A further theme is the status of women. Though Luo women are not yet standard bearers of the Women's Liberation Movement and though some stories are little more than war cries in an ancient sex battle which the men are winning, the tales as a whole suggest a markedly fair attitude towards the ladies. Plots are often dominated by heroines, and there are cases, such as a tale in which a certain Apiyo defends her children against hyenas, where the woman is not only heroic but morally dwarfs her husband. Again, in the story of Nyamgondho, a poor fisherman who rises from rags to riches, it is a woman who brings the wealth and embodies precisely the humility and gratitude which Nyamgondho at the denouement lacks.

For the most part the Luo tales are clearly not of modern origin, though particular stories have absorbed modern material. But the tradition is still alive and while syncretism is one sign of this, firmer signs are offered by rumour. There are, for example, two popular rumours which have currency in modern Luo society. One claims that a demon woman is abroad in Nyanza lying in wait for male victims. She is found in distress on lonely roads, is irresistably lovely, and has a preference for cyclists who are educated; but once given shelter, she turns into a hyena and tears her victim to pieces. Luo sources suggest that this is a very recent rumour, but it sounds like an updated version of the *femme fatale* idea put about by men fighting for continued domination over the ladies. Another rumour is palpably more modern. A Luo youth and his girl-friend, after living together in Nairobi and thus breaking tribal rules, decide to return home for a customary form of marriage. Arriving in Nyanza, they go to their separate homes to begin the marriage preparations. The same night, drinking in a local bar, the youth falls in with a lady of easy virtue, plies her with drink, commits fornication, and arranges to meet her again some weeks hence. On the day both families meet for nuptial discussions, the youth is happy to find the bar-woman in his girl-friend's party; but delight turns to horror when he discovers she is actually the girl's mother! He rushes off and hangs himself.

These rumours are a useful testimony to the surviving power of tradition. Even in the age of the printed word, and among a generation increasingly gaining its knowledge through the eye rather than the ear, oral tradition lives on. Indeed it is perpetuating and adding to itself, for these hearsay accounts of the fatally beautiful woman and the blindly criminal youth are nothing less than modern tales-in-the-making, new-fashioned instruments for preaching traditional attitudes and values. Oral conventions not only survive but possess the resilience and flexibility to update themselves. The two rumours above show how modern ways and settings have their impact – there were no bar-frequenting women in the ancient stories – but the pull of the old morality remains strong. The heinous offence in the second example is as outrageous in the 1970s as it ever was before.

It is a sign of how infectious such material can be, and how fast it can spread through modern Africa, that the second rumour, carried south to Malawi and mentioned in a lecture there, has already been woven into a short story called 'The Wrath of Fate' by the young writer Paul Zeleza. Appearing in his collection *Night of Darkness* (1976), it is given a Malawian setting and told on a bus to horrified passengers journeying home from work in the industrial area of Blantyre.[25] Nor is Zeleza's an isolated case, for if undergraduates too often undervalue their heritage, the new writers at least feel its pull and value. The swelling ranks of vernacular authors gain most directly, but those using English benefit too. These already include dramatists like East Africa's Robert Serumaga and Tom Omara; Central Africa's Steve Chimombo, James Ngombe, Joe Mosiwa, and Lance Ngulube. Among the poets are Okot p'Bitek, Jared Angira, Okello Oculi, and Joseph Buruga. To take an example from prose writers, Kenya's Grace Ogot draws an abundance of themes and inspiration from the traditions of her Luo people. In her short story collection *Land Without Thunder*, pieces like 'The Rain Came' and 'The Bamboo Hut' stand very close to tradition, while her grisly story 'Tekayo', exploring the taboo on cannibalism and set in the Southern Sudan, stands as one of the most powerful reworkings of an oral tale yet achieved. In the manner of

25

traditional tales, her story 'The Green Leaves', which preaches against the sin of stealing from the dead, ends with a song:

> My lover the son of Ochieng'
> The son of Omolo
> The rains are coming down
> Yes, the rains are coming down
> The nights will be dark
> The nights will be cold and long...[26]

In *Land Without Thunder*'s title story the influence of tradition can be felt in one of its most poignant insets. Owila has been brought alive from the lake after a fishing disaster; but his cousins are dead and will, according to custom, be buried on the shore:

> His cousins were being abandoned at the lakeshore to lie there for ever. Their souls would bathe in the morning breeze, and listen to the lullaby of the laughing waves.[27]

Thus the form, content, and general inspiration of Grace Ogot's heritage are being put to work in the modern short story. But even her undervalued novel *The Promised Land*, describing Luo settlement across Lake Victoria in Tanzania, uses the motif of migration, still powerfully resonant in the memory of a people who arrived in East Africa centuries ago after a traumatic exodus and who still say of themselves: 'We are like water which keeps flowing until it has found its own level.'

# 2

# Developments in verse

In one of his gloomier moments, George Orwell reported on the state of English verse:

> It will be seen that I have been speaking as though the whole subject of poetry were embarrassing, almost indecent, as though popularising poetry were essentially a strategic manoeuvre, like getting a dose of medicine down a child's throat or establishing tolerance for a persecuted sect. But unfortunately that or something like it is the case. There can be no doubt that in our civilisation poetry is by far the most discredited of the arts, the only art, indeed, in which the average man refuses to discern *any* value. Arnold Bennett was hardly exaggerating when he said that in the English-speaking countries the word 'poetry' would disperse a crowd quicker than a fire-hose.[1]

More recently, George Steiner has offered similar findings:

> Like far galaxies bending over the horizon of invisibility, the bulk of English poetry, from Caxton's 'Ovid' to 'Sweeney Among the Nightingales', is now modulating from active presence into the inertness of scholarly conservation...[2]

The gloom is unrelieved by allusion to the alleged poetic revivals of Canada and America or hint that verse is serpenting back into society's heart through the voices and lyrics of the pop bards. Apparently, neither the campus circuit crowds nor the magazines that bloom and wither in a season have improved matters much. Eliot and Auden, Spender and Hughes, despite their labours, have left poetry with little currency in the community at large. And it is more than likely that the long silence of a poet like Empson, who seems now to prefer to speak through essays and journal letters, stems from a feeling that British verse in the twentieth century, no matter how clever or happy in its inspiration, is a craft resembling topiary and thatching, practised by an eccentric few for a dwindling clientele. A gulf has opened up between the poets and a public which has simply stopped listening.

Orwell and Steiner of course were talking about verse in Britain, North America, and Australasia; but their comments are relevant because they describe a hazard already looming in Africa, even in the midst of seething poetic activity. My earlier comments on oral litera- ture were partly meant to suggest that verse at the moment enjoys a fairly full life in African societies as a popular art, an integral part of people's daily lives. Oral poets can still address a whole society which will respond and show no hostility to this type of communication. The problem now, in the midst of frantic social and linguistic change, is how to ferry this old poetic health across the river into an urban modernity. Here is a complex problem in cultural logistics requiring bold initiatives and men skilled enough to shift the blocks and weights the change involves.

The signs are not all propitious. The new poet, though caring and responsible, is already partly divorced from village society. His sense of belonging to a larger world and choice of an alien tongue for his art drastically reduce his ability to address the traditional pre-literate community of which he was once a part. He might still be a social artist, but of a different sort from his brother poet in the village; and he is constantly in danger of drifting into those same zones of isolation where the modern western poet resides. Moving to the towns, he sets an example others are quick to follow, and while a literary critic has no business telling people to stay on the land while he sits cosy in the city, it is hard not to feel that the fragmenting effects of urban drift already threaten the health of an ancient poetic tradition. Francis Berry, a British poet constantly working to recover something of the larger life English poetry once enjoyed, has offered remarks on the scale and harmony of the village world which have a direct relevance for the poet's sense of role and audience:

> With the destruction of the villages, where individuals, their ancestors and descendants too, lived together, bound together by continuous economic and emotional relationships, came the end of the only kind of organic society (which was also a figure of mankind in its diversity of sex, age and occupation) which the human being has so far been able to comprehend emotionally.[3]

28

The implied indictment of urban drift puts a finger on a modern truth, for already accusations are heard throughout Africa (still massively rural) that the new city-dwelling writers are betraying the people and indulging a selfish westernism. While outsiders see the new writing as a pioneering venture adding a new dimension to world literature, African writers themselves are increasingly having to explain their work to a society asking sharp questions about modern needs and imitation of the white man. Certainly, as new patterns emerge, many poets appear to be adopting a private posture, with all this means for the sterility Orwell was lamenting. Ali Mazrui had this in mind when he wrote *The Trial of Christopher Okigbo*, a book debating the whole question of private and public art and the rights of society against the rights of private vision. The charge against Okigbo is precisely his exclusiveness, his writing poetry 'for fellow poets rather than for ordinary men', and Mazrui has him shrewdly defended by Wole Soyinka, whose *Idanre* epic has much to say about the importance of private vision.

Dr Angus Calder meanwhile is inclined to blame it all on colonialism, capitalism, and the European. Discussing the verse of Brew and Echeruo in a *Busara* essay, he added some general comments on the isolation of the new poets. His argument, alas, ignores the idea of modern poets inheriting an art and role from the past and suggests that the new writers are men practising a craft imported comma, line, and stanza, from the West:

> Trade followed the flag, the missionaries often preceded it, and Western poetry came along much later, but as part of the same package deal of colonialism and exploitation. The modern Western poet is isolated in his society; when his isolation is exported with his poetry to Africa, the African poet who sees in this medium a chance of self-expression is lonelier still.[4]

After stating that poetic isolationism has steadily advanced in Europe over the last three-and-a-half centuries, Dr Calder draws up a ledger of isolation's achievements, comparing it with the ambivalence of the capitalist system itself, which he attacks as the real villain of the piece:

> Isolation produces the triumphs of poetry; working alone, the writer, Keats or Okigbo, discovers and opens up a whole new territory of the human consciousness, and is dismissed as obscure until his discoveries are applied and understood. It also produces

what Okigbo might have called the big white elephants of poetry – rhetoric shouted across a vast gulf but falling on the ears like cold porridge on the stomach; or the wanton obscurity of sections of Wordsworth's *Prelude* and of most of Pound's *Cantoes*. Its ambivalence is that of capitalism, which has produced technical advances, and also untold and increasing human unhappiness. And it is intimately bound up with the rise of urban society, which in turn is intimately bound up with the rise of capitalism.

This shows too much faith in the infective power of Western verse and too little in Africa's growing immunity to it. Calder yields to despair, saying, 'We have arrived at a position where individualism is too deeply rooted to be abolished...we are all individuals now, for worse as well as for better: none more so than Communist poets like Brecht and Neruda.' Thus we are left with no alternative to isolation with its triumphs and white elephants, no matter what political order the poet is working under.

The same problem was raised by the African-Scandinavian Writers' Conference held at Stockholm in 1967, where the main theme was 'the Writer in modern African society, his individuality and his social commitment'. Wole Soyinka, Alex La Guma, Ngugi wa Thiong'o, Lewis Nkosi, Awoonor-Williams, Dennis Brutus, Eldred Jones, and Ezekiel Mphahlele were among those present. But though the exchanges were lively, they were marked more by a variety of attitude to the problem than by unanimity about its solution. Even Soyinka's familiar dictum that 'the artist has always functioned in African society as the record of the mores and experience of his society and as the voice of vision in his own time' drew censure. Lewis Nkosi boldly deromanticised the writer's social function ('Writers simply are not unacknowledged legislators'), questioned whether they were even socially necessary, and then roundly asserted that the idea 'that poets in Africa should and are going to provide a vision of what is to happen is false and misleading. Writers are going to do no such thing.'[5] The problem, meanwhile, remains: writers become more individualistic and grow away from a major part of their potential audience. But there are signs, fortunately, that some of East Africa's writers, and especially Okot p'Bitek, might be drawing up the blueprint of one possible solution.

*East African beginnings*

It is common knowledge that East African English writing began later than its West African counterpart and that the 1962 Conference of African Writers at Makerere was an important watershed. Writers constantly hark back to this event and Ngugi speaks of being 'overwhelmed by the literary turbulence in West Africa and Southern Africa' reflected by it. But the picture of Taban Lo Liyong in his apartment at Howard University, head in hands, wondering how to solve the problem of East Africa's literary barrenness, has also become a treasured holy image:

> I walked to my apartment, threw my briefcase on the bed and sat next to it. I then held my big head between my powerful hands. I squeezed it, and squeezed it hard, till it thought. When thoughts came, they poured like tropical rain: big and fast. I pulled out a pencil and a paper and wrote fast, capturing every drop of thought.[6]

There has been a squeezing and pouring ever since, and whether in answer to the call of Taban or the conference, the number of writers offering their wares in East Africa has grown very swiftly indeed. They include, in addition to Taban and Ngugi, Okot p'Bitek, Jared Angira, R. C. Ntiru, John Mbiti, Edwin Waiyaki, Amin Kassam, Lennard Okola, Eneriko Seruma, Robert Serumaga, Everett Standa, Kimani Gecau, David Mulwa, Sam Mbure, Leonard Kibera, Samuel Kahiga, Charity Waciuma, Okello Oculi, Joseph Buruga, Austin Bukenya, Grace Ogot, Magaga Alot, Mwangi Ruhini, Albert Ojuka, Meja Mwangi, Godwin Wachira and Charles Mangua. Through the daily press and a variety of journals such as *Zuka, Darlite, Penpoint, Ghala,* and *The East African Journal,* through such publishing houses as Oxford, EAPH, EALB, and Heinemann, these are the writers making East Africa's contribution to the new literature. The scene has changed so fast that those who still believe West Africa makes the running might dwell with profit on James Currey's claim in *The Guardian* (October 1974) that Nairobi now has more writers, artists, and critics than any other city on the continent.

The work of this new generation is confident and assertive, even when it is imitative. Authors are sure of their targets, aware of pitfalls, decisive about matters of form, and, like an argumentative clutch of Renaissance artists, acutely aware of what rivals finished this morning

31

or will publish this afternoon. Because of the nature of East African colonialism (Ngugi's work alongside Achebe's sketches the differences well enough), the new literature, and verse in particular, is more strident in tone than its early West African counterpart, more protesting, more certain of where it wants to move. Significantly too, there has been a greater emphasis on critical work, designed to stimulate new writing and debate matters of literary moment. Typical of many who insist on fighting critical battles as well as pioneering new directions in creative work is Okot p'Bitek.

## Okot p'Bitek and the Song school

Okot's whole career as poet, scholar, singer, and raconteur has been concerned with the problem of making tradition meaningful to modernity and avoiding Western solutions to African problems. Significantly his first publication, a novel called *Lak Tar*, was written in Luo not English; and later, after careful research into traditional modes, he wrote his *Song of Lawino* also in Luo under the title *Wer pa Lawino*. His career has been a model of what negritude apostles preached but did not always practise. He first achieved fame with an English version of *Song of Lawino*, a poem so immediately successful that it became at once the chosen model for a whole school of writing. Okello Oculi wrote his *Orphan* in frank imitation of it; Joseph Buruga's *The Abandoned Hut* is in the same form, and Okot himself has followed *Lawino* with *Song of Ocol*, *Song of Malaya*, and *Song of Prisoner*.

The song has been a truly seminal development and its success stems in part from its relationship to oral tradition. It is a form similar in general conception to the blues, calypso, and the ballad; but Okot has borrowed from none of these since he had the lament of his own Acholi people as a model before him. Okot's achievement is that, better than most African poets, he has created in *Song of Lawino* a form which is popular and the outgrowth of a home tradition. Equally important, he has fashioned a popular alternative to the private hard verse favoured by many of his colleagues. Ngugi wa Thiong'o, not given to overstatement, makes a firm comment on this achievement:

> *Song of Lawino* is the one poem that has mapped out new areas and new directions in East African poetry. It belongs to the soil. It is authentically East African in its tone and in its appeal. This can be seen in its reception: it is read everywhere, arousing heated debates.[7]

Ngugi's enthusiasm is echoed in fulsome manner by Okello Oculi, who stresses the social significance of the work:

> *Song of Lawino* touched exactly that nerve which we had been arguing. The response of Kampala was so spontaneous...He (Okot) confirmed this yearning we had for self-assertion, not only self in terms of ourselves, but self in the collective sense, what we felt was the African sense of assertion.[8]

Okot's song is an ideal poetic vehicle for a society poised between the oral world and literacy. Its written form bears the marks of a strongly oral life within it; nor is it, like the ode, elegy, or epic, tied to any particular class or level of incident. While it is true that the lament vein runs strongly in it, Okot has in fact created a medium capable of bearing every variety of mood and event. Already the *Song* has carried much of the normal freight of the novel. Issues commonly explored in African fiction – the fight between old and new, town and country, flesh and spirit, bureaucrat and peasant – these have all figured so far in the song form. Nor is character an obstacle, for we are already as intimately familiar with Lawino and Ocol as we are with Okonkwo, Jagua, and Kihika. Might this then be a home-grown rival for the novel, the African way of saying, in a preferred poetic mode, what the novel in its westernness has been trying to say?

Whatever the case, the song is an ideal form through which a literate artist can remain in touch with his pre-literate society. The difference in mnemonic effect between verse and prose is crucial here, for the song drives its lines into the memory in a manner alien to the nature of prose. Prose holds language too slackly to achieve the memorable effect of song. Event, scene, tone, atmosphere – these are remembered from prose, but rarely individual words and phrases. The rhetorical potential of the song in an oral society is therefore very great. Worlds apart from the hard brilliance of *Idanre* or *Heavensgate*, the song is an excellent tool for writers anxious to engrave on the collective memory of a people grammars for a new way of life. Criticism has claimed for a variety of African poets that they sing for a whole community even while singing for themselves, that the lyric 'I' is really the collective 'We'. It is not to deny the truth of this to suggest that no poet in Africa has succeeded so far in speaking to and for his people in the way Okot and his disciples have done. For the song is deliberately popular in conception and is meant to be understood easily. It is the plain man's literature that does not, however, deny a place to

33

subtlety, extended metaphor, or recondite allusion. Okot's aims can be gleaned from a *Busara* essay written in 1972:

> Literature is the communication and sharing of deeply felt emotions. The vehicle of this communication is words. The aim of any literary activity must be to ensure that there is communication between the singer and the audience, between the story-teller and his hearers.[9]

The song, then, is literature for the whole community, literature that reads swiftly and smoothly. Where Okigbo and Soyinka are clever and tortuous, the songs are open and easy, yet rejoicing in a lyricism that creates the warm immediacy of a real human situation.

The organisation of *Song of Lawino* is simple and effective. Like Clark's *The Raft*, its basic situation is at once commonplace yet reflective of wider issues only loosely tied to Lawino's plight; indeed issues of which the heroine might not even be aware. Lawino is a traditional wife despised by her husband Ocol, a graduate who spends most of his time in the city philandering with a certain Clementina, who is seen by Lawino as little more than a whore. Lawino resents Ocol's attitudes and, despite her denials, is jealous of Clementina's success. The conflicts of an age-old triangle are played out in a modern African setting.

Lawino may be read, performed, and remembered on this level alone. But such is the poem's nature that while Lawino laments her fate to an absent husband (whose voice we never hear), her dramatic monologue rises to, first, a massive attack on westernism, and secondly a defence of the whole gamut of traditional beliefs and postures. It is not, therefore, simply a private grief made public, for while it is specifically the deterioration Lawino sees in Ocol which matters most, it is the business of the poem to lament the broader Acholi and African deterioration which Ocol's case reflects.

This prepared attack-and-defence covers crucial areas and aesthetics, religion, politics, language, diet, and concepts of time are among them. Lawino loathes the way English has become a toy for social climbers; she finds western medicine fussy and often useless; western cooking is complicated; time has been seriously tampered with; literacy has castrated a generation; Christianity is all alien mysteries; politics is simply jobs for the boys and keeps her husband from home; western dancing is vulgar and disgusting. And with every thrust

34

there is an assertion that the Acholi equivalent is satisfactory, has
served the people well, and should not be reviled. The poem at times
assumes even a racial complexion, becoming not just an Acholi, East
African, or broadly African statement, but a statement for black people
everywhere.

The dangers in an exercise of this kind are obvious. For example,
does the detail flow as part of a spontaneous outpouring, which is
what the poet wants, or is it manifestly contrived? Does the defence of
tradition get mawkish and sentimental? Must a traditional narrator like
Lawino know too much about the new world to seem an unschooled
representative of the old? What, in reality, would be her normal range
of insights, concepts, and vocabulary? If such questions can be raised
as substantial charges, there might follow a related complaint that
Lawino is too obviously a mouthpiece for Okot, that the act of parturition has left something of her still living in the poet's mind. While there
are times when we do not willingly suspend our disbelief and feel that
the voice modulates into Okot's own, broadly speaking Lawino is a
convincing figure. There is the further point that the task of creating
a lady character who holds the stage for so long is not easy for a male
poet, presenting a tough test of whether he can make crucial imaginative leaps. Yet even here the warm response of so many lady readers
and listeners is proof of a broad measure of success.

Lawino's lament is partly lyrical, in that it is a subjective outpouring
of personal pain, partly a dialogue-of-one in which a wife addresses
an absent husband (gaining point and sympathy from his desertion
of her), and partly a plea to an unseen African audience, a 'jury' in
the wings who will nod and say 'Yes, Lawino, you are right.' This, I
take it, is what the frequent invocation to the clansmen is meant to
mean. Part lyric lament and part cool rhetoric, the poem has been
designed with astute care. With so much to say, how can Okot so
express himself that he will hold a reader's attention and deliver his
message in neat portable units for the memory? How can he make a
long poem that people will begin, persevere with, and finish? The very
idea of so large a vehicle for new gospels would be considered by most
scholars as itself a recipe for disaster. Yet *Lawino* is a great popular
success, among the best-selling English poems this century has
produced.

How can this be explained? Presumably those who dismiss the
question of style would argue that it is the poem's content that appeals.
Yet the debates of *Song of Lawino* are a mere commonplace of African

writing. Where is the writer who has not explored them in one form or another? If, then, there is nothing original in the substance of Okot's poem, we are left with the idea that its success after all concerns style and poetics, the way Okot's material is organised and set forth. Nor should the choice of a lady protagonist be overlooked, for Okot knows well that while African audiences might turn a reluctant ear to even the most eloquent male, deep cultural forces condition them to listen closely to the lament of a woman and mother, especially one ill-used by the world. Okot knows too what African writing has constantly revealed, that the mother-image towers like a colossus over the whole life of the continent. Where is the writer who has dared to attack the shrine of African motherhood? *Lawino* herself declares:

> No one looks down
> On his mother
> There is no medicine in the hospital
> For a mother's curse.

Having settled his broad strategy, Okot approaches tactical questions with a craftsman's resourcefulness. A professional raconteur and singer, he has a natural talent for the arts of language manipulation; his ear is sharp, his sense of timing exact, his ability to tease and shock renowned. He creates, however, a surface plainness which can deceive the unwary, fox the speed-reader, and cause heartache to the imitator. Natural talent and expertise in oral-formulaic device combine with skills sharpened during Okot's triple training as lawyer, scholar, and teacher – skills designed to prove a point beyond reasonable doubt, to teach lessons, paint verbal pictures, assault the emotions, and persuade a jury where justice lies. Thus Lawino's argument is arranged with care. The verse is broken into handy blocks of matter like some well-organized lesson so that reader and listener can absorb and respond to all that is said. Order here satisfies the demands of both rhetoric and aesthetics; nor is there room for cloudy language, far-fetched image, or anything to block the highway of plain powerful statement. Each point is made firmly and lucidly, yet often, echoing oral practice, providing a deft variation of its predecessor, a restatement in fresh terms with perhaps a bold image for illustration. Thus the song's flow is sustained as each idea pushes the argument a step further.

36

The opening lines set the poem spinning with life:

Husband, now you despise me
Now you treat me with spite
And say I have inherited the stupidity of my aunt;
Son of the Chief,
Now you compare me
With the rubbish in the rubbish pit
You say you no longer want me
Because I am like the things left behind
In the deserted homestead.
You insult me
You laugh at me
You say I do not know the letter A
Because I have not been to school
And I have not been baptized[10]

At once we feel caught, drawn on by the smooth hurried flow of the lines, engaged by their easy lucid style. A fast pace, plain style, an urgent female voice, and what Fleet Street would call a human interest situation – they all conspire to pull us into the rapids with the river waters leaping and swirling all round us; and though we can sometimes snatch a glance at the sky overhead or the changing scene on the riverbank, we know in our bones there is no escape, for we are doomed to see, hear, and feel it all and drown in the deeps of Lawino's lament. The poem drives onwards, as Lawino appeals to her clansmen (37):

My clansmen, I cry
Listen to my voice:
The insults of my man
Are painful beyond bearing.

My husband abuses me together with my parents;
He says terrible things about my mother
And I am so ashamed!

He abuses me in English
And he is so arrogant.

He says I am rubbish,
He no longer wants me!

*Developments in verse*

Okot likes a short line with rare variation in length and rhythm, for a slack obesity would obstruct the surge and sweep which are crucial for the urgent attack Lawino is after. Who would listen long to a lament moving at the pace of a philosophical treatise? The very rush of the lines is suggestive of female hysteria, and this is a deliberate effect of the iron control Okot keeps on the poem's shape and direction. Line and tempo stand artistically united with the aim and subject of the verse. Equally, Okot's use of repetition and parallelism not only serves to drive home Lawino's complaints, so that finally we are forced to sympathise; it also creates the illusion of fierce domestic argument, as if Lawino is ranting at Ocol, preventing any interruption, and leaving him standing before her dumbstruck. Yet the controlling devices are always there, holding the poem together, giving it shape and supporting its rhetoric.

Given the nature of Lawino's complaint, it is significant that scenes from traditional life are among the finest segments of the song. The poet's imagination takes fire at these moments for Okot relishes Lawino's attacks on Ocol's westernness, and when his heroine sings of tradition, conjuring scenes from the age-old life patterns of her people, his heart sings with her, abandoning itself to a feast of nostalgia. Let Taban Lo Liyong rave about modernity, the author of *Lawino* will fight for tradition. He has laboured with love on the following passage, describing Acholi dances (48):

> When the drums are throbbing
> And the black youths
> Have raised much dust
> You dance with vigour and health
> You dance naughtily with pride
> You dance with spirit,
> You compete, you insult, you provoke
> You challenge all!
> And the eyes of the young men become fed!
> The son of a man
> And the daughter of a man
> Shine forth in the arena.
> ...   ...   ...
> The tattoos on her chest
> Are like palm fruits,
> The tattoos on her back
> Are like stars on a black night;

38

> Her eyes sparkle like the fireflies,
> Her breasts are ripe
> Like the full moon.

And on this fragment from a rural scene (67):

> And when you balance on your head
> A beautiful water pot
> Or a new basket
> Or a long-necked jar
> Full of honey,
> Your long neck
> Resembles the *alwiri* spear.
>
> And as you walk along the pathway
> On both sides
> The *obiya* grasses are flowering
> And the pollok blossoms
> And the wild white lilies
> Are shouting silently
> To the bees and butterflies!

Recalling the halcyon days of Ocol's wooing, before the present decay set in, Lawino's memories ring like echoes from a prelapsarian dream, remembered fragments of a world of innocence, a world gone for ever (58):

> When Ocol was wooing me
> My breasts were erect.
> And they shook
> As I walked briskly,
> And as I walked
> I threw my long neck
> This way and that way
> Like the flower of the *lyonno* lily
> Waving in a gentle breeze.
> And my brothers called me Nya-Dyang
> For my breasts shook
> And beckoned the cattle,
> And they sang silently:
> *Father prepare the kraal,*
> *Father prepare the kraal,*
> *The cattle are coming.*

39

> I was the leader of the girls
> And my name blew
> Like a horn among the Payira.
> And I played on my bow harp
> And praised my love.

It scarcely matters that amidst this arcadian splendour a nagging question arises about its purpose. Who is to be informed, Ocol or the reader? One might reply that it is simply the core of what Okot wants to be seen and admired; yet the question remains and Okot's wallowing in the sunbeams of a golden past leaves the poem briefly drifting. We know from Lawino that both Ocol and the peasants are well acquainted with Acholi traditions, so why rehearse them? Presumably, they are in the nature of joys recollected in adversity and designed for Lawino's, or the poet's, emotional therapy, as the aged might dream of their youth and vigour.

A risk in any poetic defence of the past is that it will involve a romanticised picture built more from dreams than fact. All too easily, as Soyinka suggests, the past can become a bolt-hole of escape from the present. Okot has resisted this temptation for he displays no uncritical acceptance of the past, even when passionately keen to defend it. He knows well enough that old Africa was not a tropical Arcadia. Hence evocative scenes from harvest time, moonlight festivals, and courting rites are balanced by allusions to squalor, sickness, witchcraft, and death. Lawino, for example, scorns the idea of a homestead where

> Children's excreta is
> Scattered all over the swept compound
> And around the granaries

and freely admits that in the traditional order

> Some clumsy and dirty black women
> Prepare food clumsily
> And put it
> In dirty containers.

The sheer speed of *Song of Lawino* makes it hard to watch for a detail like the poet's use of tense, which is related to both poetic strategy and the poet's broader aims. When Lawino recalls her courting days, when, as she puts it in a sudden shift of appeal from Ocol to the jury, 'This man crawled on the floor! The son of the Bull wept', the tense is naturally the past. But at other moments, when, for example, Lawino describes a rubric for traditional dances, the tense shifts suddenly from past to present. '*You dance* with confidence', she says, '*You do not come* to the arena drunk', '*You adorn yourself* in Acholi costumes', 'A young man *wears* the odye and lacomi', 'It *is danced* in broad daylight.' Likewise on Acholi aesthetics (65):

> No-one, except wizards
> And women who poison others
> Leaves her hair untrimmed!
> ... ... ...
> Young girls
> Whose breasts are just emerging
> Smear *shea* Butter on their bodies,
> The beautiful oil from Labwor-omor.

Or perhaps in a description of domestic life (81):

> And when my sister
> Is grinding simsim
> Mixed with groundnuts
> And I am grinding
> Millet mixed with sorghum
> You hear the song of the stones
> You hear the song of the grains

What is virtually a vivid present here has the effect not simply of bringing remembered scenes close to us, and hence vitalising the narrative at this point; it is also a reminder that traditional life is present fact, a surviving reality, not merely a corpse awaiting the morbid pathologists. Artistic and social aims merge in the poet's grammar as Okot reminds us that some of the old ways are still a choice for the modern world, that the life Lawino hymns, with its love of ceremony and intimacy with soil, season, and landscape, lives on beyond the office blocks of Nairobi and Kampala.

The subtleties of time are also among likely victims of yielding to the rapid flow of Lawino's lament. Yet these are a base on which some of the poem's major structures are built. Time merits a special discussion in John Mbiti's *African Religions and Philosophy* because he feels it is crucial to an understanding of his people. 'The concept of time', he says, 'may help to explain beliefs, attitudes, practices and general way of life of African peoples not only in the traditional set-up but also in the modern situation.' In the traditional view, he says, there is 'a long past, a present, and virtually no future'. This, while obviously

41

a simplification, casts a good deal of light on the conflicting worlds in Okot's poem. Lawino is deeply involved in the present, in Acholi life as it is lived here and now, and she is also in touch with the cells of an inherited life. Yet apart from her desire for Ocol to mend his ways, she expresses little interest in the future. She does not dream of what she or her family *might become* at some future time. Her verb tenses encompass past and present, but rarely reach out to the future: speculation has little place in her mental life. Ocol, however, in Mbiti's terms, has undergone a massive shift in mental orientation, for his concept of time has been radically changed. He has turned his back on the past, seeing it only as a nightmare from which he must close off his mind. His reaction to a world-view gazing always behind it has been a leap to the future. What sociologists call a peasant 'circular' view of time has given way to a 'linear' view associated with science and the West. What dominates Ocol's whole posture now is the future – the repository for all revolutionary zeal. Lawino's amazed reaction to Ocol's outlook can now be understood. Since in the old view the future, because it has not yet been experienced, does not, strictly speaking, make sense, then men like Ocol must appear to verge on lunacy, absorbed in unreality and a hunt for phantoms. Perhaps this is too crude a distinction, but it helps to explain the sheer width of the chasm that has opened up, actually and symbolically, between Lawino and her husband. Random lines from Ocol's reply show how verb forms shift violently from past and present into a passionate affirmative future:

> We will plough up
> All the valley
> Make compost of the Pumpkins
> And the other native vegetables,
> The fence dividing
> Family holdings
> Will be torn down,
> We will uproot
> The trees demarcating
> The land of clan from clan,
> We will obliterate
> Tribal boundaries
> And throttle native tongues
> To dumb death.[11]

Little wonder that Lawino finds her husband strange. How can a man so newly shaped fit into a world dominated by the time concept Mbiti describes?

The time element also informs the whole texture of human behaviour and habit, especially in Lawino's world. A more humane time-flow than the unfeeling ticking of a clock decides when a child should be fed or when harvesting or sowing must begin. The sun is nature's clock, and so is the moon, whose place in the people's minds is captured in this simple statement from Lawino:

> We all know the moon –
> It elopes,
> Climbs the hill
> And falls down;

But for the Ocols, mechanical time is all-powerful and Lawino's response to it is one of amusement (89):

> On the face of the clock
> There are writings
> And its large single testicle
> Dangles below.

This is merely lighthearted description, but it paves the way for the serious charge that Ocol has become the servant, rather than the master, of time. This too marks a radical shift in human habit:

> Time has become
> My husband's master
> It is my husband's husband.

And then comes a line whose simplicity might mask its aim of pressing the attack on modernity a step further. Lawino quotes a cliché she has heard Ocol often use:

> Time is money

In Western conversation it is heard so often that it is accepted without murmur, and usually without reflection. It is one of the linguistic niceties of African literature, however, that the impact of so trite a remark in the local context is vastly more explosive. That even the sacred gift of time should be shackled by the money ethic of the west is a suggestion of horrifying magnitude. Yet this cliché, dropped almost casually into the middle of the poem, foregrounds a central

43

feature of the order ushered in by the white man and embraced by Ocol.

A word about *Song of Lawino*'s diction. Just as Okot's lines are largely free of inert language, so his actual choice of diction shows a preference for the plain and common core. Though written verse, we must see it as conceived partly within the realms of 'orature', where poetry, as Francis Berry points out, needed 'a simple boldness of diction and simplicity of syntax', for convoluted constructions or thick, gorgeous 'Keatsian' adjectival and adverbial compounds would have muffled the hearers' understanding of what the poem was, or what it was about...' Hence the simplicity of Lawino's words on literacy, that solitary-practised, family-breaking skill shrewdly pilloried as perhaps the greatest devil of change African society has encountered (190):

> For all our young men
> Were finished in the forest,
> Their manhood was finished
> In the class-rooms,
> Their testicles
> Were smashed
> With large books!

Since Okot's literary career was born in reaction to western culture, there was little risk that he would follow those colonial romantics who decked their verse in imagery culled from British sources. Ngugi in *Homecoming* claimed that Eliot, Yeats, Hopkins, and Wordsworth were still 'the main inspiration for East African poets'; but his remarks were based on *Drumbeat*, a pioneering anthology published in 1967. Okot, however, flies straight to the home scene for his imagery without stopovers in Europe, as he must do if his writing is to be authentic and persuasive to a local audience. When Lawino walks past her husband, 'He hisses like a wounded *ororo* snake'. When the youths are waiting to see the nubile maidens we find them 'Lurking in the shades/like the leopardess with cubs'. They argue among themselves and 'bite off their ears/like jackals'. To Lawino, her rival's hair looks like 'the python's discarded skin'; her head 'smells like rats/That have fallen into the fireplace'. Ocol's political words are 'Itchy like scabies,/Itchy like scabies on the buttocks'. He is now at odds with his brother, so harmful is the new order to family ties; yet once upon a time 'They were as close to each other/As the eye and the nose'.

Christian notions rendered in the vernacular idiom cast a fresh light
on the collision between two worlds of theology. The Credo's opening

> I believe in God
> The Father Almighty
> Maker of Heaven and Earth

becomes (132):

> I accept the Hunchback
> The Padre who is very strong
> Moulder of Skyland and Earth

which describes how Nilotic people see creation as a moulding, a
potter's work done with clay. The prayer *Glory Be To The Father*
becomes:

> Glory shine on the body of the Father
> And on the body of the Son
> And on the body of the Clean Ghost

*Song of Lawino* is a bold experiment, successful as an English version
of the vernacular, or, as Okot puts it, an eagle with clipped wings. The
poem's moral strength becomes clear as one gradually hears Lawino
as a representative voice of the majority – the peasant mass who still
live in her world. The song has an obvious structural unity, its thirteen
sections cohering impressively, and it has achieved its distinction
through a combination of poetic skills, rhetorical management, and
social sensitivity. Its main fault perhaps lies in its length, its determination to go on until all has been said. Okot must have believed he
was writing his *magnum opus*, a once-for-all statement, unaware that
Lawino's success would call for at least three further exercises in the
same form.

The successor to *Song of Lawino* came in 1970 with the publication of
*Song of Ocol*, the necessary reply from the defendant to complete the
hearing. Yet *Ocol* seems to have been fathered hurriedly, as a response
to Lawino's success rather than as a logical sequence in a pre-arranged
pattern. Indeed, the impression that *Lawino* was a once-for-all effort
is so strong that there is no surprise in *Ocol* being a slimmer work,
uneven in tone and texture and rather light in its argument. It is as
if Okot was caught unprepared, with his imagination exhausted by the
herculean labours of *Lawino*. He has worked so hard to show that

45

*Developments in verse*

Lawino is right that it is virtually impossible to show now that she is wrong.

Thus, where *Lawino* seemed a wholly sincere performance, straight-faced, passionately argued, with constant appeals to our sense of justice, here a new element enters, an unsteady, shifty tone that arises from the poem being partly an exercise in irony. Okot has too much sympathy for Lawino to build a successful case for Ocol, though he gives him some splendid huffing and puffing. He tries manfully, however, and his best passages possess an extraordinary energy. At several points early in the poem a fierce stridency erupts, a verbal lashing impressive enough to make Ocol's case seem superbly exciting if nothing else. But the strain is too great; the pull of Lawino's cause gnaws Okot's conscience and modifies his writing. He cannot in the end allow Ocol to get away with it: the risk of a single reader mistaking where truth and justice lie becomes too acute. As a result the poem finally sabotages Ocol's case. Okot will, for a time, roar convincingly through Ocol's mask, but then must peep out from behind or else suddenly drop it, anxious to assure us that all this sound and fury is really a bad joke. Sometimes it feels as if the whole song is designed to cheat Ocol and deviously support Lawino, as if Okot, like some expert judo man, is using his opponent's weight to let him destroy himself.

The ambiguity is felt most when Ocol's imagination takes wing over precisely those areas of tradition he affects to despise. Nostalgia rises, a glow bathes the verse, whenever dance, song, and story are recalled. He sighs at remembered pictures of girls going to the well or striding along rural paths to the river. He recalls wistfully, like some fervent negritudist, the land's cool stillness at dawn and the easeful way his people wake into it. He admires – one feels it in every word – the Suk, Turkana, Kipsigis, Kalenjin, and Maasai, all those in fact who cling most fiercely to old ways. He loves their haughty independence, their scorn of modernity, their bravery, warrior classes, marital codes, and manliness. So when he shouts 'Away with it all', we can't for a moment believe him.

One might argue that Ocol and his type are simply the classically split African, modern men with a lingering affection for the past. This is well enough, if we can ignore the idea that this is the answer to Lawino's lament. The basic trouble is that Lawino has painted her husband in such garish western colours that we expect him at least to mount an attack that is deeply felt. Indeed the whole drift of *Lawino*

46

prepares us for a defence of modernity as sincere as the wife's lament, not for a song that becomes a further plea on her behalf.

These issues aside – and one accepts that they are fundamental – *Song of Ocol* claims a special place in Okot's development; for the poem is conceived in English not Luo, leaving the poet free of the restrictions involved in translation. In a sense, then, *Ocol* rather than *Lawino* is the true test of Okot as an English-language poet. Scrutiny reveals that at least at the technical level of linguistic manipulation, the poem succeeds, for it contains some of the poet's finest writing. From the opening lines:

> Woman
> Shut up!
> Pack your things
> Go!

free now from translation's grinding problems, Okot skips off at a dizzy pace, creating with superb ease, enjoying the sheer verbal spin of it all. There is a sense of a lighter atmosphere and an untrammelled spirit at work. The poet is wielding a familiar, well-honed weapon, and wielding it with verve and virtuosity. One sign is a bubbling sense of humour, sharper than in *Lawino*, and at its most outrageous suggesting the influence of Taban Lo Liyong. It can be lightly ironic, scornfully bitter, even self-mocking, making Ocol's reactions less predictable than Lawino's, full of that sense of surprise one expects in good art.

A second sign of development is Ocol's more compressed verse. In order to tighten his style and achieve maximum impact Okot takes Lawino's thin line and makes it thinner. This partly involves abandoning simile for plain bold metaphor. Hence lines such as these from *Lawino*:

> It goes this way and that way
> Like a sausage fruit in a storm

or

> Her eyes sparkle like fireflies

give way typically to a more compressed statement:

> Your song
> Is rotting buffalo
> ... ... ...
> It is pork gone rancid,

47

It is the honeyed
Blooded sour milk
In the stinking
Maasai gourd.

The poem's opening salvoes succeed best. Broadly free of tonal ambiguity, they are a brilliant display of abuse, male chauvinist scorn, and revolutionary fire. The verse shows no sign of strain as Ocol's venom starts to pour (199):

Woman,
Shut up!
Pack your things
Go!

Take all the clothes
I bought you
The beads, necklaces
And the remains
Of the utensils,
I need no second-hand things.
There is a large sack
In the boot
Of the car
Take it
Put all your things in it
And go!

There is an illusion of simplicity here as though the words find their own way into a scheme for expressing violent spitting anger. Staccato imperatives inform stanzas that speed to a 'thumping' close, like blows delivered in a quarrel.

In lines heavy with allusions that Lawino will appreciate, her song is dismissed in an avalanche of rhetoric (199):

Song of the woman
Is the confused noise
Made by the ram
After the butcher's knife
Has sunk past
The wind pipe,
Red paint spraying
On the grasses;

48

It is a song all alone
A solo fragment
With no chorus
No accompaniment,
A strange melody
Impossible to orchestrate;

As if in echo
Of women's wailings
At yesterday's funeral
Song of the dead
Out of an old tomb,
Stealthy cracking
Of dry bones,
Falling in of skulls
Under the weight
Of earth;
It's the dull thud
Of the wooden arrow
As it strikes the concrete
Of a wall
And falls to earth

Once more, the verse draws us on so fast that we risk missing its felicities. Lawino's song is consigned to the realms of all that is dead, gone, and useless: a mere echo from a tomb. But notice how Okot gives Ocol an appropriate range of material and reference to describe the failure of an *oral* phenomenon, which is what Lawino's song is. Hence, 'the echo/Of women's wailing'; the 'Song of the dead'; the 'stealthy cracking/Of dry bones'; and the acutely effective 'dull thud/Of the wooden arrow/As it strikes the concrete/Of a wall/And falls to earth.'

Ocol's opening charge is that Old Africa is dead and buried and that appeals to it are like echoes from the tomb. This is shrewd, for once it is established, it has the effect, first of suggesting the futility of Lawino's lament, and second of hinting that all those traditions Lawino defends, however strong, were unable to resist the swelling tide of modernity. Tradition's death is the surest sign that Lawino has no case. In one sharp thrust Lawino's whole world is discredited, leaving a triumphant Ocol free to stroll casually through its ruins and outline various details of his vision. His pronouncements ring out like shrieks from a negritudist's nightmare (209):

*Developments in verse*

> To hell
> With your Pumpkins
> And your Old Homesteads,
> To hell
> With the husks
> Of old traditions
> And meaningless customs,
> We will smash
> The taboos
> One by one,
> Explode the basis
> Of every superstition,
> We will uproot
> Every sacred tree
> And demolish every ancestral shrine.

The *tabula rasa* solution, bewailed by Césaire, will be applied with a vengence and, of course, with twentieth-century efficiency (213):

> We will arrest all the witches,
> Wizards, evil-eyes,
> Sellers of fetish bundles,
> Bones and claws,
> Dealers in poisons
> Extracted from plants
> And venoms from snakes...

A police state approach will be adopted to all purveyors of traditional culture too:

> We will arrest
> All the village poets
> Musicians and tribal dancers,
> Put in detention
> Folk-story tellers
> And myth makers,
> The sustainers
> of village morality;

Steadily, Ocol insists on a rejection of all things African. Those who study the African past will feel the wrath of the new order. Schools of African Studies will be closed, their professors hanged, and a bonfire

50

made of all anthologies of African writing. The apostles of negritude
will not escape either (214):

> Where is Aimé Césaire?
> Where Léopold Senghor?
> Arrest Janheinz Jahn
> And Father Placide Tempels,
> Put in detention
> All the preachers
> Of Negritude...

Ocol at this point sees Africa through the eyes of a completely bleached
modernist. His training has taught him to reject his background
utterly. Feelings of disgust, shame, and despair fight one another for
prominence (206):

> What is Africa
> To me?
> Blackness,
> Deep, deep fathomless
> Darkness;
> Africa,
> Idle giant
> Basking in the sun,
> Sleeping, snoring,
> Twitching in dreams;
> Diseased with a chronic illness,
> Choking with black ignorance,
> Chained to the rock
> Of poverty

The African is always laughing and dancing in his chains; baring
white teeth that won't bite; seeing snakes in the whirlwind and in the
rainbow; carrying his gods on his head as he roams the wilderness;
feeling pride in his absurd, toylike weapons; clinging fearfully to
mother, brother, uncle, and clan; afraid to boldly innovate. Ocol curses
it all and in a resounding *cri de coeur* asks:

> Mother, mother,
> Why,
> Why was I born
> Black?

*Developments in verse*

African audiences tend to react mirthfully to all this, as though detecting even here a tonal ambiguity; as if they can see traditionalist Okot smirking behind a mask he has borrowed for the occasion from his modernist colleague Taban Lo Liyong. Meanwhile, Ocol outlines his futuristic dreams for East Africa in a strain of verse best described as Nuclear Age Marlovian (245):

> We will uproot
> Each tree
> From the Ituri forest
> And blow up Kilimanjaro,
> The rubble from Ruwenzori
> Will fill the valleys
> Of the Rift,
> We will divert
> The mighty waters
> Of the Nile
> Into the Indian Ocean

Ocol urges Lawino and her people to accept the Deserted Homestead (a favoured symbol among the Song school) and march off to the City Gate. But it is a prospect that does not leave even him entirely unmoved (247):

> Weep long,
> For the village world
> That you know
> And love so well,
> Is gone,
> Swept away
> By the fierce fires
> Of progress and civilization!

The wistful note in a passage like this contrasts sharply with the apocalyptic style of the opening, as if the revolutionary is already suffering the inevitable sea-change to a traditionalist. We hear it again as Ocol conjures more vignettes from the rural past (247):

> That walk to the well
> Before sunrise,
> The cool bath in the stream,
> The gathering of the family
> Around the evening fire...

That shady evergreen *byeyo* tree
Under which I first met you
And told you
I wanted you,
Do you remember
The song of the *ogilo* bird
And the chorus
Of the grey monkeys
In the trees nearby?

It is among these final sections of the poem that we find the plainest shift of allegiance. Caught by anxiety to assert his private vision, Okot at one point manufactures an opportunity to attack a betrayed Uhuru, with its broken promises and corruption, and the general chaos of an era which began with a golden dawn and somehow sank into nightmare. Alluding to 'fat black capitalists' and bishops in golden crowns, and then describing for a poor woman the riches he has enjoyed since Uhuru (they include a Mercedes, a well-stocked farm, and a town house nestling in bougainvillaea), Ocol asks, with tongue in cheek (235):

Is it my fault
That you sleep
In a hut with a leaking thatch?
Do you blame me
Because your sickly children
Sleep on the earth
Sharing the filthy floor
With sheep and goats?

Meanwhile Senghor's dream of African Socialism is now only 'a faint flute/Playing in the moonlight', Nyerere's vision of *Ujamaa* only a 'distant drum'. Ocol asks an African ambassador at the UN to explain, in 'English or in French', the local foundations on which the new Africa is being built. He asks a sweating scholar to explain to the world the African philosophy being used to reshape the continent. The implied comment (which is now frankly Okot's not Ocol's) is that nothing is being achieved in either area. By this time any attempt to sustain a truly Ocolian point of view has been abandoned, and there remains only a pathetic Ocol, part sentient strawman, part burning revolutionary, and part homesick traditionalist; a bundle of conflicts and contradictions, whose final irony might be that he represents a modern man intended by Okot to look like this from the start.

*Song of Prisoner* and *Song of Malaya* appeared in 1971 and are the most recent pieces from Okot's pen. *Song of Malaya* (i.e. *Song of the Whore*) can be quickly dismissed as a Rabelaisian *jeu d'esprit*, a holiday from commitment and a wasted opportunity, for Okot either refuses to see, or will not examine, the agonies of one of Africa's most distressing human problems. What is offered is a fleshly revel designed to annoy Sunday School teachers.

But *Song of Prisoner* is a different matter. Not only is the subject weighty, its treatment tells us so. Here is a cause to rival Lawino's and the poet applies all his strength to support it. The theme of post-colonial disenchantment, hovering in the background of *Lawino* and briefly raised near the close of *Ocol*, now gets undisturbed attention. The anger of the poor, who helped to win freedom only to be beaten down by the violence and the trickery of the new élite, is the theme of Okot's angriest poem. The theme is not new, for many writers have explored it since the early 1960s. Okot's introductory paraphernalia (the poem is dedicated to Patrice Lumumba) suggests a generalised satire, which on scrutiny, however, turns out to be a work rooted firmly in recent East African history. The poem in fact appears to have been inspired not so much by Lumumba's imprisonment and death in Zaire as by the shooting of Tom Mboya in Kenya.

A man is in jail. He has no name, which makes him at once pathetic and symbolic. He is married with children and comes from the village of a minority tribe who inhabit the shores of a lake. Once a runner, hunter, and boxer, he sees himself now as a 'young tree' burnt out by the fires of Uhuru. He played a part in the struggle for Independence, though his precise role is not specified, and the post-Uhuru period finds him speaking up for the rural poor, neglected minorities, and the unemployed. His outraged sense of justice has provoked him to assassinate a leading political figure, someone he identifies with the post-colonial conspiracy to grind the poor and enrich the elite. For this he has been arrested and beaten, and now lies cold and hungry on a cell floor with no hope of justice from his captors.

The poem gives us a powerful account of the conditions, man-oeuvres, and trickery which pushed the prisoner to his act of despera-tion. His account is personal but meant at every point to record the suffering of a whole class of people, including not only minority tribes but even the neglected among the governing group. Like *Lawino*, this is another dramatic monologue; and the court-room feel of the first poem returns as the prisoner justifies himself to various auditors, including the jailer (to whom he refers throughout as Brother), a judge before whom he will appear, and the reader who, though not addressed directly, listens as the prisoner sends his litany of woes echoing round his cell. The whole poem becomes a plea at the bar of humanity. The accused won't admit guilt for the murder of the politician, but confesses to other crimes, such as impotence within the new order, deafness, blindness, fear, joblessness, landlessness, sickness, orphandom, and hatred of those who exploit the poor.

In a sense the poem is misnamed, for this is a song not of one prisoner but, as it turns out, of two; for in addition to the main voice there is heard in a section ironically styled 'Voice of a Dove', a quite different one. This is apparently a device to drive home some of the arguments the main prisoner is raising and also to impose a measure of symmetry on the plot. The second voice belongs to a prisoner who has also committed assassination; but where the first has killed a leading member of the ruling group, the second appears to have shot a minority leader. As prisoners before the law, they are both, in theory, equal; their crimes are similar, their rationales almost identical. Their prospects therefore should be equally bright or gloomy. But it is precisely the poet's point that their situations are no more alike than a scaffold and a bed of roses. The first prisoner, badly beaten and bleeding, will certainly hang. The second has been arrested only to create a legal charade. He is well treated in jail and secure in the knowledge that the ruling group, who are his brothers, will ensure his release. To further scar the face of justice, this man will go free into the luxuries of a new life bought with the money powerful men have paid for his crime. He can relax in his cell and dream of a large farm, a rural haven where he and his family will never want again, where all past hardship will be erased in an era of peace, comfort, and plenty.

The opening section, which shows a further tightening of Okot's style, reveals the prisoner suffering in his cell. Discreet alliteration and vowel harmony produce a chilling sense of the man's discomfort:

> She kisses
> My bosom
> My neck
> My belly button
> My back
> My buttocks
> And shoots freezing bullets
> Through my bones[12]

55

The prisoner is rigid with anger, his throat burns, his heart is riddled 'With the arrows/Of despair'; he is 'drowning/In the deep Lake of hatred'. Bruised and bleeding, he asks the jailer why he stooped to such depths of brutality against a man so poor and

> Weak
> Hungry like an empty tomb,
> A young tree
> Burnt out
> By the fierce wild fire
> Of Uhuru.

He then turns to the imaginary judge and asks (16):

> Your Honour
> Why do they beat me
> With their clubs
> And tie my hands
> And feet
> With this rope?
> Why do they box
> And slap me?
> ... ... ...
> Why do they
> Punish me
> Before I plead
> Or am found
> Guilty?

During the prisoner's vigil, his imagination takes flight and conjures pictures of the world outside, a vein of extramural images and narrative which are an important part of the poem's structure. This has several functions. First, it provides a link with events which have brought the prisoner to jail. Secondly, it is the natural reflection of a man denied his liberty and the mind's way of mitigating the horrors of prison. It lets the soul fly beyond the walls to scenes and people conjured by memory and imagination, thus keeping the prisoner anchored in sanity. While he feels the freezing floor, his captors' blows, and the cell's drabness, he can vicariously enjoy the warmth and love of life in the home with his family and friends. It recalls similar flights in the prison verse of Wilde and Brutus, or the rural Ireland with roses blowing in the rain that O'Casey slips into the dreams of the Dublin poor. Insets of this sort also provide, in a rather Romantic way, a moral norm against which inhuman behaviour can be judged. Finally, unrelieved focus on a prison cell would rapidly become an artistic liability, risking the attention and sympathy of the audience. It refreshes the reader to encounter scenes from rural life, especially when a poet points them as well as Okot. It is a relief, for example, after preceding horrors, to have section Six open with (49):

> A bird's song
> Breaks through the high ceiling,
> It is the ladybird
> Collecting nectar
> From the banana blossom
> And flying back
> To her nest.

But notice that the inset also suggests a level of freedom in nature which some of the poem's human representatives cannot begin to match. The insets, however, cannot all be Arcadian and near the start especially, when Okot is at pains to draw the full dimensions of the prisoner's plight, they are dark with horror (17):

> My children howl
> like mad dogs,
> A lullaby is stuck
> In their mother's throat.
> My father
> Is asleep
> In the stomach
> Of the earth
> Unseeing
> Unhearing
> Undreaming.
>
> Listen to the footsteps
> Of the wizard
> Dancing on my father's
> Grave.

Similar pictures are scattered throughout the second section, 'Wounded Crocodile', whose atmosphere has the latent force of a tornado. A Chief's dog is heard barking, and the prisoner, echoing a standard anti-colonial taunt, asks how much meat and milk the animals of the élite get daily. He then asks if we have seen 'The mosquito legs' of his starving children, their pot bellies and red hair. His family are glimpsed at home awaiting a daily meal that lacks both meat and milk, and which today will not come at all.

Their plight mingles with their father's to produce deep pathos in this section. The prisoner is haunted by their cries; his brain is battered by the laments of his mother and sister until he feels driven across the borders of madness:

> I plead insanity,
> I am
> Mad,
> Can't you see?

Meanwhile nature itself seems affected by his plight. Night creatures reject their normal behaviour and time itself slows up as the section sputters to a close (24):

> The owls
> Keep silence,
> Cocks refuse to crow,
> Bats clap their wings
> Against the black mud
> Of the night
> In which
> The eagle
> Of time
> Is stuck!
>
> And I
> Trembling,
> Hungry,
> Mad,
> Sit,
> Spit,
> Shit,
> Hate,
> Wait...

The brooding atmosphere continues in section three as the poet describes the prisoner's helplessness before the steely might of the

élite. A contrast is drawn between the rural world and a central
government that will brook no opposition. The verse carries images
of carnivores, corpses, and shadows. One of the poem's finest sections,
there is perfect harmony between message and poetic strategy. While
a brutal interrogation proceeds, the prisoner sees his mother screaming her sorrow at a black sky and his sister who

> . . .mumbles a dirge
> And rolls herself
> In the dust.

He hears an alarm raised in the village, a sign that the peasant order
is girding itself to help him. Drums and horns sound forth; clansmen
gather with sword and spear. But it is a futile gesture, meaningless
in a world of machine guns, tanks, and bombers. It is part of the poet's
aim to show not simply how the peasants have been neglected, but how
enfeebled they are in terms of military might and political power. The
verse here makes the point sharply. The clansmen's swords and spears

> Embrace the faint moonlight
> And dance like butterflies
> Over the corpse
> Of a rat.

Butterflies do not agree with moonlight; but with their innocence,
weakness, and lack of claws they make an excellent figure for a feeble,
decorative old order. The new age, according to the poet, is all
darkness, and here are creatures doomed scarcely to survive the
lengthening shadows of dusk. Subsequent imagery is in the same
mould, serving to point up both the futility of any attempt by the
prisoner's people to help and the basic weakness of the order they
represent. But their serious concern and ancient unity are fused in
an image which makes well the point about their impotence (31):

> The warriors
> Push the dark wind
> With their buffalo-hide shields. . .

There is a sense of close-ranked solidarity here, of shoulder-to-shoulder
energy and forward sweep. But it is an empty gesture, a tilt at the
wind, and soon both prisoner and warriors are subsumed under the
symbol of a sacrificial lamb torn to pieces by marauding carnivores
(31):

> Old hyenas
> Fight over the remains
> Of a lamb,
> They suck
> The eyeballs
> And tear painlessly
> At the tongue,
> Penis,
> Testicles...

Yet despite the peasant's impotence, the central power will take no risks. Hence the ludicrous despatch of tanks, which, in a mocking echo of Conrad's colonial warship (and with all the suggestions of a people's resilience that go with it), they ring the village, flatten the crops, and, like 'steel rhinoceroses', sneeze 'molten lead' into grass-thatched huts. Aircraft roar overhead to complete from the sky what tanks could hardly fail to do on the ground. Hence a renewed emphasis now on the prisoner's smallness. Before the ruling power he stands and declares (33):

> I am a mere
> Pygmy
> Before your
> Uniformed Power
> Which towers like
> Mount Elgon
> And covers the Land
> With its dark shadow.

He is an insect trapped between an elephant's toes, an earthworm grovelling in the mud, and, lower still:

> The wet dung
> Of a chicken
> On the floor!

The village world lies smashed and defeated in section four, a bloody fulfilment of the Ocolian apocalypse. The tanks and bombers of central government have done their work, leaving behind an obscene display of their might (35):

> The setting sun
> Pours blazing oil
> Into the Lake,

60

The water is covered
With the blood
Of dying hippos,
Crocodiles, fish
And fishermen...

But the poem now turns to an attack on tribalism and nepotism. The prisoner addresses his father, reviling him for not marrying well. If only he had eloped with a girl from the 'Right Clan', all this pain would have been avoided. The prisoner here is morally at his nadir, for pain has throttled his idealism and brought him as low as his jailers. But for an accident of birth, he too would have been comfortable and well-fed. There is an echo of Taban Lo Liyong's *Meditations in Limbo* in Okot's lines:

You
My old man
Rotting in the earth
What an idiot
you were!

For failing to guarantee his son's birth into the Right Clan, the father receives a most unfilial threat. Committing enough sin now to get himself a haunting all the way to eternity, the prisoner shouts:

Listen
You fool,
When I get out
Of this hell,
I will exhume your bones
And hang you
By the neck...

Nor is this all, for he will dig up his father's parents too and make a bonfire of their bones.

The raw-nerved intensity of Section Three returns in 'Sacred Rock', a section where we share the prisoner's indignation as he sees a Mercedes Benz sliding through the dark carrying one of the élite to seduce his wife. Few barbarities could stoke the boilers of hatred better than this and the sense of chained fury frantic to burst its fetters grows dramatically. We hear the limousine sliding through the night, singing its song of luxury to the countryside (43):

> A black Benz
> Slithers smoothly
> Through the black night
> Like the water snake
> Into the Nile

But so vile is its mission that nature itself opposes its advance:

> The grasses on
> The pathway
> Hiss in protest,
> The shrubs scratch
> Its ribs
> With their nails,
> Foxes hit the windscreens
> With their laughter,
> Dogs whine
> And sharpen their teeth...

But the car sweeps on to its destination and as our bourgeois villain enjoys the prisoner's wife, hiding his 'shameless face' between her breasts, the verse surges to a climax with the Prisoner's fury breaking loose (45):

> My anger explodes
> Like a grenade,
> And destroys like a hurricane,
> My jealousy is darker
> Than the coming storm
> And madder than thunder...
> Cut off this rope,
> Free my hands and feet,
> I want to chase
> The thief,
> I will smell him out
> And smear the road
> With his brain...

The verse reflects a violent sense of the Prisoner's passion as he spits out his crude deluge of hatred (46):

> His spittle covers me
> Like dew

And makes me stink
Like gonorrhoea
He wipes his arse
On my head
And plucks off
All my feathers...

In section six the prisoner pleads sickness and says he is a victim of all his society's diseases. Then, in lines which smother those not-so-old dreams of negritude, he cries that he is (50):

Crippled by the cancer
Of Uhuru
Far worse than
The yaws of
Colonialism,
The walls of hopelessness
Surround me completely

The cancer of Uhuru is tribalism which causes unjust distribution of wealth, rule by a clique, and development aid channelled into cities while the villages rot in neglect. Tribalism has caused the despair, the utter hopelessness, of the Prisoner's family and clan. In a newly liberated nation, brother already scorns brother as foreigner and fool (52):

They call me
A foreign bastard,
They describe my Clansmen
As fools and weaklings,
Can you hear them saying
That my clan
Will never rise to Power,
And I will die in deep poverty
And my children
Will become thieves?

In 'Voice of a Dove', a new voice is heard, vibrant with hope and confidence. Is this a new prisoner? If so, there is no anouncement of his arrival: we have not been told he will be coming. Indeed, it might be that Okot intends no new voice at all, but only the first voice continuing in a different strain. Perhaps we are meant to see the

63

prisoner as some vaguely composite figure like Eliot's Sweeney or else as a man who has lost his mind under pressure and is now, like some Jacobean madman, conjuring a perfect reversal of his situation – what *would have been* had he belonged to the Right Clan. There is much manufactured mist here, doubtless because Okot is coming close to the nerve of recent East African history, and at this point the poet surrenders a clarity which is one of his major assets. While all three interpretations – new man, composite old man, or old man dreaming in madness – make the point Okot is after, let us conveniently imagine that a new prisoner has arrived.

It appears that, as a hireling of the ruling group, he has just assassinated the leader of a minority tribe. His conditions under arrest state afresh the injustice which is the poem's central theme, for while basic features remain constant – a prisoner, a cell, wife and children at home, the mind flying beyond the walls – the drift is entirely changed. Prison and judicial prospects hold no terror for this man. Word of his arrest, he says, should be 'great news' for his wife and family. The opening vignette of a rural scene with the *lagut* bird carrying grass to the thorn bush, where she will nest and bring forth her young, is not sketched as a contrast to the horrors of prison; nor has it the ring of a desperate bid to stave off madness. It projects instead tangible post-prison rewards this man will enjoy when he spends the money his hirers have paid him. The *lagut* bird's nest prefigures his own, which is a thousand-acre farm in a fertile valley. This is no yearned-for gift, the object of speculation in the grammatical moods of doubt, but an actual purchase already made. 'I have bought/A farm' he says, addressing his wife, 'Your house stands/On the crest/Of a small hill. Your bed is soft/Like the voice of a dove'. The only future tense used is a firm indicative in the middle of this Arcadian sketch (60):

> The crested cranes
> Dance love dances
> By the stream
> That flows gently
> Through our garden,
> Our children will play
> And swim in the stream
> And hook fish
> For the afternoon meal...

There is no *might* or *could play* here, but only a definite *will play*, which demonstrates the supreme confidence that he will escape the rope and

go free to his rewards. He has earlier stated his position quite baldly
(59):

> I will not be hanged,
> I will plead
> Not guilty,
> The best lawyers
> Will defend me,
> Our black nationalist judges
> And those who hired me
> Will set me
> Free...

The point is clear: for the right kind of prisoner there is one law, for
the member of a minority tribe another.

By section Eleven, Okot has escaped a tight situation, the mist melts,
and we see again the main path of the poem. A familiar voice is heard
pursuing a familiar line of complaint. The prisoner is demanding
release, for he wants to tell the world's news agencies that the light
of Uhuru has gone out, that ordinary men are not free when walled
in by fear and suspicion. His mind carries him again into the countryside as he yearns to taste anew the joys of fresh air and freedom. These
are lines of a relaxed easy sensuousness, romantic balm for the wounds
of jail (91):

> I want to wake up early
> Before the morning birds
> Begin to sing
> And swim in the naked air
> Of the dying night
> ... ... ...
> I want to sleep
> With the sand
> At the sea shore
> And expose my belly
> To the spears of the sun
> And swallow the boiling air.

One of the moral strengths of *Song of Prisoner* is that it does not
stagnate in mere passionate protest but rises to an affirmation of
human hope. After an epic litany of woes, the poet transcends the
negative and purely local and sends the prisoner's thoughts soaring
beyond East Africa and out round the globe. In a sort of Ninth-

*Developments in verse*

Symphony choric ending, the prisoner sings an ode to joy, a hymn
to affirm the brotherhood of men against the petty sordidness of the
local scene. He wants to join the great Dance of Humanity, to sing
wild songs to the beauty of creation. He would hold hands with Arab
and Israeli, sword dance with a Russian, sing German beer-songs,
dance with colonialist and capitalist, hear the Eskimo play his 'snowy
song', and dance his 'whaley rhythm'.

### Okello Oculi

...So I wrote and I must say at the time, the first nonsense I wrote
was immediately after *Song of Lawino* by Okot. *Song of Lawino*
touched exactly that nerve which we had been arguing. The
response of Kampala was so spontaneous that we thought we
were on the right side.... He [Okot] confirmed this yearning we
had for self-assertion, not only self in terms of ourselves, but self
in the collective sense, what we felt was the African sense of
assertion...

For me at the time my argument was: 'why can't I be a disciple
of Okot? I'm not going to have any sense of apology about
writing, especially in the way Okot wrote, in verse form and
having one character singing all the way. I decided that I might
as well be an interesting disciple in the sense of adding something
new, hence the structure of *Orphan* with so many characters
running around looking at this one character...

Somebody for generations worked to maintain that society that
gave the artist birth. I think his first allegiance, his first sense of
responsibility, is to that society, to play his own part. That's his
gratitude... It would appear to me that the link between the artist
and society – it's primordial. It is so biological that I do not see
the artist suddenly jumping up and looking at himself as somebody who is somehow aloof from the problems of a particular
society.[13]

Okello Oculi's interview with Marti Mueller and Laura Tanna is one
of the better items in Killam's *African Writers on African Writing*. Oculi's
candour and modesty ensure that he will reveal much about his vision,
his influences, and his image of himself as a writer. When poets (inside
Africa and out) take themselves so seriously and scholarship wears so
often a furrowed brow and unsmiling eyes, it is refreshing to come

across a man who can call his work 'nonsense', laugh at Shelley's exaltation of poets, and blithely swear ignorance of what verse really is. A warm generosity comes through also; Oculi registers his gratitude to the society which produced him, and acknowledges an obligation to help with its problems if he can. He is also charitable towards his colleagues and warmly acknowledges Okot p'Bitek as his master. And when, elsewhere in the interview, Oculi says he's a disciple of Okot and not of Shakespeare, Lawrence, or Pope, he is testifying to the new independence of African writing becoming evident everywhere. Born in 1942, Oculi comes from the Lango people, a group closely related to the Acholi and the Luo. He read Political Science at Makerere and then worked as a journalist for Uganda's newspaper *The People*.

*Song of Lawino* appeared in 1966, and *Orphan*, Oculi's imitation, in 1968. But this is not simply another *Lawino* under a different signature. An important truth to grasp about Oculi, even in the face of his modest disclaimers, is that he is a strong-willed, independent writer, who might not even appreciate the range and potential of his own talent. He is a natural poet, in the sense that his response to life seems spontaneously to take a metaphoric form; and his declared ability to 'think in images' suggests a reason for the highly visual quality of his work.

Oculi's mind is either more complex or more cluttered than Okot's. The blend of image and association that informs his verse, its tight, teeming quality, and the energy that heaves in every line, suggest a complicated vision, as if existence for Oculi is more chaotic than his colleagues find it and must be recorded like that. Less kindly, one might suggest that his verse lacks the artistic restraint necessary to capture the deep simplicity of his master's songs. Whatever the truth, it is clear that while Oculi has chosen to imitate Okot's form – indeed is sparked into poetic life by it – what he has poured into the borrowed mould is a highly personal substance. It is not simply that Oculi has introduced a whole cast of figures to comment on his hero's situation, thus marking an attempt to develop his inherited form. The very texture of the verse, its bone and tissue, is new. A cluster of passages written in frank imitation of Okot are rare exceptions to the claim that Oculi, while writing in the *Song* tradition, has produced a work of distinct originality.

Oculi does not call *Orphan* a song but a 'village Opera'. Each character, he says, 'performs a drama' for the orphan boy and 'all of them with the orphan boy perform for you and me'. It is no reflection on the poem to say that Oculi's description is neither accurate nor

67

helpful, for he is notoriously diffident about the niceties of definition; but the word 'opera' is misleading, whether seen in *Fidelio* terms or as an East African echo of a Yoruba art form. *Orphan* is less static than *Lawino*, and the inclusion of characters extra to the central singer is part of the dynamic mode Oculi is trying for. But it is wrong to say that these figures each perform 'a drama', for they offer little more than set speeches or sermons. There is a certain sense of theatre, as there is in all the songs, and no doubt each speaker with gestures and verbal play can create a lively impression. But there is no dialogue, no plot, little hint of character inter-action, and no sense of mimesis.

After a prologue describing the basic situation of a boy left an orphan at 'cross-paths', and therefore suffering isolation (the key word in the text), the following appear and give their views: the Grand-mother of Okello's Father's clan; his mother's uncle; the village gossip; a village elder; a woman whose husband is of Okello's clan; an agemate of Okello; Okello's stepmother; a man; Okello's milk sister; and Okello's father. Whether blood relatives or close neighbours, they all provide a picture of the past and a context for the painful present. Some views are close and subjective, others coolly distant; but together they amply reflect on the orphan and his fate. There is, however, no variety of voice, for all these figures use the *persona's* register. It is the narrator's voice we hear, his complaint and his vocabulary. At least on the evidence of *Orphan*, Oculi has not yet acquired the knack of shaping varied speech patterns for varied characters.

Isolation and loneliness provide the poem's central theme, echoing a lament heard throughout modern African literature. In prose and verse, in every writer of stature, the same figure recurs: a lonely child, man, or woman who has fallen through the once secure net of tradi-tional society, a person without the certainties of the old order who flounders hopelessly on modern waters. Jagua Nana in Lagos, Obi returning from England, Laye's African Child, Armah's teacher, Nicol's judge's son, Kane's Samba, the figures of Kibera and Kahiga, Ogot, Sutherland, Aidoo, Palangyo, and Clark – their plight is the same: they are lonely people, shocked at a situation that is new.

As a theme, then, all this is commonplace, and the socio-economic arguments explaining it have been crossing the debating floors for years. Where Oculi adds freshness is in his refusal to see the problem in merely socio-economic terms, though he freely accepts the value of that approach. He is reluctant to do the economist's job and talk about cash economies; he refuses to shoulder the sociologist's burden and discuss population drift. Instead, choosing a mode alien to the world of graph and computer, he merely asserts that the colonial experience *somehow* killed that central source of pride and dignity without which human growth must die. This source, significantly, is personified as the orphan's Mother, by which one must also understand some such broad symbol as Mother Africa. Hence one of the closing sections of the poem (98):

Orphan,
Humanness and morals were known and practised
Before you began life;
Tenderness, humility and decency
By man to man in honour of manness;
All are burnt on the altars of Isolation
And on the worship grounds of aggressive
Selfishness, when a mother dies.
The agents of Europe knew this
And killed our Mother first and did all
To expel her spirit to the rough skies.[14]

This is Oculi's way of expressing the human and moral change which historic event incurs. Hence too the final exhortation, when Okello's father, after urging him to resurrect the ancestors' 'manness worship cult', closes the poem on this same symbolic note (101):

Enthrone the spirit of your mother
In the new homestead,
And let the world feel
The arrogant boast of her milk,
Stubborn woman in her
Singing of the fertility of her womb through you!

Orphan is the lost son of this symbolic figure. In him the new Africa is at a crossroads, confused and lonely in search of its departed mother.

All this might sound like an East African exercise in negritude. But Oculi possesses at once a humility and astuteness which prevent his using frayed hand-me-downs still traded in the market. To pillory European involvement as the major cause of the present problems is well enough; but it remains a commonplace, even when modestly redeemed by the idea of a throttled Mother life-symbol. *Orphan* shows Oculi seeking a kind of truth rooted in the universals of the human condition rather than in historic accident. Hence, far from simply laying the blame on Europe, or the 'false starters' as he calls the new elite, or 'the degreed wizards and head hunters/with Grand titles', who are in the same group, he accepts loneliness and isolation as a constant of the human condition.[15] This partly explains the existential overtones of so much comment from the orphan's comforters. In reply to a question from Marti Mueller attempting to link *Orphan*'s loneliness with the poet's stay in the West, Oculi replied that man is basically lonely and isolated, and that a good deal of culture is simply designed 'to make people feel that this isolation is not there'. From his position on the fringes of the traditional world, Oculi has looked back and felt with shrinking horror that even the solidarity and community of that world were more social expedient than basic reality. As he observes, 'Even twins get born differently'. Faced with the bleakness of human isolation, society tries to counter it with the idea of love or clanship. 'These', says Oculi, 'are an attempt to create an ideology that tries to get hold of this isolation and contain it.' But he feels that Western society (from which he would presumably exclude areas such as rural Spain, Italy, Portugal, and Ireland), has now lurched to an extreme, sanctifying the idea of isolation and using it as a principle of social organisation. 'People are baptized in it', he says, and capitalism is a manifestation of it.

Yet the socio-political reasons for Africa's orphandom are not neglected either and provide a counterpoint to Oculi's more timeless concerns. He cites Kenya as possessing many 'orphans' quite simply because colonialism there meant land-dispossession. When the white man comes and drives a peasant off his land, the settler's victory (itself a monument to the individualism or 'isolation' which western culture has sanctioned) 'breeds an orphan'. But the orphan problem has not been cured by independence. The masses are still not a party to decision-making because they are kept out by someone infected with the western bug of isolationism, who says, 'They're not part of me. I am alone. I am isolated from the peasant. I am educated and have wealth. I am more intelligent...' It is against a background of this sort, part socio-political, part morally poetic, that *Orphan* must be read. And Oculi's humble vision is strongly stamped on his poem. This is no simple, cut-and-dry reaction to experience but one whose honest doubt is mirrored by a complexity and untidiness in the verse. It is as if Oculi is saying, 'Life is not so simple and symmetrical as you think. It's a strange entangled affair and neat orderly verse won't reflect it.'

The style of *Orphan*, then, is at once more tortuous than any poem of the Song school so far. Okot's crisp verse with its polished surface, its lines just long enough and no more, its images always apt and lucid, its custom-built stanzas essential to the total design, its supreme simplicity of language – all this yields to a slower, dense kind of verse, a ramshackle vehicle that bumps and falters and too often veers towards side-lanes instead of facing straight down the highway; a verse that seems indifferent whether its lines be long or short, its punctuation helpful or mystifying, its stanzas shaped or shapeless, its images clear or cloudy; a verse which suggests that its maker has little concern for those questions of audience and rhetoric so skilfully handled in the work of Okot p'Bitek.

Yet Oculi's verse has its strengths and one of these is its highly metaphoric nature, at once the Oculian hallmark and a reason for his obscurity. Where Okot offers a plain medium with figurative language, as it were, applied from without, Oculi's verse seems to be metaphoric at its core. Image and metaphor erupt from within, like a kernel cracking its shell. But Oculi, alas, often loses interest as soon as the figure's basic energy is released. There is inadequate attention to what happens once the seed of metaphor has been quickened; and if the blossoming details do not seem to add much to the poetic effects he is after, if in their eruption they destroy the outer shell of his verse, then Oculi doesn't mind. The heart of the matter is living and beyond that he cares not.

A similar unconcern is evident elsewhere. Oculi doesn't distress himself over line length, appropriate rhythms, or the importance of keeping images unclouded. The rhythms jerk awkwardly as if beyond control with Oculi seeming to care only that his metaphors are on the boil. And caring too about another quality he admires and cultivates: energy. Who would doubt that Oculi ranks among Africa's most energetic poets? He is a poetic heavyweight with massive punching power and a savage aggression that he applies to the received forms of the language.

It is as if Oculi were embarrassed over the niceties of verse: care for the minutiae of stress, balance, and organisation. Not for him the *labor limae* of revision and more revision. The pots of boiling metaphor spill over where they will, causing too often a confused effect where figure and allusion fight each other, their independence compromised, their potential and actual strength diminished, their singularity and vividness smoked-round by vague language or inept jargon.

71

*Orphan's* opening lines illustrate some of the poet's typical strengths and faults (11):

> The woman whose breasts I sucked
> Is gone to the worms!
> Before we talked she went with the milk,
> Cushion soothe fill of soft bellies,
> Balm of unspoken yearn in screaming lips.
> Born to earliness's helplessness
> I found they had taken her woman to the soils.
> I am only her absent existence,
> Memory's lubricant
> Weighted under loneliness's gall pool,
> And soaked in the dew of tongues free now
> In her goneness,
> Only uncertain in dreams
> And in debts still in the nursing of forgetful minds.
> The woman whose tender care,
> Like the termites that come when the hens
> Have wiped their beaks for the day,
> I missed,
> Left me to the whims of kites' appetites
> While she eloped with the Wild Cat.
> Deaf to my screams of goodbye unintended,
> She left me to the cuddle of loneliness.

The fierce fleshly opening, screamed with pain and protest, is Oculi at his best. Its violent birth-death yoking, so that the raw sucking of breasts blends with the earthy horror of those same glands being sucked and eaten by the worms, carries remarkable power. The smell of mortality and the ring of timeless statement are underpinned by a strong rough rhythm. The third line also possesses the virtues of clarity, concreteness, and colloquial rhythm: 'Before we talked she went with the milk'. Oculi works well at this elemental level; and the passage contains further good items too, each of them a reminder of Oculi's natural poeticity. 'Cushion soothe fill of soft bellies' is clever and apt; so is 'Memory's lubricant'. The termites coming 'when the hens/Have wiped their beaks for the day' strikes very sharply and 'She left me to the cuddle of loneliness' shows how effectively Oculi can blend the tactual and the abstract.

But there is much else in this stanza, not all of it quite so fine. The

concreteness of the opening lines gets forgotten and their homespun
mode discarded as though an embarrassment – as though Oculi loses
his nerve and leaps to a more scholarly pitch. So we meet lines that
hide vividness behind screens of verbiage. The abstract takes over and
orphan begins talking like a befuddled Aquinas or an African Talcott
Parsons. 'Earliness's helplessness' is not a success; neither is 'In her
goneness' or 'debts still in the nursing of forgetful minds'. When the
tactual blends with the abstract, there is potential for depth and power.
There are, for example, the lines:

> I am only her absent existence,
> Memory's lubricant
> Weighted under loneliness's gall pool.

These almost succeed and in their metaphoric complexity show how
remote the typical Oculian mode is from Okot's; but they fail, I think,
because their meaning within the poetic context is not immediately
clear. Where this fusion of the tactual and abstract does work is in the
closing line where the meaning is immediately apparent because the
image is plain and unclouded:

> She left me to the cuddle of loneliness

This is also good because it evokes the poignancy of the situation.
Orphan's need for the physical reassurance of touch, of warm
motherly comfort, is answered by the cold abstract embrace of 'loneliness'. But such strokes are constantly spoilt by the vague or the inert,
leaving us with a feeling that a distinguished poem – distinguished in
substance and form – lies just below the surface. If only Oculi would
return to *Orphan* later, carefully revise it, shake out the dross, sharpen
each image, polish each line, check all rhythms, attend to punctuation
...But Oculi would scorn the idea.

The clouding effects in Oculi's style mean that much of *Orphan* (it
improves markedly towards the end), lacks the quality of clear exposi-
tion. The cluttered style brings *Orphan* closer to Okigbo than it is to
Okot, Oculi's professed model. Much less 'popular' than Okot's verse,
the average reader must find *Orphan* hopelessly obscure. Oculi is
obviously sincere in his social commitment and genuine in his desire
to address his people; yet he chooses a dense, elliptical mode that even
critics and students find difficult. Style and social aim, therefore, do
not meet harmoniously in *Orphan*. Indeed they do not meet at all.

Yet fitful flashes of genius somehow carry us through. If Oculi's romantic unreliability often precludes lucidity and smoothness, it holds out at least the hope of surprise, of graces snatched beyond the reach of art. And the poem is indeed replete with touches that put Oculi firmly among the original poetic talents of modern Africa. In the opening section, for example, he talks about the orphan's mother's birth pangs. She suffers, he says (12):

> Under insults of terrored midnight nerves
> And clang yells of tingling metals
> To pull her out of labour's depths
> And scream me into existence...

The agonising 'scream' in the last line, stamping the hallmark of pain on the moment of birth, strikes a keynote for the whole poem; and the excerpt also shows how Oculi can invest his verse with a sense of muscular movement and make sound an echo of sense. In the same section the Old Man speaks to the infant Okello, explaining that his birth signifies the return of ancestors. He closes his comments with the blunt command:

> Okello, suck your mother – grow up to bury us!

Readers, both African and alien, might feel that this raw language is not at all the register of respectable middle-class poetry. Wordsworth and Coleridge, who promised common language in their verse, never uttered anything so blunt. There are English parallels, though much further back; for what Eliot said about Metaphysical poets and Elizabethan/Jacobean dramatists often seems fitting for Oculi: 'They possessed a mechanism of sensibility which could devour any kind of experience' and showed 'a direct sensuous apprehension of thought'. Notice too the poet's pushing together once more of the ideas of birth and death, his juxtaposition in a short line of the two major facts of human existence. Apart from creating an effect of compression, this brief imperative represents a community's whole vision of life; for the old man is expressing a basic idea of his people, that man is born to grow, procreate, bury his elders, and be buried by his own offspring. This is a nine-word sketch, with an aptly built-in rise and fall, of a community that makes up the world of the village.

Okello's Mother leaves him an orphan at birth, and the idea of a child being left defenceless to face the unknown (unthinkable in real traditional society) is expressed with power:

74

> She left my screams to frighten nibbling
> Rats under bushes

where the threat posed by the nibbling vermin, which represent a hostile future, is the more sinister because felt to be stealing malevolently in. She went 'jostled away from the echoes of the questions/In my screams', which is a nice capturing of death's rough indifference. And then she left her son

> To face alone
> The darkness hidden behind the glare of
> The mid-day sunshine.

At such moments one feels the force of Oculi's natural talent. That they should be commonly followed by lines such as these from the grandmother

> Real in the reality of unreality
> And lasting in unlastingness

is simply part of the price paid for the occasional delights the poet serves up.

Good writing is also plentiful in the section called 'Village Elder', where Oculi uses gnomic material with its own form, rhythm, and 'truth'. An old man lectures Okello on a familiar strain of African stoicism. Life is hard, but therein lies its challenge. Those who reject hardship as a chance for growth remain humanly stunted. The old man emphasises too the idea that all men are doomed to a degree of loneliness and isolation. This is part of his cold gnomic consolation, and a feeling that he has tested his views in the fire of experience saves his words from sententiousness. Using an extended metaphor, he explains his previous lack of communication with the boy (27):

> I do not hear your wails;
> The sap flow in the tree trunk
> Bypasses the withering branch,
> And the flamboyant bloom in the flowers
> Unnotices the thirst to death
> Of a leaf.

His way of describing how one creature finds it hard to feel another's suffering is expressed in a further image of fine casualness:

75

*Developments in verse*

> The courting grasshopper chirps in a sun bath
> Oblivious to the pangs in the body
> Of a vagabond dog dragging along
> Against the weight of creeping rot in a limb.

But it is inept to have the old man speak first in this rustic way and then suddenly shift to the register of philosophy, as he does now. We are all, he says, 'Trapped within the walls of localised awareness' – which is perhaps true, but hardly a village elder's way of saying so. Nor is it convincing to have him explain nature's indifference by saying that we

> All move within unbridged selves
> And the ethic of indifference accepted in
> Resigned imitation.

This curious mixture of the earthy and the socio-scientific spoils an otherwise fine section of the poem. And yet, in typical fashion, such lapses might be followed at once by a stroke of sheer brilliance; perhaps an image struck off with lofty ease or a remark cast in a mould perfectly suited to the speaker's status and background. Here the old man suddenly refers to

> The melancholy chat of flesh in the cooking pot

where the fate of the organic world is portrayed in fine grisly fashion. Ancestors' bodies buried in the homestead carry the same reminders:

> The disposed-of bones in the homestead,
> Scattered in a jumble, question the fate of
> The flesh that once walled their unity
> And sing the credo of the final isolation...

which is well enough except for the liturgical metaphor that ends it. In the meantime, everyone knows that

> Happiness is no kinsman
> No twin brother to share a termite's head with.
> They know suffering is life's
> Smile in the dark.

The old man ends his sermon on a strong existentialist note, urging Okello to

> Learn the alphabet of life,
> That we are born with the indelible

Sin of Isolated Selves,
To remain perpetual tourists
To each other
Along life's pathways!

Yet orphan must not lie passive before this truth. He must assert his right to life, his right to grow as an individual. Nothing should hold him back. Hence the old man's allusion to a song the living sing to the dead seeking freedom from the haunting of a disgruntled elder's ghost – a song affirming the pre-eminence of the living and the primacy of their desire to go about life's tasks with a light heart and a decent chance of success. The dead have their rights; the past has its claims; but the present and the living count most of all (41):

I have a right to be
I esteem myself highly
I came from the womb of a woman
Before the false morning glows
Before the reddening of the horizon
Not from a cursed marriage because
My mother did not elope
I must have come for a purpose, not
Of your making
I must have come for a reason higher
Than your usage, for you did not design
My coming and the world
It is no prerogative of yours
To reject or
Accept me
Leave me alone to live my turn.
For you
I exist.

Central to Oculi's style is his irreverent freedom with language. Unwilling to prostrate before the idols of conventional usage, he asserts a poet's right to resurrect old words and put them to new work, or strike off new creations of his own. This is not unhealthy, even if the record so far suggests more adventure than achievement. But too often his experiments appear unsightly or unnecessary. The negatives created by his freedom with the prefix *un-* are a case in point: sometimes they are successful, sometimes not. When Oculi writes in the Prologue, 'In the village the problem of unnoticing is still minimal',

77

the word 'unnoticing' slips by, paining neither eye nor ear. Even when it appears in a verbal form (27):

> And the flamboyant bloom in the flowers
> *Unnotices* the thirst to death
> Of a leaf

one feels little reason to object. Yet a similar effort with the verb *to look* doesn't succeed, as the following lines show:

> Present of racing to catch our inner selves
> Unlooking at the patchwork of modernity

It is also hard to see aesthetic reason in Oculi's fondness for inflicting plural forms on abstract nouns, as he does with *sleep* in 'Things of shame on her children in their/Half sleeps', or with *vigour* in 'Having returned with new *vigours* and/Ammunitions', though here it might be argued that the poet is trying to suggest vigour of different kinds. *Despise* is normally a verb and when Oculi makes it a noun the result is more daring than effective. Its appearance in the lines below merely prompts the thought that a shelfload of alternatives would have served him better:

> And a poor teacher shouts and terrorises
> Against the cold silent despise in the
> Eyes of pupils

Why not *scorn, contempt, hate, odium, loathing,* or *hostility,* to mention a few? But happier experiment can be seen in the use of *wizard* as a verb in 'She lies and wizards', in the rare use of the verbal form of *scream* in the powerful line 'And scream me into existence', and in some delightful play with *nativity* when he writes (55):

> All of them in the Exclusive Club
> Are allergic to my village simplicity,
> To my crude pride in myself and my *nativity.*

Presumably, if Oculi had wanted to convey the plain idea of *birth,* he would have used that word. 'Nativity' is good not simply because it rhymes with 'simplicity', but because it teasingly suggests a particular kind of birth, either one like Christ's or, more probable, one carrying all the colonial-psychological freight that the idea of 'native' has brought down to us. The poet's invention of *dejuiced,* used in the line 'Fur-coats and Limousines and dejuiced accents' has visual merit, but will be understood aurally as *deduced*, which is rather different. But the unusual form *coldened*, in 'As *coldened* hunters do when ill omen's spear/Passes them by in a narrow miss' is a very happy stroke of invention.

Oculi has not been well served by his editors. Indeed a marked feature of African writing so far has been the low level of its editing. When a script is handled in Europe or America, distance and cultural ignorance might well create such a weakness. But this can hardly hold for African publishers, where editors understand a broad range of cultural reference, and can more easily work with the author on cases of difficult interpretation. Editorially, Oculi's *Orphan* is as bad as it could be. There is little to excuse the following blunders:

> In uncoordinated excitements (59)
> Liquids that are with a fire that never die; (94)
> The labour of my ribs
> And of my freckled hands, were robbed (52)

where in addition to the word *were* being wrong, the comma before it makes no sense.

> When I leave this house
> And the men refuse.

is offered as a complete sentence, when it is clearly lacking a main clause.

> Without a drop of a grumble
> Breathe in,
> Latrine odours oozing out of a drunken husband (95)

This example shows how a single comma, at the end of the second line, has completely destroyed the sense of a comment, suggesting that the third line, which is meant to provide the object for the verb 'breathe' is really unrelated to that verb. In the following excerpt, a possessive pronoun causes damage (98):

> Europe's propaganda and onslaughts at
> My pride and core corroded my manness,
> While she gloated at success and
> Desecrated the sanctity of manness with
> Growing expertise and awarded degrees
> To *its* planners,
> And pet-named her guilt 'profits'.

This reads more or less clearly until we trip on 'its', a possessive pronoun unrelated to anything that has gone before. It cannot refer to Europe, since the feminine pronoun 'she' has already been used. It cannot refer to 'sanctity', 'manness', 'expertise', and 'degrees' since, presumably, none of these is being 'planned'. Poor editing has left the problem with the reader.

Oculi deserves better than this. A poet possessing such rich talent should be able to rely on the kind of careful editing and continuous criticism which will encourage his talent to blossom. Oculi's wild horse needs control and training. Its feats after such attention would, one imagines, be truly remarkable.

### Joseph Buruga

Oculi's *Orphan* appeared in 1968 as an acknowledged imitation of *Song of Lawino*. Joseph Buruga's *The Abandoned Hut* came a year later in 1969.[16] It would be fair to say that Buruga has been undervalued as a poet and when his poem first appeared little more than a polite yawn was heard. Wasn't it, after all, just another 'song'? Wasn't it yet another imitation? Didn't every young poet in East Africa have a similar piece ready? Hadn't it all become too familiar after *Lawino*, *Ocol*, and *Orphan*? Buruga suffered a further disadvantage. No one seemed to know who he was. Even at his Nairobi publishing house information was scarce. One editor thought he had seen poems by him published *somewhere* but couldn't be precise. Another had seen him at a conference but felt sure he was not there to read verse since everyone else was talking science. Yet a third, once at Makerere, thought he remembered him but couldn't recall the year. Buruga was not preceded by a reputation for involvement in a writers' workshop, nor had he caused much stir in the pages of *Penpoint, Darlite,* or *Nexus.*

It was all rather sad and *The Abandoned Hut* seemed like a grossly inauspicious title. Critics and reviewers left the work alone, preferring to wait for Okot's next song, discuss new poets like Angira, or read the latest outrage from Taban. *The Abandoned Hut*, while not a distinguished poem, is a better work than its reception suggested. Clearly Buruga has learnt from both Okot and Oculi, for his poem in many respects is much the same as theirs: the hut, the homestead representing tradition, has been deserted, as it was in *Lawino* and *Ocol*; the *persona*, Mediye, has been abandoned too, just like Lawino and Orphan. But particularly, Mediye has been abandoned by Basia, either a Kakwa version of Clementine, or a female version of Ocol, a modern, unprincipled woman, and a materialist. The formula thereafter is the same: Mediye descants on his traditional Kakwa life-style, lamenting how moderns like Basia have devalued it. Both mould and matter are then all too familiar. We are getting another *Lawino*, this time coming from the Uganda Kakwa, close neighbours of Okot's Acholi.

Yet the poem has its own merits. This is not Okot writing, nor Oculi, but a man with a quite different sensibility from theirs. Buruga is simply another poet working with the song form, in much the same way that European poets once clustered in admiring waves round the sonnet, using a common medium for personal and highly individual-ised expression. Buruga has a different ear from Okot and Oculi; his cultural formation, his education (in the sciences), his home back-ground, his vernacular language, are also different from theirs. So too is his moral sense and view of what is worth admiring or rejecting in the past. It is unwise, therefore, to dismiss Buruga's work as merely another song, just another *Lawino*, *Orphan*, or *Ocol*.

Mediye has been in love with Basia since childhood, when they tended cattle together by the River Oru and played games through the long warm afternoons. Basia, however, has now been trained in western ways and has slowly grown apart from her lover. Infected with the germs of materialism, she now despises Kakwa customs, scorns Mediye, his name, and his affection for tradition. She works in an office, throws herself gracelessly at the feet of every plutocrat who appears, has a most un-African horror of babies, takes the pill, wants a church wedding, loves cars, likes to be seen on the telephone, and loathes playing host to her extended family. She burns midnight oil, crawls the bars, and offers no hope whatever of Mediye winning her back to his vision of the world. In its way, this is a *Song of Lawino* in reverse.

The verse moves fast and appears at first to be as smoothly light as Okot's and to share the same clarity of image. But it does not withstand the same scrutiny as Okot's verse and what is revealed is the work not of a poor craftsman but of a very good apprentice. Where Buruga fails in *The Abandoned Hut* is not in his handling of verse – the basic skills are there ready to mature – but in his want of invention. His sense of the fitness of word and phrase, his ability to shape an image and organise an effective stanza, are all adequate. But his basic store of ideas, his ability constantly to create new situations or strike off original reflections – these seem just now to be weaker than in his fellow poets. There is not with Buruga, as there is with Okot or Oculi, that sense of a teeming imagination at work, of his being able to go on spinning, pouring, and conjuring ever-new ideas and images. His imagination is modestly fertile but not prolific. Poetically, he values restraint over freedom, correctness and polish over dynamism.

Buruga cares about line length, tempo, and the framing of a suitable verse paragraph as the basic unit of his poem. He seems to arrange that each stanza will carry a statement of event, an image for illustration, and a closing comment weighty enough to achieve a clinching effect. Typical is the following stanza describing how Basia lured Mediye into love and infatuation (9):

> Like the mirage
> To a thirsty man
> You made me believe
> There was water:
> When I drew near
> I found none.

Simile, statement, and closure – the pattern recurs roughly seventy times throughout the poem and both event and reflection are usually offered against a background of rich natural imagery.

The opening lines are an example of how Buruga, in imitation of oral practice, likes to illustrate a situation from a variety of angles (8):

> A woman
> An ordinary woman,
> That's what you are.
> Your enchanting smiles
> Lured me into a trap.
> Your looks
> Hypnotized me
> Like a mamba
> Ready to strike.
> I stood and stared
> I was bitten
> The venom spread rapidly
> I collapsed.
> Like the spirits of the river
> You bewitched me;
> Like the giant spider
> You knit a cobweb

I was caught.
I struggled,
Struggled hard
To free myself
But failed.

On it flows for several more stanzas, all of them in their own way
describing Mediye's abandonment. Her smiles trapped him; her looks,
mamba-like, first hypnotised, then poisoned him; she bewitched him
like the river spirits which drown people; she caught him fast in a
spider's web; he fell into the raging waters of a swollen river and was
swept away; he was thirsty and she lured him like a mirage in the
desert; like the cobra, she spat venom in his eye, blinding him; able
to reject him at any time, she waited until the planting season when
he was dizzy with thoughts of growth and procreation; she stabbed
him with the knife of love and the blood poured forth profusely; her
tongue cut him like a hunter's knife; and now he is desolate, like an
orphan. And so on. It is hard to object to this elaboration, for the basic
situation must appear worthy of the long lament which is to follow.

One can detect even here in the opening lines an occasional awkwardness, perhaps a beginner's hesitation; and punctuation (neglected
as trifling by too many African poets) does not display that creative
use it enjoys in the hands of an Okot or Soyinka. The virtues of clarity
and vividness, however, are sometimes compensations for otherwise
hesitant writing, and these Buruga often displays. But we don't simply
get verse whose visual qualities have received careful attention; Buruga
has a sensitive ear too, quite as sharp as Okot's, and he has toiled over
the verbal harmonies of his work. Take for example the following
evocation of the love-fraught childhood of Mediye and Basia (16):

Then our love was young
Like the new moon
On a cloudless night
Throwing its gentle rays
On the green grass
Of the rolling plains
Of the River Oru.

The effects of discreet alliteration, vowel harmony, colour and rhythm
combine to produce a stanza both 'visually' and aurally satisfying.
Nor does Buruga's skill equip him only for nostalgic indulgence: his

verse accommodates a variety of emotion and situation. For example
(17):

> I can still hear your oaths
> Like echoes in a forest;
> I can still hear them
> Like the wailings
> Of a hyena
> In a dark cave.

For an image designed to be aural rather than visual it matters little
whether the cave is 'dark' or light; but the adjective adds to the horror
Mediye now feels when he reflects on Basia's treachery. Oaths once
sweet to the ear, like music, have now modulated to gloomy, fearful
sounds, 'Like echoes in a forest' which frighten the lost, or 'the
wailings/Of a hyena' which threaten cruelty and cunning from the
darkness.

Too often, however, Buruga's care for detail fails him, and we find
imagery, superficially flawless, faulty when given close attention.
There is a slight blemish, for example, in the extended simile describing the impression Basia made on Mediye in the early years of their
love (16):

> Like the flower
> Of the water lily
> Opening in the morning
> As the gentle ripples
> Of water
> Flow past them,
> You brought hope
> Into a lonely heart
> You brought life
> Into a lifeless heart.

This is well enough, even when one has sensed near disaster in the
last line when 'lifeless desert' seemed in the wings waiting to destroy
the whole stanza. But the simile is not absolutely right, for it lacks that
final attention to detail necessary for perfect realisation. First, Basia
is not, surely, like the 'flower of the water lily' which opens when the
water flows by, as the stanza seems to suggest. She is really like the
water itself, which brings life to the lily, the symbol for Mediye's heart.
Furthermore, whatever the interpretation, *them* is obviously the wrong
pronoun for 'water lily'.

84

In another imperfect simile, the poet has chosen a bad vehicle. He wants to say that Basia caused love to grow in Mediye's heart and that this was a piece of falseness (16):

Ah!
Womenfolk are truly
Mendacious.
Oh, Basia,
Like a mushroom
Growing on an ant-hill
You grew love
In the garden of my heart.

The basic elements of this simile produce a picture neither clear nor apt. Leaving aside 'truly/Mendacious', perhaps an accidental piece of word-play, mushrooms on ant-hills are at odds with the image of flower-like love growing in a garden, which the poet presumably wants. Again, as with the water-lily, there is confusion over the subject of the main verb. Is Basia or her love like a mushroom? These are imperfect passages which reveal their flaws only under careful scrutiny; but they are, unfortunately, common enough to damage the overall impression of the poem.

An important distinction between Buruga and Okot, and a mark of how independent a pupil can feel from his master, lies in their choice of what to defend in traditional life. Okot singles out the vitality of the old music and dance, the warm togetherness, the night stories, the joys of an intensely physical rural life under the sun. An important choice for Buruga, and a sign of his moral cast of mind, is the old Kakwa attitude towards virginity, birth, abortion, and contraception. Two central sections of the poem upbraid Basia for adopting Western attitudes in these matters and Mediye argues his case humanely. Moral anger is particularly strong in Mediye's complaint against abortion. Basia has conceived a child but destroyed it because it has come too soon to let her fully enjoy her career of selfishness and hedonism. She has discarded it like so much refuse (36):

A life,
An innocent life
That's what you destroyed.
That's what you threw
Into a rubbish pit
Like waste paper
Of no value.

> That's what you threw
> Into a drain
> Like a thing
> That's not a being!

Mediye's disgust and the moral squalor of Basia's action are rendered in terms of basic local philosophy, which puts human life in a very different category from non-human and inanimate objects.

Buruga's defence of virginity is equally sincere, but less persuasive since it comes across as male special pleading rather than a hymn to virginity in itself (39):

> I do not understand why
> A man must walk through a path
> Trodden down for him
> By other people.

> I do not understand
> Why a man should not
> Experience the thrill
> Of exploring
> The virgin forests
> And savannahs.

A further indication of Buruga's moral concern comes with his comments on the place of the aged in the traditional world. This is shrewd commentary because it points a finger at both an accepted strength in traditional society and an obvious weakness in the Western code so widely copied. Buruga's *persona* reaffirms the importance of basic filial relationships and argues for a continuing value on personal involvement in society and family life from youth to old age. What Buruga knows is that the richer Western societies are in effect truncated or headless because the senior age-group, far from being reverenced for its wisdom and experience, and far from continuing to fulfil a vital role in the proceedings of society, is driven from family circles, diagnosed as useless, and shunted off to the geriatric palaces of Hastings or Florida. By comparison, the society Buruga talks about is strikingly complete. The aged grow more important with the years, their life efforts are rewarded, they continue to play a meaningful role in their community. Growing old in familiar surroundings, they die at home where their life has always derived its significance. There is then a good deal of weight in the following lines (81):

86

Basia says
My kinsmen smell
Like the *juju* rat.
She says
They are dirty
Like pigs.
When Basia says these things,
I feel sorry for her.
How can I reject
My own people?
If my father is blind,
I do not throw him away.
It is through the eyes
Of my blind father
That I see:
If my mother has *ridi*,
I do not reject her.
She has brought me up,
She reared me.
How can I shut her out?

The poem ends with Mediye planning to 'fatten/The goats of love/On new pastures'. Like the mudfish, he will swim into the depths and burrow into the muddy earth. Perhaps when the new rains come, and with them a new season, he will emerge and try the waters of a new lake.

*The Abandoned Hut* shows that Buruga is a serious poet, with a good ear, a developing skill in imagery, and a strong moral commitment. There are marks of apprentice work here – passages not fully realised, inconsistent and awkward punctuation, an occasional lurch into cliché, and a tendency to go further than inspiration will carry him. But the signs of strength are tangible enough to mark out Buruga as a promising poet and to further illustrate the flexibility of Okot's poetic creation.

### Interlude I

The closing months of 1968 were momentous for the history of African Literature and for the struggle to Africanise strategic areas of the continents' educational programmes.

Present in, or working near, Nairobi in 1968 were several scholars with firm ideas about changes they wanted to effect on the local scene. They included Ngugi Wa Thiong'o, home from Leeds, flushed with the success of *A Grain of Wheat*, lecturing in the University's English Department, and mulling over ideas for his book *Homecoming*; Taban Lo Liyong, pursuing research on the Maasai in the Institute for Development Studies, furiously writing *The Last Word*, his first book, together with long poems such as 'Thoughts from Limbo' and 'Student's Lament', and already preparing his second book, *Eating Chiefs*. In the same Institute, toiling along the labyrinthine paths of Luo history, law, and musicology was Henry Awuor Anyumba, and only blocks away from University Avenue, in Nairobi's commercial section, Philip Ochieng worked for the *Daily Nation*, fresh from studies in America, full of energy and ideas, and writing a weekly column as splendidly outrageous as the Tai Solarin journalism that used to stir Nigeria. Up-country meanwhile, working for the University Extramural Department and preparing for the Kisumu Festival of December 1968 was Okot p'Bitek, modestly aglow with the success of *Song of Lawino*, and with Ocols, Malayas, and Prisoners, boiling fiercely in his head.

This group's common interest lay in changes they desired in the University's Department of English. All literary men, they felt that here was one small yet crucial corner of the national scene that they could usefully modify. With Professor George Wing, eulogised in Mphahlele's the *Wanderers*, vacating the chair for a post in Canada, the group decided that the time was ripe for root-and-branch change in the Department's structure and curriculum. Identifying the University as the focus of Kenya's cultural aspirations, they argued that one of the main Departments within it was in the hands of strangers using as their sacred books a body of literature totally alien to the African mind. In rather blunt comment, one of them called it 'the whitest Department north of Pretoria'. The group adopted a careful strategy: Ochieng would use his press column for a frontal attack on the Department, and his fellow shock troops (Ochieng's term) would carry the fight into the University's committees and debating halls.

A series of articles in the *Daily Nation* followed, calling for the complete Africanisation of the University and particularly of its English Department. It urged the seizing of an historic opportunity to change the English syllabus so that British Literature would be pulled from its pedestal and be replaced by African Writing.

88

On 20 September 1968, the Acting Head of the English Department, Dr J. E. Stewart, also anxious for relevant change, presented a paper to the Arts Faculty Board on possible developments within the Faculty at large and particularly within subject areas covered by the Department of English. The growth of the French Department, a satellite of English; the possibility of developing a Department of Linguistics and Language; a future Department of Religion and Philosophy; the future of African languages, especially Swahili – all these were discussed in Dr Stewart's paper, from which the following are extracts:

> From the earliest planning days it has been emphasised that the University College must be in a real sense an African institution. This clearly includes the active study of the African world in all its aspects...

> The time is especially opportune for the planning and gradual formation of [a Department of Language and Linguistics] since we have here at present distinguished linguists with the Language Survey, including our Visiting Professor Whiteley.[17]

But though the paper was wide-ranging and even, at the time, quite visionary in its thrust, it did not meet with universal approval.

In a paper dated 24 October 1968, titled 'On the Abolition of the English Department', Ngugi, Owuor Anyumba, and Taban Lo Liyong replied in vigorous terms to Dr Stewart's paper. Their argument boiled down to a suggestion that while Dr Stewart's paper contained interesting ideas, it was really spoiled by the sort of thinking which had long ensured that Nairobi, and all African Universities, would carry at the heart of their programmes the culture and philosophy of the West. Though there was a commitment to increasing African content, this would happen only as a sort of grafting onto the main stem, which would remain Western and European. They quoted in particular the following points from Dr Stewart's paper:

> The English Department has had a long history at this College and has built up a strong syllabus which, by its study of the *historic continuity of a single culture throughout the period of emergence of the modern west*, makes it an important companion to History and to Philosophy and Religious Studies. However, *it is bound to become less 'British', more open to other writing in English (American, Caribbean, African, Commonwealth) and also to continental writing, for comparative purposes.*

To this group, Dr Stewart's paper represented basically a no-change situation: all would remain the same, at heart, whereas what they wanted was radical change. They seized on what they felt was the central weakness of Dr Stewart's paper:

> Underlying the suggestions is a basic assumption that the English tradition and the emergence of the modern west is the central root of our consciousness and cultural heritage. Africa becomes an extension of the west, an attitude which, until a radical reassessment, used to dictate the teaching and organization of History in our University. Hence, in fact, the assumed centrality of the English Department, into which other cultures can be admitted from time to time, as fit subjects for study, or from which other satellite departments can spring as time and money allow.

Fastening further onto Dr Stewart's arguments, they asked: 'If there is need for a "study of the historic continuity of a single culture", why can't this be African?' They suggested that merely because English had been kept on as an official language for political reasons, this should not be a reason for substituting a 'study of English culture for our own'. They added bluntly, 'We reject the primacy of English literature and culture', and asserted that their basic aim was 'to orientate ourselves towards placing Kenya, East Africa, and then Africa in the centre. All other things are to be considered in their relevance to our situation, and their contributions towards understanding ourselves.' The main practical idea was that the Department of English be abolished and a Department of African Literature and Language be set up in its place.

Other comments from the paper are worth noting, for they reflect the thinking of an influential group of African scholars not simply about a Department of English's place in independent Africa, but about their view of the whole function of a literature department:

> The primary duty of any literature department is to illuminate the spirit animating a people, to show how it meets new challenges, and to investigate possible areas of development and involvement.

On the thorny question of literary excellence, a standard expatriate objection to localising the syllabus, they were equally firm, insisting that this in the first place is a highly dubious and subjective area of concern, and then that there are other considerations which must be given priority:

> The question of literary excellence implies a value judgment as to what is literary and what is excellence, and from whose point of view. For any group it is better to study representative works which mirror their society rather than to study a few isolated 'classics', either of their own or of a foreign culture.

They closed their case by stating that they wanted to establish 'the centrality of Africa in the department' so that, once priorities had been properly fixed, 'after we have examined ourselves, we radiate outwards and discover peoples and worlds around us'.

The debates sparked by this document were long and fierce. They continued in common room and lecture hall; and across the road on the Norfolk Hotel verandah the triumvirate shot down white arguments where once Lord Delamere shot elephants. The press side was kept bubbling by Ochieng, who was eventually able to report in a *Sunday Nation* column for 6 April 1969 that victory was in sight:

> Being a tolerated eavesdropper, I have been able to gather that very drastic changes are in hand for the English Department at the University College, Nairobi. The proposed changes, a little bird tells me, have been accepted in principle by the Faculty of Arts Board, and should be effective next Academic year...Our University must begin to produce citizens of the world, and not parochial Black Englishmen. And the best way to 'reintroduce the African Man into the world' must first be to introduce him to himself and to his environment.

The result was precisely the reshaping that had been sought. The Department of English became 'The Department of Literature', so that its British and English connotations disappeared. African literature became the focus of the programme and from there the line moved out in appropriate culturally-connected directions. Whatever one's views of the debates, few would deny that Nairobi is now firmly established as the most dynamic and productive Department of Literature in East, Central, and Southern Africa.

Nor does this complete the scene. While writers' workshops flourished at Kampala, Dar Es Salaam, and Nairobi, attempts were under way to provide better outlets for their work. The magazines were especially active. *The East African Journal*, taking a greater interest in literary matters, was already publishing a regular supplement, *Ghala*, devoted purely to literary work. Oxford University Press enlisted the aid of Ngugi to get its new journal *Zuka* established, and EAPH, proving its continued confidence in local writing, was planning the first volumes of its *Poets of Africa* series. Nairobi's *Nexus*, Kampala's *Penpoint*, and Dar's *Darlite* were all enjoying a renewed life. The determined activity surrounding *Nexus*, the literary journal of University College, Nairobi, was typical. Financial and professional assistance from EAPH put the magazine on a better footing. Its title was changed to *Busara*, a Swahili word meaning criticism or judgment, and more prominent coverage was given to criticism since it seemed that East African writers, now adequately catered for, lacked an atmosphere of sharp, articulate criticism. Grace Ogot, the Kenyan novelist and short story writer, kindly allowed her name to be placed on the editorial board, and at EAPH itself, the Ugandan writer Enriko Seruma and Lennard Okola, the Eliot scholar and editor of East Africa's first anthology of verse, *Drumbeat*, both watched over the new magazine's fortunes.

The new journal had a happy birth. On the creative side it published poems by Everett Standa, E. Overton Colton, Daniel K. Gekonyo, Michael Cullup, and Parvin Syal, short stories by Joseph Kimura and Amin Kassam, critical essays by Angus Calder, James Stewart (an evaluation of Ngugi's *Grain of Wheat* and Soyinka's *The Interpreters*), and Taban Lo Liyong's massively provocative 'Tutuola, Son of Zinjanthropus'. Of special importance, however, was the appearance in the first issue of the poet Jared Angira.

### Jared Angira

Angira's emergence was sudden. A Luo student from Kenya's Siaya District, he was completely unknown to *Busara's* editorial staff, perhaps because he was studying Commerce not English. At the magazine's first editorial meeting, much writing passed from hand to hand; but the firm confident verse of Angira struck everyone as distinctive. Across the room, impressive in their freshness, flew quotes such as these:

My oily face
reflecting the lakeshore sun
my rainbow beads
singing around my waist...

92

my ankles bangled copper
my wrists bangled ivory...

While revealing, naturally enough, some of the marks of an apprentice (not every poem was fully realised and at this time Angira had been writing only for a matter of months), the sheer competence of the verse announced a poet already beyond the rudiments of his craft; a poet with a flare for combining rich sensuous description with discreet moral statement. Ulli Beier recalls how *Black Orpheus* was happy to discover for its first issue the Nigerian poet Okara. *Busara* in turn was lucky to discover for its first number the youthful poet from Nyanza.

Angira's career has swiftly exfoliated. Appointed *Busara's* editor in 1969, he also founded Kenya's Writers' Association, and was for a time Africa's representative with the World University Service. Sensing his potential, EAPH published a collection of his verse, *Juices*, in their *Poets of Africa* series, and Heinemann followed with *Silent Voices* (1972). *Soft Corals*, Angira's third book of verse, was published by EAPH in 1973.

A curious aspect of Angira's career is that his first appearance in *Busara* (his work had gone unnoticed in the *Daily Nation* and the *Kenya Weekly News*) was accompanied by a review. The sense of discovery among the editorial board encouraged Angus Calder to mark the poet's arrival in original fashion: hence his 'Postscript on Eight Poems' printed alongside the verse.

Of the eight poems chosen, 'The Undressing' was printed first, mainly because it displayed those qualities of firm sensuousness and moral bite which had announced Angira's emergence. A figurative account of Africa's meeting with the West, the poem is conceived in terms of a Luo girl from Angira's home embarking on a journey to a sordid baptism:

They
(who I knew not)
called me to Kisumu
with my oily face
reflecting the lakeshore sun
my rainbow beads
singing around my waist
better than the love songs
better than the songs
of Victoria Nyanza.

93

I came to Kisumu
my ankles bangled copper
my wrists bangled ivory
my mango breasts left
staring at the beauty
of Victoria Nyanza:
my posture
feeling the beauty of 'apala'
whose life was lost
for the bridal carousing.

They
(who I knew not)
ordered my neck bands
my waist beads
my copper bangles
my bridal dress
all to be cut
and rombled
into Victoria Nyanza....

Good clear imagery, a gift for compression, lyrical delicacy, anaphoric echoes of tradition, moral concern, and verbal innovation combine to produce highly effective verse. Similar strengths inform the following lines from 'Dusk in my Village', a rural picture that might easily have slipped into a negritudist mawkishness:

The western skies
turn soft and orange
as gentle rays
gently strike
the calm leaves.

The sweating faces grow cold and gummy
and the sun
puts east on the shadow.
...   ...   ...
Green girls in salad time
from the waterholes and rivers
proudly climb the gentle slope
with quiet pots
as shepherds count
the beads on their waists.

The feeling of language tightly controlled and skilfully exploited is strong here. The decision to risk two versions of 'gentle' in the opening stanza (from which most young poets would have shrunk with fear) creates an air of confident smoothness and simplicity, yet the soothing flow of the verse almost masks the care with which the scene has been created. This is no simple picture of an African Arcadia – sweating faces growing cold and gummy suggest too much of hard peasant reality for that. The impulse towards Romantic nostalgia has been checked, the temptation to wallow in sentiment resisted.

A modest complexity marks 'Mtwapa ferrymen', a poem on the history of a creek ferry north of Mombasa:

> Once it was sentenced to fate
> later to fortune
> and finale came
> with attribution to nature
> that such men
> smiling
> chests as wide as granary
> hopeful
> should be harnessed
> to the boggy-ferry!
>
> Songs ooze from
> those soft mouths
> where one would imagine
> butter shall never melt
> despair is exiled far
> happiness with songs
> happiness with jobs
> slowly the boggy is towed
> slowly the creek is crossed.

The first stanza's enquiry into why human beings should be yoked to a ferry typifies Angira's compassion and reflectiveness; and while the first four lines of the second stanza are less than inspired (even if the butter allusion is really about economic status), the two closing lines succeed well in their mimesis of the men's strained tugging and the boats' movement over the creek.

The theme of 'Nationbuilders', the final poem of the eight, struck a note which has sounded repeatedly since: the familiar strains of post-colonial disenchantment as a young man attacks fat administrators who preach industry, stoicism, and frugality. The figure painted here is unoriginal – nor is the poem as a whole memorable – but this has become a stock target in Jared's campaign to defend the poor and attack the rich:

> Ah
> I see him come
> bulging like a comic image
> of michelin tyre
> compact
> large
> breathing in agony.
> ... ... ...
> Aha
> He comes chewing gifts like curd
> grinding wealth like a caterpillar
> and storing bribes
> like the ancient granary
> to build the nation in a socialist state.

Angus Calder's 'Postscript' to Angira's eight poems pinpoints the young Luo's strengths:

> His poems seem remarkable for many reasons. In the first place, though their author has been writing for only a few months, he already possesses not merely one technique, but several.

Calder further argues that Angira seems 'able to come fresh to each poem as a new technical problem to be solved in a new way', and from the eight poems he chooses 'Mtwapa ferryman' for special praise, citing its oblique opening, its sensuousness and irony, its appeal at once to mind and senses, and the poet's refusal to indulge in blatant moralising which might have marked him as merely a second-rate talent. More crucial is the evidence of a highly fertile imagination at work. Angira has 'plenty of impressions and ideas forcing their way into poetic expression, and he therefore has not needed to rape his subjects in search of excitement'. 'Postscript' ends however on a cautious note: 'Perhaps such praise at this early stage is dangerous: but the writer who can compel it must be aware of its dangers.'

'Manifestations', Angira's manifesto preface to *Juices*, while redolent with youthful outrage, is tonally at odds with much of the book's material, its shrill anger suggesting that it would have been more suited to the verse of *Silent Voices*. This apart, its style suggests that by 1970

Angira had caught the germs of a raging Menippean – Butlerian – Shandean fever which Taban Lo Liyong had been spreading abroad, for here is precisely that *pot pourri* of verse and prose served up with grins and grimaces that Taban was making so fashionable. Angira's piece, however, displays a nice rhetorical ambiguity, being at once a flattering imitation of Taban and a gentle satire of him. Taban's mode was admired for its bold iconoclasm and for the chance it gave to display one's learning, to kick and splash in the waters of new-found scholarship. Angira's imitation is sincere enough, but he is also saying, 'See, Taban, I too can manage your virtuoso stuff, and frankly, it's easier than you want people to think!'

Arguably, 'Manifestations' was triggered by a 1969 incident, when, for reasons more expedient than humane, Nairobi City Council destroyed the tin-and-cardboard shantytown of Mathere, where thousands of poor folk eked out a dismal existence. The operation was painfully swift, and as an example of bureaucrats bullying the weak it sparked fierce protest from young men like Angira and Ngugi. 'Manifestations' begins near Mathare and Kaburini (the second name meaning cemetery) and the speaker, strangely learned, represents the underprivileged:

> Now each time I stand before the red carpeted dais listening to some upgraded being of the upward order tell us to be quiet; with coiled intestines, to sleep on the moonlit lawn 'cause houses have collapsed, Sam Butler waves up his *Hudibras* and shouts between my thighs:
>
> He that complies against his will
> is of his own opinion still. . . .

And in acknowledgement I say between the speaker's underpants:

> The trouble is that I have
> white hair
> I have yellow teeth.
> I have wrinkled skin
> I am waiting for the powercut
> I am waiting for the powercut-cum-eclipse
> then I'll raid humanity's plantation
> and rape the King's virgin daughter
> after all her thighs are inducing
> after all these, there will be no more power
> and I'll go back to the land.

97

The closing line of this prophecy of universal revolution is the poor man's reply to Kenyatta's constant refrain that city folk should go back to the soil, which is the nation's bank. This man's futile hopes – and his place in a broader pattern of misery – are stressed by a suggestion that the poor can enjoy only pre-natal dreams. Parturition destroys all illusion and eight hours later the poor child is screaming from a latrine pit's depths, its figurative home for the rest of its life:

> the intercourse between life and fortune
> is abortive
> Fate brought the death-syphilis
> Nature's underpants went gummy and wet
> the odour poisoned the hair
> he sat on the chair and left the leakage

Like Soyinka's Half-Child in *Dance of the Forests*, the infant here symbolises the grim present and a hopeless future.

After an attack on the government for building, amidst squalor and raging opportunism, a casino and skyscrapers, those handy symbols of an immoral capitalism, the focus shifts to the safer ground of literary jest. Chaucer has invited the poet to his birthday party, along with a Tabanic list of other guests who include Shakespeare, Milton, Lawrence, Owen, Yevtushenko, Plato and almost everyone else except Greene, Forster, and Housman. Apart from its indication of Angira's own reading, and his possible sources of influence, this section is really a blithe attack on Taban. Exception is taken to his habit of swamping opponents by the old trick of arriving in court a minute before lunch with binloads of reference and learning, the very sight of which crushes all opposition. Boccaccio says he would prefer to be left in peace while Beethoven suggests a new list of new names or at least a list of old-undiscovered ones.

The title of Angira's second collection, *Silent Voices* (1972), suggests a concern still with the inarticulate masses for whom the poet sees himself as spokesman. Familiar practice survives from *Juices*: a short, tight line is still much in evidence, a vehicle suited to the urgent speech of youth rather than mature reflectiveness. Expanded here, however, is Angira's vision of himself as a member of the world family of poets ancient and modern. Where in *Juices* he appeared at Chaucer's party among a wide and glittering company, he now claims (in 'Epilogue' and 'Me and Chris') friendship with the late Okigbo, a poet for whom he has the deepest affection. Though they never actually met, they are imagined as facing the world together, sadly tramping a road from Guernica and Flanders to Vietnam and Biafra. Lines from 'Epilogue' strike a worshipful note:

> I'll carry the wreath
> to the gold laden lair
> where you lie
> in royalty.

In 'Meeting' Angira includes Milton and Owen. Where the Puritan poet is seen commanding an Olympian height for his sweep over humanity, and where Owen unearths truth from the mud of Flanders, Angira and his migrant Luo are blown by stormy winds down the Nile to his present home – suggesting that his shaping forces and present directions are more random, more haphazard, than those experienced by these English poets.

Poems of madness also occur. Given Africa's cultural vertigo, it should not surprise if a poet lurches towards the bolt-holes of madness or responds with sympathy to signs of madness in others. In 'Femi-Aura' the village idiot dies bloodily, courting a leopard instead of a belle, while in 'Convulgence' Paulina Muga wears her husband's shirt, puts waist beads round her neck, cooks chicken in a fish pot, and sleeps with her own son (29):

> Paul is crazy
> and her daisies
> grow flowers with thorns

'The Country of the Dead' also stands close to the borders of madness. Partly about the hereafter, this is also an account of the poet's response to a living world fraught with despair, where one speaks and gets no answer, weeps and wins no pity, listens and hears no sound, shouts and stirs but echoes. A desolate image closes the poem, after the *persona* has searched in vain for an escape route (30):

> I've searched the exit
> But heard no owls
> no parrots, the waves beat afar
> on wrecks of ships
> the sand stares with me
> the country of the dead.

Developments in *Soft Corals* (1973), Angira's third collection, are both technical and thematic. More often now the short tight line gives way to something longer, resulting in a noticeable slowing of the poet's characteristic tempo, as youthful impatience yields to mature reflection. Thematically, along with a self-critical attack on academic poets and desk revolutionaries, there is now a concern with universal problems: man's basic idiocies rather than local African villainy. This more global reach is seen in 'Thoughts in December Night', a bitter contrast of lunar triumph and earthly woe, and in 'The Woodman', a poem inspired by the Polish economist Oscar Lange, in which a doomsday picture is sketched of an earth finally ravished to emptiness (59):

> The woodcutter is dead
>     the wood itself is dry
> The end of the *te deum*
> The final *nunc dimittis*
> And we must sing psalms
>         for the woodman
> Canticles for the wood
>         the last collect
> Farewell for the woodman
> In the denudation of the wood...

Okigbo's voice, echoing here, is formally announced in the opening poem, 'Singing Along the Palmbeach Road', epigraphed with Okigbo's words *The Moonman has gone under the sea the singer has gone under the shade,* and basically a spry imitation of *Heavensgate* complete with gateman and (Luo) Mother Idoto, but with Palmolive soap instead of oilbeans and a quail instead of a sunbird. Its opening catches well the distinctive tone of Okigbo's poem:

> In the palm is the palmolive
>         soap
> Palming off the fortune
>         and I here
> Wiping off
>         the palmoil
> To embalm
>         the dead shadows
> Forgotten...

Angira, however, has not yet Okigbo's casual detachment, that knack of making verse that seems free to wander where it will. Passionate enough to die for a moment of history, Okigbo at his best wrote verse that breathes a cool timelessness, the traced enigma of inscriptions on an ancient monument. When needed, the Nigerian poet could keep his artistic and political self under separate controls, a technique Angira finds hard when the quiet music of eternity is so repeatedly drowned by the raucous din of the present. Hence, even in the middle of the Okigbo imitation, his sudden attack on the dogs and vultures tearing at the independence cake.

*Soft Corals* is a disappointing volume. Offering much competent verse, it suggests on the whole that Angira's output has outstripped his inspiration. Protest themes remain, pursued more thoughtfully, their illustrations more recent, and with wider allusion to the high priests of revolution. But these are veins by now worked pretty thin. Only when Angira trades abstract social debate for specific human detail does his verse regain some freshness. It is hard to move readers with rhapsodic flights on Marcuse and Fanon, but the wretched life and death of Winnie Okech in 'Hollow Bones' provoke an instant response including anger at the evils that have destroyed her:

> It is not odd
> > daughter of the land
> That you should laugh
> > at the gale of unfulfilled
> It is not sin
> > daughter of the land
> That you should flee
> > from eroded suitors
> It is not banned
> > daughter of the lake
> That you should object
> > to swimming naked
>
> For in the brief encounter
> Beholding our earthly patience
> Begging our confused pardons
> Swallowing our own scum
> We have wept
> > at things we adored
> We have laughed at inopportune moments
> We have slept
> > at the graveside mourning

A new strain is heard here, the tone of a mature diagnostician who has studied a disease, knows its symptoms well, but knows from long

101

experience that the prognosis is gloomy. Winnie Okech's life is a figure for the lives of a whole generation, born into poverty under colonialism, sustained by the hopes of Uhuru, and dying in bleak despair. Only in poems such as this does *Soft Corals* have its moments of grace.

## Interlude II

There are many other poets at work on the East African scene. But some resemble those initially promising West African writers John Ekwere and Mabel Segun, who appeared early with good work and have not been heard of since. In East Africa Walter Bgoya, a Tanzanian, began well and then, at a point when he might have established himself, decided his work with the East African Community was more important. A volume of his verse, long promised by EAPH, has never appeared. Edwin Waiyaki, a Gikuyu who has studied in Paris, is also the author of some fine verses. But again a long-promised collected edition has not been forthcoming and one has to trek through the journals to dig out his scattered pieces. They are in *Nexus* and *EAJ*, and a couple in *Drumbeat*. Cook and Rubadiri chose just one of Waiyaki's poems for their anthology *Poems from East Africa*, which one would have thought was scant recognition of a poet who has responded poetically to the landscape of Kenya so sensitively as Waiyaki. Samuel Mbure has published verse in *Zuka*, *EAJ*, and *Busara*, and more recently has appeared in a volume of verse edited by Chris Wanjala. Mbure is a promising poet, who writes tight, firm verse with a better sense of rhythm than many and a command of image as good as most. His piece 'All That We Can Do' (*Busara II*) is a case in point:

> Hastily, hastily the night comes on
> And I, one of her prisoners,
> Chained hand and foot
> And led to plead my charges;
> Wish, lust, desire, longing, dreaming,
> These all have I committed.
> Oh, here inside my dark cell
> What meditations rage,
> What fires burn, persecute
> The slumbering heart!
> Oh, what fires...
> All that we can do

Is lift the rod together
Strike the serpent's head
And then remake Eden.

A poet doomed for the dishonour of prophets in their own land
is Albert Ojuka. By any computation Ojuka is the most prolific poet
in East Africa, outproducing even Okot, Oculi, and Angira. Ojuka is
Kenya's poet laureate, except that instead of waiting for the truly great
occasion, he has been producing public poetry to order for the *Sunday
Nation* weekly for many years, in addition to literary criticism and book
reviews. Occasionally he attacks vociferously what he sees as the
Literary Establishment in East Africa, complaining that in some respects it is still in a milk-stop spoon-fed stage. In turn the Establishment
seems to ignore him, and his poems have not been published in a
collected edition. This is not surprising, since the bulk of Ojuka's work
has a hand-me-down hackneyed quality about it. Whether the subject
is Biafra or the Arusha Declaration, the verse tends to live on the
surface, dealing out platitudes in a style that is trite and anaemic. Of
late, however, he has begun to plough a deeper furrow, turning up
richer soil that promises a more provocative and memorable style of
verse. His poem '*Pedestrian, to Passing Benz-man*' is a case in point:

You man, lifted gently
out of the poverty and suffering
we so recently shared; I say –
why splash the muddy puddle on to
my bare legs, as if, still unsatisfied
with your seated opulence
you must sully the unwashed
with your diesel-smoke and mud-water
and force him buy, beyond his means
a bar of soap from your shop?
a few years back we shared a master
today you have none, while I have
exchanged a parasite for something worse.
But maybe a few years is too long a time.

## Developments in verse

### Onyango Ogutu

A particularly interesting career is that of Onyango Ogutu. Born in the Alego location of Siaya district, Western Kenya, and thus a Luo, Ogutu left school before A levels and worked in the spares department of a Nairobi motor firm. Writing a mode of verse inspired by Tennyson and Browning, and usually on the reverse side of receipts, chits and invoices, Ogutu first came to the attention of the Nairobi English Department at Paa Yaa Paa Art Gallery, during a film show devoted to the career of Malawi's David Rubadiri. The contact led to Ogutu's verse appearing in *Busara*, and subsequently in many journals and anthologies. As though to secure the advancement others got through College at Makerere, Dar, or Nairobi, Ogutu has achieved prodigious feats of writing, wide reading, and private research on his own people's culture.

Ogutu's verse has undergone a sea-change since 1968. A dreamy vapid mode has made way for a tougher local and modern statement as the influence of Tennyson yielded to the influence of Soyinka, Okot, and Angira, and as a strongly personal posture emerged with developing poetic confidence. Ogutu has flirted casually with the song form of Okot and would like to use if for the great Nilotic epic that is waiting to be written. But the shorter, more compressed lyric statement seems to suit him better and he would be wise to avoid adventures of an *Endymion* kind.

Stylistic and thematic change have come together. A rather sloppy concern with romantic love has changed to a fierce commitment on the standard modern issues of Pan-Africanism, social conflict, political injustice, and corrupting modernity. But in keeping with his passionate care about the nature of his own society, the home tie stays strong. The landscapes of Nyanza, the Luo homesteads with their euphorbia-fenced dwellings, the hot Nandi hills, the fertile land and lakeshore – these all feed his imagination and his poetic energies. Significantly, he made his first public appearance in his home area at the Kisumu Festival of 1968, organised by Okot p'Bitek, reading a poem called 'Flags of a House', later published in *Ghala*. The shy, scarcely audible delivery hid a poem touching on the conference theme through poetic play with points of Nilotic linguistics but moving also to broader continental concerns by making linguistic similarities a basis for cross-continent artistic relations, addressing Okara and Achebe, and speculating on how the great diaspora occurred. It was an origi-

nal, if tentative, search for an artist's way of giving substance to the
political doctrine of Pan-Africanism. Here are brief excerpts:

> Which beyond my fate
> True origin claimed
> Yoruba?
> Acholi?
> Ibo?
> Dinka?
> Nuer?
> Luo?
> ...   ...   ...
> As my song mysteriously goes west
> For okebe Achebe a word –
> You are ours, Brain and Pen
> Though no longer you think of me
> Okpara
> Okara
> I sleep to the rhythm of . . .
> 'The Voice'.

Ogutu's first published poem was 'Queens', appearing in *Busara*
(Vol. II, No. 2). Exploring the rather commonplace subject of city girls,
the poet's view is part warning, part derision, and part sympathy.
Though the dealer in the opening lines is meant simply as a man who
knows the town, Ogutu's background in spare parts inevitably intro-
duces overtones of the motor trade:

> A dealer knows the date my girl
> A dealer knows the date.
> Your lips redder than oxpecker's bill
> Your body soft like silk and wool
> Your hair a puppet of fitful wind
> Black cloud flying high aloft.
> Black, black . . .
> Your head adorned with horse-hair ligisa
> Ligisa of the dead.

The allusion to the ligisa or headgear of the dead sounds a note of
pathos and moral censure, and also points to the doom that waits in
the final stanza. Meanwhile, Ogutu's bold image of his whore in the
third stanza is evidence of how sharply visual his best poetry can be:

105

> City girl, you bleach God's blackness
> You slough your dress of chameleon hue
> You stand there, Queen of heart and purse
> Big wheels swinging at your ears.

The dénouement, comprising a metaphor of impressive moral and aesthetic power, is built with images of water and shipwreck from the Nyanza home area. These are among the best lines Ogutu has written. The Queen's career is in the city; but her ultimate ruin is seen against her home background:

> And lo you are gone! Gone with the waves of life.
> Queens are waves of the lake
> Rippling lovely with minor winds
> And ending on rocks and lake banks
> Splashing with a violent life.

'Kisumu', published in *Ghala*, July 1970, is in a more compressed vein. Kisumu is for the Luo what Ife is for the Yoruba, a 'sacred' city by the lake. Before it is the open blue of the lake; behind stretches a plain edged by the boiling rocks of the Nandi Hills. The more elliptical style here reflects Ogutu's discovery of Okigbo, and the stanza's physical shape owes something to Angira:

> tattered, subdued, waterwetted
> plains genuflecting before the hills
> unholy spearing God's dwelling high
> your shrine
> plated with silver
> sacred on floor
> scattered
>               ribbon
>                      embers
> on threshold of night
> mirage –
> Luminous darkness' cowries
> living rivers crisping
> whining bibing
> brittle rays striking
> mossy rocks on
> homesteadless
> hills.

'Cattleboy' recalls a boyhood spent tending cattle in the Nyanza countryside, a song of innocence hymning halcyon days spent under sky and sun. The poet and his friends would

> quench
> Afternoon heat on
> Crisp laughing brooks:
> Clear sky and birds
> On still pool reflecting.

Then in a stanza distantly echoing lines from Soyinka, he describes boyish sunset games:

> In cornfields, tassel maize
> Tall maize with yellow powder
> Dusted us, trailing goats astray.
> Sun's eye red ember
> Sent long fingers of shadow
> After lowing bell-cows

## R. C. Ntiru

Another poet of Ogutu's generation, R. C. Ntiru, a Ugandan, works with Ogutu at the East African Publishing House. Unlike Ogutu, however, Ntiru is a university-trained academic poet. He took a First in English, is learned in the main areas of world literature, and fostered his creativity within the academic environment of Makerere's writers' group. He edited the *Makererean* and *Penpoint* and managed the Makerere Travelling Theatre. He has written a radio play, short stories, some good criticism, and is completing a first novel. His verse collection *Tensions* was published third in the *Poets of Africa* series and his *Lifelines* will be number six.[23]

The University, English Departments especially, brings mixed blessings to aspiring writers and Ntiru's work is sufficient proof of this. He appears in some of his early poems to be too 'correct', as if he is seeking full marks from an examiner. In these pieces, he stands as a poet who knows all the rules, respects them to the point of fear, and will not countenance breaking them. Ntiru's early verse therefore often has the polished correctness of an Honours English chore but none of that explosive freedom that announces independent artistic life. If only, one feels at such moments, he could trade his correct-

107

ness for Oculi's wildness. Proper concern over diction and rhythm; anxiety lest he write a bad line (he does in fact write some very slack ones), literary echoes of the English syllabus, that indefinable trade whiff that blows off academic poetry everywhere – it is all there, with the qualification that Soyinka and Okigbo are echoed as much as Eliot or Auden.

The mind that carries off a First might predictably be more at home with the intellectual rather than the physical world; and certainly there is not much sense of the physical landscape in Ntiru's early work. The content, the themes, are African, but it is exceptional to find a particular atmosphere or sense of locale. Where in Clark and Okara we have the rivers of Ijawland, where in Kofi Awoonor the Atlantic visibly washes the coasts of Ghana, where Angira and Ogutu constantly reflect the shape and feel of Western Kenya and where Okot, Oculi, and Buruga reflect the rolling grasslands of Uganda, in the early Ntiru all this is lacking. The home landscape has either made no impression on him (which is unthinkable) or it represents an area of his memory drowned for the moment in a flood of academic and philosophic matter.

Nor does the humorous find much room in Ntiru's work. The mirth of a Soyinka in his comic mode or the bitter laughter of an Okot or Angira are not heard. For Ntiru life seems a gloomy, rather joyless passage through time. There are serious flaws in man's vision and it would be immoral to laugh and let them pass. If modern man can wallow in wealth while his brother starves, he must be told about it; and this is how Ntiru's art is defined, for its basis is moral rather than sensual, its urge is to censure rather than to celebrate. Modern man is discarding a joyful response to the mystery of birth and cultivating the murderous practice of ripping children from the womb. He must therefore be upbraided for it. The world failed to understand the justice of the Biafran cause and must therefore be scolded.

Yet according to Ntiru's 'Portrait of the Little Self', neither the poet nor his censure can change much, for this piece gives us a picture of frustrated ambition, cancelled initiative, useless speculation, and a web of those tensions implied in the volume's title. The poet can neither laugh nor cry to any effect. He can neither address society with profit nor usefully stay silent. What remains, according to the poem, is for the artist to lie in a narrow bed and contemplate the 'silence beyond silence' of the grave (53):

What can I do that matters?
If I laugh, my puny laughter
is drowned by the multitudinous laughters
of the self-assured transclass men and cosmopolitan women.

The third and fourth lines here are unhappy, suddenly swelling with
a bad dose of gout. The second stanza is a little better:

If I cry, my lonely tears
are drowned by the larger tears
like a drop of dew
washed down by an April rainstorm:
the larger tears of those who suffer the double pain
of losing what they never had.

But the third stanza again sickens as the temptation to be scholarly
suddenly grows irresistible:

What can I say that will be heard?
Or not say that will be missed?
If I open my mouth, my feeble word
fades behind the deafening echoes of the more
          deafening applause
of the emphatic coryphaeusque speeches of the men
who have hijacked the course of human history:
and the wind blows the words back to my mouth.

Men hijacking human history is sharp, modern, and potent: it is also
part of a line that has shape and controlled movement. But it fails to
pull off the rocks those two lines beginning 'fades behind the deafening
echoes', where the idea of poetry as patterned and ordered has been
temporarily abandoned. 'Emphatic coryphaeusque speeches' gives
readers a chance to rise and walk to a dictionary; but it gives them
little else. Better than this is the penultimate stanza, where clear images
give a better picture of what the poet is trying to say:

If I look at the sun,
it shoots deadly life-arrows at my eyeballs,
and when I turn aside,
I see beneath the protective back of my hand
the sun capsizing into the ocean.

Ntiru is better elsewhere and it would be unfair to suggest that this poem is typical of *Tensions* as a whole. The more tangibly human, earthy subjects suit him better, even if he believes that his strengths run towards a more abstract style of verse. One example is 'The Happiness of a Mother', written *for aborters and abortionists who take Malthus seriously.* The joy of birth is described as something at once intensely private and personal, yet social too, and the point is made that life, even crippled life, is always better than the tomb (89):

> Even when she was still pregnant,
> loving her husband with that strange hate,
> sweating at the nose and hating peas,
> the grinding stone heard her chant to
> to the enclosed life, built on hope:
> the cripple is better than the tomb.

The birth guarantees family 'immortality'. The clan and tribe will survive and continue with the new children. Hence the social joy:

> This mother's pride is nothing private.
> Her mother saw the child and sighed in tears:
> my intestines, my husband! I die, I live!
> The climactic quintessence of a mother's happiness
> is the birth of a husband, a grandchild.

It is a pity that an otherwise fair stanza is spoilt by a 'climactic quintessence' which strikes the one hollow note in the entire poem.

The image of poverty amidst luxury is apt to spark a strong response in Ntiru. The language of 'The Pauper' is concrete and visual, and the whole portrait is edged with a colouring of human sympathy. The poor man leans 'on a leafless tree/Nursing the jiggers that shrivel' his bottom. He trudges on 'horny pads', 'Gullied like the soles of modern shoes', all under the eye of an inscrutable God. The poem gets most vivid in stanza four (35):

> You sit alone on hairless goatskins
> Your ribs and bones reflecting the light
> That beautiful cars reflect on you,
> Squashing lice between your nails
> And cleaning your nails with dry saliva.

'Morning Arrows', dedicated to Okello Oculi, upbrades the sun for unveiling each day a world filled with pain and frustration, shining a fierce light on every wart that scars mankind's face. This is a good imitation of the hectoring Oculian style, but gaining from its control under the reins of Ntiru's discipline. The rough and tumble energy is here, the bold phrasing and repetition; yet the poem enjoys a restraint, a submission to discipline and decorum that makes this essentially an Ntiru poem. Oculi's strong tones are heard in the opening lines (69):

> I have squinted in your pointblank accuracy
> and like my friend I hate you

And again in stanza four:

> I fear the boldness of your forefinger
> that points with ominous accuracy
> to the mutual illusion of the insincere love
> to the cracking of the believed lie

Even here, alas, the writing grows slack as the lines lose their vitality – though this erratic strain is authentic Oculi too! But the inset of an old woman glimpsed through the crack of a mud wall, struggling with her short blanket in the dawn of what might be her last day on earth, is exceptionally well done:

> Through a crack in the caking wall
> an old wailing woman
> struggling with her wraith for the short
>     tattered blanket
> sees your blinding fatal approach
> in a vision of the blistering journey
> from warm womb to cold cradle

Further Oculian echoes occur when Ntiru talks about 'the lostness of her unfathered son', the 'pastness of things', 'the goneness of peace', 'the brokenness of pots', and in paradoxes like 'certain in the uncertainties', 'immortal in the deaths', and 'unexpectedly bring us expected death'. The poem ends with a direct reference to *Orphan* and a prayerful plea to the sun:

> Give us the guts to moult
> Give us courage in the cyclic ritual
> of being orphaned
> Teach us to love our adopted parents.

111

An idea here which recurs throughout Ntiru's work is that of
sloughing off the skin, of peeling off an old coat. Hence the line 'Give
us the guts to moult', which carries a plea for the strength necessary
for continual personal and social renewal. The snake metaphor is
interesting in that in an African context it is usually optimistic promising immortality and perpetual renewal. Conditions would be better
if only the courage to renew were achieved. This is hardly a vision
of the New Jerusalem but it lightens the gloom a little. In 'At the
Crossroads' he writes (63):

> Had I the nerve
> to peel off my public skin
> and silently slough off the premeditated phrase...

which comes in a poem sketching the necessity of making hard decisions about personal rebirth and changing old habits and attitudes.
Mid-life sloughing is clearly Ntiru's preferred mode of change; but
if timidity prevents it, he can rush for escapist bolt-holes, there to
dream of a return to innocence which will fire his poetic imagination
even if it will not change his basic condition:

> Give me my innocent days
> of the bees in the nectar garden
> of our naked bodies
> in the first rains

'The Gourd of Friendship' asks how the world has changed since
the old days and works in a style reminiscent of traditional oral
practice (62):

> Where is the curiosity we've lost in discovery?
> Where is the discovery we've lost in knowledge?
> Where is the knowledge we've lost in communication?
> Where is the communication we've lost in mass media?
> Where is the message we've lost in the medium?
> And where is the community we've lost in all these?

Apart from the nice irony of Macluhanesque phraseology woven into
a written form echoing oral practice, it should be noted that Ntiru has
seized a point from the more humane Marxists, that the West's contribution to Africa has involved a massive erosion of human community.
Community, as expressed in attitudes to one's neighbour, is the theme
of 'The Gourd of Friendship'. It is easy to go to the moon, because

no one is there, easier, far easier than the basic business of building
human togetherness:

> But the road to your neighbour's heart –
> Who has surveyed it?
> The formula to your brother's head –
> Who has devised it?
> The gourd that doesn't spill friendship –
> In whose garden has it ever grown?

In a review of *Tensions* in the *Pan-African Journal*, Mauri Yambo
described the book as the best collection of poetry yet to appear from
East Africa. Better, that means, than *Drumbeat*, better than Mbiti's
*Poems of Nature and Faith*, better than Angira's *Juices*. This is a strong
claim. Clearly, as Yambo points out, Ntiru is a poet with a good deal
of development ahead of him. It will be interesting to see whether he
develops into a poet of the first rank or rather, as some suspect, a
first-class critic.

### Taban Lo Liyong

> I, as all the parish knows,
> Hardly can be grave in prose:
> Still to lash, and lashing smile,
> Ill befits a lofty style.
> ...   ...   ...
> Safe within my little wherry,
> All their madness makes me merry:
> Like the waterman of Thames,
> I row by and call them names:
> Like the ever-laughing sage,
> In a jest I spend my rage:
> (Though it must be understood
> I would hang them if I could.)                              (Swift).

*This complete gentleman you see here has collected too many beautiful
feathers. Resplendent in borrowed over-coats, he looks bigger than life.
That means he is so small.*                                    (Taban).

*The salvation of Africa lies in the hands of misfits. Misfits who have
complete abandon.*                                             (Taban).

*Friedrich Nietzsche is my greatest European hero. Followed by Karl
Marx. Then, Adolph Hitler. For, between the three of them, African
independence was born.*                                        (Taban).

## Developments in verse

*Do I contradict myself?*
*Very well then I contradict myself*
*I am large, I contain multitudes.*                    (*Taban* – after Whitman)

It is as hard to write about Taban Lo Liyong as it is to write about
Amos Tutuola, for these two writers are Africa's greatest eccentrics.
If, in Taban's phrase, the Yoruba writer is the true Son of Zinjanthropus, then he himself is his delinquent nephew. Faced with either
case, literary criticism is not sure where to start; and Taban's career,
even more than Tutuola's, is deliberately designed to ensure that no
critic ever will finally get at the truth about him. What Taban is or
represents, what he wants to be or appears to be – these are as hard
as deciding where to fix Tutuola on the merit table, or into which
pigeon hole his work should be squeezed. Teacher, researcher,
marathon walker, polymath, eater of library books (and shelves), born
cynic, utopist, bibliographer extraordinary, reformer, journalist,
essayist, professional devil's advocate, catalyst, midwife, prophet,
dabbler in riddles, poet, pop philosopher, brother to Ocol (secret lover
of Lawino), Voltaire to Okot's Frederick the Great, Whitmanesque
gadfly, modernist, traditionalist, sociologist, individualist, iconoclast,
sententious elder of 36. Which of all these is he, at heart? In which
role would he like to be remembered? Chris Wanjala has rightly noted
that 'his works are full of the proud and grateful consciousness that
he is a synthetic being', and perhaps this is as good a description as
one could find. But whatever the answer, there is no doubt that Taban
is the most chameleon figure in East Africa today. But of course all
the critics say this, and it would be a relief simply to leave it there and
get on with Ngugi or Kibera. Yet Taban's impact on the modern scene
has been too great for so brief a dismissal: it won't do simply to label
him as some weirdly synthetic chameleon.

Fixing five epigraphic quotations to the beginning of this section is
a despairing gesture, though designed to suggest what might be
pretty firm characteristics in Taban's writing. It is a gesture of
despair because one of the curious facts about Taban Lo Liyong is that
for the critic to give a faithful account of his work every comma,
syllable, and dropped apostrophe would have to be quoted. Yet
Taban is as much an 'experience' or phenomenon as a writer of texts
to be analysed. As with sodium on water, you see him burn
and race; but analysing the effect is a dull chemical exercise. The
parts are dead matter on the critic's dissection slab; yet the living

114

whole is all brightness and energy. Or is it? Taban's career, though it shouts to be analysed, isn't ready for analysis yet. 'The mortar is not yet dry', in Okigbo's phrase. But it never will be, and a start must be made.

An Acholi from Uganda, after teacher training at home, Taban studied quietly in America, at Howard and Iowa, disturbing few people there, and only occasionally ruffling the water back home with letters to editors that reflected the curious directions his thoughts were taking. During the long winters of Iowa, instead of dreaming over its wintery landscapes, as Okara did, he closed the blinds, locked his door, and moled his way through five boxes of books delivered daily from the library. His voracious reading, which has inspired countless African undergraduates, would have put even Macaulay to shame; and it is rumoured by one American who breached the sanctity of the Tabanic cell that on every wall was written the Latin adage CARPE DIEM. Teachers' college, Howard, and Iowa – this was not the royal road of Makerere, Leeds, or Oxbridge his colleagues had walked. It was by no means a fashionable avenue in the Uganda of the early Sixties and it is interesting to speculate if this has fed the titanic drive which has marked Taban's career so far.

Like a prophet emerging from the desert, Taban returned home determined to do all in his power – by cajolery, coercion, provocation, and intellectual freedom-fighting – to transform East Africa and end its literary drought. After dipping his head deep into many wells of modern thought, he would, furthermore, return with no fixed position visible to readers, colleagues, or critics. His choice of a confessional strain, a stream-of-conscious-tell-it-all mode suggesting an honest mind's encounter with a myriad viewpoints, looks like a quirk of temperament; but it was also a preferred way of releasing the maximum latent energy in the home scene and of placing before his community the widest possible range of ideas on which planning for the future might be based. Hence the persistent and deliberate contradictions; hence the love of paradox and Swiftian lists. Certainly East Africa's current position as the matrix of the continent's fiercest and most creative debates can be ascribed in generous measure to Taban's influence. His arrival from Iowa changed the local scene like magic. The words began to pour, essays, letters, poems, longer poems. Then books. First *The Last Word*, perversely titled because it was his first word (in book form) on African problems. Then came *Fixions*, comprising work arising from research into oral tradition;

*Eating Chiefs*, more work in oral literature; then *Frantz Fanon's Uneven Ribs*, a book of verse; and most recently, still more verse, *Another Nigger Dead* and a *pot pourri, Thirteen Offensives Against Our Enemies.*

Initial response to Taban's writing mixed astonishment with disbelief. Astonishment at the jesting freshness of it all, disbelief at the violence of Taban's attacks on a herd of sacred cows including negritude. There was a problem of appropriate response to writing whose viewpoint always shifted, never settling long enough to be pinned down or explained. The show kept moving at speed, and masks worn during the early performances were thrown from the caravans as the circus headed up the road to a new pitch. A show over, what it had offered had to take its chance, either to live or die. The new reality, the current show, mattered most. Audience and disciples, gathering in droves, faced an impossible task trying to keep up and understand.

What emerges from behind the masks, and from writing that runs simultaneously in a dozen different directions, is a mind of Olympian independence, which refuses to be reduced to a formula, together with a comic attitude that cries plague on everyone's house, including the writer's own which he is just about to burn down. In the guessing game Taban's work sparked, it was fashionable to blame it all on Nietzsche, especially when an adulatory Goethe Institute lecture by the author coincided with published work revealing dream-visions of a super-modern Africa, a new economic and military giant. But it is not in Taban's nature to be the prisoner of one influence. A fuller picture emerges from seeing him as partly a gifted (and highly assimilative) child of Nietzsche, and partly as a child of an ancient tradition of world satire. The lineage is familiar enough. Beginning with Menippus, it comes down through Rabelais, Skelton, Cervantes, Butler, Swift, Pope, Sterne (Taban often whistles Uncle Toby's signature tune), Voltaire, and Carlyle. Writers in this tradition often serve up satire in a narrative framework, despise – or appear to despise – formal principles, rejoice in rollicking wit, cock a snook at orthodox style, love exaggeration, delight in the grotesque and caricature, and work from values very hard to fix. It is the mad world of Jolly Rutterkin, Martinus Scriblerus, Gulliver, Tristram and Uncle Toby, Candide, and Professor Teufelsdrockh, a world where anything goes, or seems to go, except orthodoxy and stuffy conventionality.

Unfortunately, it is not a tradition famed for spectacular success in verse. And certainly there have been voices raised, in private and public, parodying Pope's remark to Swift, 'Cousin Taban, you'll never make a poet'. His piece called 'The Best Poets', in *Frantz Fanon's Uneven Ribs*, provides part of his answer (36):

> Ask not
> reader
> if this be
> poetry
> or not
> because it isn't.

Taban dismisses poetry because nobody speaks it; its thoughts are arranged unnaturally. But prose is too wordy and time-consuming for the reader, and Taban will offer something in between, which looks like poetry but isn't. It is simply a mosaic made up of single thoughts set out simply:

> I would be dead
>    before
> poetry rule-full I learn.
> ...  ...  ...
> call it
> what you may.

Certainly there is little of the conventionally 'poetic' about Taban's verse. There is not much to transport us into a larger and lovelier world. There is little concern for verbal beauty or compression. Constructive rather than creative, it is verse conceived in the wits rather than the heart, though more recent work has taken on a nostalgic colouring.

The burden is on argument more than wordplay, on rhetoric more than description. Not strongly visual poetry (there are few memorable images to delight the eye or sink anchors in the memory), there was initially much inert language, giving rise to slack writing, though of late there has been a definite stylistic tightening, a concern for verbal cleverness, and an epigrammatic strain which has brought the writing closer to the norms of verse. In his early work, Taban needs time and space to get an argument moving. He is, here, a thinker, a controversialist, an *agent provocateur*, an essayist rather than a poet in the conventional sense.

His choice of verse as a medium is puzzling. Perhaps, like Swift, he argued, 'Truth shines the brighter clad in verse'. Possibly he imitated the example of Okot's 'simple' songs, whose immediate success with the public gave their author's ideas wide and rapid currency. Certainly, for an artist committed to fostering creativity and debate the question of audience is crucial. There is no doubt, for example, that more East Africans read, or heard, *Song of Lawino* than Taban's prose work *The Last Word*. If Okot could reach so wide an audience, perhaps Taban, versifying his gospels, might get the same response. Hence this torrent of confessional material, which normally would have been poured into prose, is channelled into a verse at once intensely private and intensely public, reflecting the character of its author who is by turns both introvert and extrovert to a high degree.

Taban, perhaps more deliberately than any of his colleagues, is writing not only to change the world but to record his response to life and his assessment of himself at given moments or crises. An urge to record his own development, to practise a creative diary-keeping, is strong in him. Words help both to grapple with experience and to record one's deep responses to it. In *Another Nigger Dead* he writes:

> i review my life through the line ive written
> and pass judgement on the world around me.

By traditional gauges Taban's career is still young. Yet, possibly because of its meteoric nature, and partly because its products are so many, one can already identify specific phases, though at the risk of imposing a pattern on a career whose aim has been partly to break, and keep breaking, patterns wherever they appear. Useful background for the early period can be found in 'Wanted (Dead or Alive) Black Orpheus', first published in *Transition*, and reprinted, to confuse the critics, as the Prefatory Statement to *Frantz Fanon's Uneven Ribs*. This was the famous lament over East Africa's literary barrenness. Taban bewailed the fact that though the area could boast many mute inglorious Miltons, there was not yet even an Uncle Remus or a Tutuola. There were epics as lofty as the *Odyssey* waiting to be written down, but no one was concerned to do it. He asked (2):

> When will the Nile basin find a Dickens? Or a Conrad? Or a Mark Twain? Or a Joyce Cary? Is a Rudyard Kipling coming to Mowgli our national parks? Will the muses living on the Mountain Moons; will the dwellers of Kere-Nyaga; will the skyscraping Kilimanjaro acquire lyricists, poets, musicians to sing to them? When come you Omar Khayyam?

118

He praises Robert Ruark for writing about East Africa when locals could have done so and didn't. He castigates the descendents of the Bagandan Kings who refused to record the life of Buganda and took to whisky instead. The Huxleys and Karen Blixen are thanked and Okot too for his *Lak Tar* (his only production in those days) and Grace Ogot for shaming the men with her short stories. He seeks the help of Ezekiel Mphahlele (then living through the Kenyan chapters of his novel *The Wanderers*), the midwiving skills of Ulli Beier (whom he wants to imitate), and the scholarship of Gerald Moore. It all ends on an optimistic note appropriate for Taban's opening phase of euphoria and exhortation. The new writers will come (4):

> They will learn the language. They will come in procession. They are coming: Homer in khaki shorts; Virgil in monkey toga; Dante in a witch-doctor's garb; Shakespeare who speaks a little Karamojong, less Agikuyu, Swahili and Runyankore; a Milton without the eye handicap; a T. S. Eliot who knows Etesot.

Exhortation and optimism dominate Taban's early pieces which are vibrant with the promise of change. 'Student's Lament' is an example. Its Augustan epigraph reads: 'Being a lament upon a letter written by a sympathetic East African lady author thanking this poet for an article of his published in *The East African Journal*, November 1966, which was called "difficult" by certain readers.' The poem begins in frankly provocative style with a joyful reflection on early colonial days when fathers herded their children to the mission schools, thus allowing the first generation of young Africans to have the outside world revealed to them. This, says Taban, was fine, but the trouble now is that

WE DON'T CULTURE

because politicians whose training ended at Primary Four make cultural decisions with insufficient knowledge. These men have 'perverted' Capitalism, 'placated' Communism, and called the result 'Socialism and African'. What is needed is an articulate opposition to show where the mistakes are being made, and Taban mounts a Miltonic plea for its acceptance (120):

> But
> They also serve the nation
> Who serve in opposition.
> *Harambee* is for heaving burden
> Not for lugging captain.

119

> A saying No with reason
> Is far from treason.

At this point, he hymns his father's generation as progressive for believing in education virtually without question. How tragic that after independence (itself one of education's results), the new élite should stop progress and become tradition-hugging conservatives without vision and taste for further growth. Echoing his famous essay 'Negritude is Crying Over Spilt Milk', Taban pillories Negritude again, along with all who believe that independence automatically placed their countries on the same level as any other nation. With independence wisdom flew through the window (120):

> Strange mules called Negritude
> And African Personality
> Overran the terrain
> And kicked wisdom down
> Or above our heads.

Everything ground to a halt:

> Politicians quite unaware
> How low we are
> On the ladder universal
> Decided to halt the race
> And embrace the niches sure
> Where we were stuck for the moment

Taban is determined to scourge all complacent thinking. For Africa to begin competing with nations of the developed world no retraction of horns, no fearful retreat into the past, can be allowed (121):

> Overnight,
> We aged quite a bit
> And founded heritage grand
> To last who knows till when?
> And decided we learn no more.

He parades and parodies the humane claims of Negritude, scorning the suggestion that these are enough to support new nations in the modern world:

> Weren't we humanists true,
> And hospitable too?

Can't you see life superb
In the Negro universal?
Isn't Blackness deep
And the dark skin enigma?
Heard you not of Songhai
And Leakey's Eden too?
Forget not Zimbabwe....

He dismisses this dreaming with a word on some modern realities:

YES
Forget not Zimbabwe...
Remember Zimbabwe...
And, alas,
Iron Smith too!

Africa, he argues, has too much virtue, which caused, among other ills, her submission to imperialism. She must now be as alert, nasty, fore-armed and aggressive as the rest. She must live by Moses' law (a nice thrust) for the world, alas, does not live by the values old Africa proclaims:

If the whole world were swamped
With African humanism
We could sleep assured,
In the Aberdares deep
Or Sharpeville south,
That no more slavery will come.

The remedy is obvious:

With anti-missile missile
A missile you do check;
Only foolishly sometimes
Do you use Quixotic lance.

Africa, still on the defensive, has been passive too long, and this is another condition which Taban would change. The new era must face the present and future and move to the offensive so that others can be made to help carry Africa's loads:

Why remain defensive
When you could initiate offensives?
For is it not time
Someone had carried your burden too?

121

To fight the devil properly you have to learn his ways, a sacramental truth among all liberation movements. But first you must know your own position:

> The beginning of wisdom
> Is the realisation of weakness;
> The growth of wisdom
> Is the search for true causes and effects;

The message for students is to oppose isolation from the rest of the world. They need to progress but are blocked too often by 'Toothless heroes' reclining like wood on government benches; men who refuse to let students and scholars produce the ideas which they might put into practice. The new élite are not intellectuals but men caught up in a dangerous yet comfortable conservatism. They have all, Taban says, fallen for Lawino's world:

> Then it's better they say:
> Let's strive to catch up,
> Than: We arrived long ago;
> Negritude had it all in store.
> Lawino's dirge must end
> Unless we go
> Karamojong.

The new thinking must be got right, for Africa badly needs right policies fashioned from right philosophies. Political philosophy centred on tradition and tribal gods is worthless. A modernism enshrining the law of the market and unbridled capitalism is even worse. An 'achievable Marxism' is quietly canvassed during a side-swipe at Machiavelli and Hobbes. Meanwhile, fruitful ideas will emerge only if students are kept clear of politicians (128):

> Estrange the students
> From the politicians.
> Or else they're condemned
> To mediocrity.

But not all students and disciplines are equally favoured. Sociologists are despicable and must be refused entry into the Tabanic Republic. Their sin is to be in the pay of the ruling élite whom they teach to maintain the *status quo* and to wring cheap sweat more efficiently from people already too sweated and exploited. They talk of *modi vivendi*, and are anxious not to rock boats. They have nothing to say about evil and

> In the name of objectivity
> Not a word passes their lips
> To do with value judgement.

Social scientists are thus condemned for helping to perpetuate evil systems, worse by far than armchair philosophers who at least are human at heart:

> But Marx was best
> Being many things in one.

Politicians should know their place; students must avoid politicians; sociologists must not be hired. Whence comes any hope? The stage is clear now for the African writer, a newcomer with a duty to speak up for humanity. Taban insists that writers must not be witches from ivory-towers, or 'eunuch scholars' as he calls them, nor must they have sold their manhood to bourgeois power groups. And, though writing in an age which detests sermons, they must write didactic literature; literature which instructs, lights up the darkness, and rouses people to work in right causes. He can cite perversely but conveniently the precedence of African tradition for his view (133):

> Every writing must have a moral
> Tacked at the end.
> Like stories of old.

There is no room yet for a barren intellectualism. The processes of the brain must, like the screws of a liner, engage the sea:

> Intellectualism
> Leads to the heart of darkness:
> Storeroom of overdue projects
> And agenda untouched.

Nor can a writer be allowed to exist outside society, for 'All who talk/Talk from within'. Then, with an act of faith in man's ability to discover new truths, a gesture which seems to shake a fist at the doomwatch school of thought, he declares (134):

> The best that can be known
> Is yet to be known
> As far as man's welfare is concerned.

However, while it is sometimes convenient to invoke tradition, even to the extent of suggesting that 'He soars highest/Who's deeply rooted', Taban believes here that the way forward will be managed best by burning tradition on a reformer's bonfire. Tradition can be discarded for precisely the reasons it came into existence: it arose to satisfy social needs and must die to satisfy those same needs. A central plank in Taban's early philosophy is now nailed into place: a *tabula rasa* solution to the continent's problems. The argument is simple. Africa should accept that its traditions have failed, forget the past, and make a new start unencumbered by the junk of history. This, he argues, would resemble the creative opportunity seized by Wren, who designed a whole new city after the Fire of London. In a gigantic Arnoldian culture-quest Africa can ransack the storehouses of the globe, borrowing openly and without shame. Such an opportunity would release 'from inertia energy kinetic'. Africa's cultural lag should not, he says, be mistaken for a renaissance, and there should be no sadness over the final dismissal of a useless past (139):

> Shed no tears
> For vanishing exotica.
> The African is just a man
> Participant in cultural transmission
> With his time, beat, and tempo.

And there is no room for a philosophic wait-and-see, a belief that things must get better. James Ngugi is upbraided for his soothing words to a character in his first novel: 'Weep not, Child,/This latter darkness/Shall not last for long'. This is too optimistic, too trusting in the fruits of a capricious fate. Didn't Marx make the same mistake, believing the bourgeoisie would fall like ripened fruit? A vigorously aggressive attitude must be adopted to steer Africa away from the sirens of blind hope and an insidious conservatism.

In addition Taban suggests what he himself practises: a poking, infuriating provocation to make men think, think, and think again. Meanwhile, the younger generation should openly flout traditional codes and refuse to obey their elders (presumably not the progressives praised earlier in the poem):

Children
If we continue
In traditional obedience
To elders present
The land is lost again:
Times have changed
Other things are not equal...

A government of the poor by the poor, using energy and thinking
stifled for years, must be introduced. While ministers earn thousands
a month, own their own pools, and airports', a gap is opening up
between them and the masses who shiver in the cold and have 'no land
for burial'. He asks, in disgust (143):

Is this the reward
Assigned for us
We who sprained our shoulders,
Who broke our backs
Scarcely healed
From lugging Stanley along?

And then, in threatening terms:

In the next trial by fire
When we boil up all the tortoises
We shall pick out the males
From the females

An obvious irony here is that Taban the modernist has the pride
of bearing and self-confidence of an old tribal chief whose every word
is uttered as if it is ancestral wisdom. The tone of certainty, the
hammer-stroke pronouncements that must, like Tutuola's fantastic
detail, be accepted without question, the beginnings of a gnomic strain
– they are all at ironic odds with his modernist gospels.

A clear view of Taban's attitudes to technique and the art he practises
so self-consciously appears in 'An Excerpt from an Essay on Uneven
Ribs: A Prelude'. Early in this piece he writes (41):

I intend to follow Voltaire,
And Rousseau, too,
And Byron – the Lord of Sex,
And Nijinski and Clay, the Champ.[24]

125

Also he wants to sing with Walt Whitman a song to 'the glory/Of the flesh, man' and to the thrill derived from 'spirited contest'. Meanwhile he is carving his own identity (42):

> (I create on paper
> And regard myself
> A God, and believe in myself, the best thing to do,
> Especially for those who believe in nothing.)
> For in believing in myself,
> I have substituted a personal God.
> More meaningful to me,
> Because he caters to my desires, in obvious ways,
> And I have escaped being troubled by the world,
> Which is too much with us.

Eccentricities of viewpoint and intent are given an easy rationale:

> I'd rather be bright mad
> Than dull and well
> Vegetating in a life of ease.
> My complications do me excite.
> And contradictions give me breadth and depth

It is the mirror image of a romantic rebel, forever striking off in new directions, unpredictable, always ahead of those who would pin him down, cocking a snook at man's traditions in religion and philosophy:

> The defiance of God is the best;
> The defiance of other authorities, second best;
> And of the self (meaning the accumulation of teachings
> Of others which the self has absorbed) is third best.
> ...   ...   ...
> The more we popularize
> The ways of Satan
> The nearer we are
> To the progressive minds
> Existing in the time
> When religions were born.

But Taban cannot ignore the task of communication. He must air his ideas to effect the changes he wants to make. After years in the Iowa wilderness communing with Plato, Aristotle, Aquinas, Nietzsche, Descartes, Socrates, Hegel, Kant, and their brethren, he must now

126

shout their wisdom, reforged and simplified, among the plains and hills of East Africa. A Dale Carnegie for Africa's younger generation, he will guide it through the thickets of human philosophy (47):

I bring you light
I am the writer of pop philosophy
I shall present my thoughts so simply
The professors who have lost the art of conceiving
Truths, so simply told, or teaching anything
Not couched in language elevated
Abounding in figures of speech,
Or their various journalese –
They who no longer know earthly language
Wordsworths for ordinary men –
Are no threats to my teachings, they will not
Understand it.

The fawning praise of intellectuals in 'Students Lament', when they offered a suitable stick with which to thrash the politicians, changes now to derision, perhaps because they might despise (as they do) Taban's popularising approach to cherished areas of scholarship. Another contradiction occurs here when Taban suddenly praises tradition, heaping adulation on the ancestors:

(I always insist
Our forefathers were wiser than we:
They gave us the social institutions we use
We may therefore say: Man *descended* from wise ancestors.)

The fact that only pages earlier he preached the necessity of a *tabula rasa*, cursed negritude, heaped coals on the heads of conservative politicians, urged the young to disobey parents, asserted that tradition meant cultural lag – all this is irrelevant when he wants to make a convenient point about the ancestors. The fact that, given time, energy, and much reflection, one might discover room in his strategy for both points of view, is small solace for readers promised simplicity in all things usually thought recondite. The all-change-always-change approach has its awkwardness for a man trying to do a serious teaching job, as Taban claims to be doing. It is not always easy to serve at once the needs of creative provocation and good pedagogy.

The sop to the ancestors and traditional institutions is cancelled by the drift of comment near the poem's close, where Taban begins to

127

preach the Ogunian individualism canvassed by Soyinka in *Idanre*. The relevant passages from Soyinka are worth recalling:

> It will be time enough, and space, when we are dead
> To be a spoonful of the protoplasmic broth
> Cold in wind-tunnels, lava flow of nether worlds
> Deaf to thunder blind to light, comatose
> In one omni-sentient cauldron.
>
> Time enough to abdicate to astral tidiness
> The all in one, superior annihilation of the poet's
> Diversity
> ... ... ...
> You who have borne the first separation, bide you
> Severed still; he who guards the Creative Flint
> Walks, purged spirit, contemptuous of womb-yearnings
> He shall teach us to ignite our several kilns
> And glory in each bronzed emergence.

Apart from revealing yet more contradictions, Taban's way of making the same point reveals the prosaic nature of his verse when set beside the rich density of Africa's greatest poet (50):

> What mankind needs
> Is the breakup of society;
> A forgetting of languages.
> Let each individual go his own way
> And fend for himself, protect himself, wage his own wars
> On his direct enemies and not the bogus bloodfeuds,
> An eye for an eye, so long as it is the eye of the antagonist,
> Is a better philosophy, than leaving all judgment
> To this insincere social machine;
> Man should live life like that of his fellow animals.

So much for the gospel of 'Students Lament', which taught that the way forward lay in accepting the truth that man is born into a society and that all who talk 'talk from within'. So much too for the Marxism sometimes canvassed. Rugged individualism, assertion of one's independence, and the devil take all social bonds and obligations – these, the sacramental phrases of capitalism, are what appeal now, though, in that West African phrase from the name-change columns, 'all former documents remain valid'.

In 'The Throbbing of a Pregnant Cloud', a poem in twenty-one sections, the manic-depressive waves reveal a more sombre Taban, moody, introspective, and diffident. The poet who once preached revolution is now an old man of 34, reflecting sadly on a career one might feel is finished. There is a sense of weariness and of campaigns completed. The front-runner's strains have left him exhausted. It is now the turn of others (20):

> Having attained the height eagles fly
> I might as well die, tomorrow
> ...   ...   ...
> All the rest now depends on others
> I have set fire to the house
> And fashioned wings for flight.
>
> My task is done
> My fuel is running out
> I give up.

His vision is no longer clear, his zest for life has gone, his creative well is drying up. In two antique-toned stanzas he reflects on his lost youthful energies:

> In the days when I was young
> And my voice was loud
> Cassandra's role I'd have played
> To awaken heaven and hell
>
> But many a day has passed
> And our sights are red
> And no more terms are left
> With which to call
> The word BLOOD.

Section V continues the mood of gloom. The poet is a prophet ignored at home, a thinker before his time; the ideas he has propagated have not taken root. There is a blank wall before him, blocking new paths. Without drastic action, all is finished. Even the writing itself leaves him dismal, for in Section IX he writes (25):

> Don't be mad man
> All this is prose

> Plain plain old prose
> You are not suited to poetry
> Perhaps you are a poetaster
> But really man this is prose stuff
> And prose it is man

Section XII takes him even deeper into gloomy introspection. He diagnoses schizophrenia, saying that the outward show he offers the world is jaggedly at odds with his inner self. Like all good clowns, while he laughs outwardly, there are tears and tragedy within. But this is worse, for he kisses with a bite, jokes with corrosion, mixes venom in his mirth. His two selves are always struggling to meet; yet the completed circuit would trigger final destruction. Apart, they are slowly tearing him to pieces. The section ends on a note of resignation. Two lines record this low moment in his career:

> One thing I know
> My best days are over

Campaigns once keenly anticipated are behind him and yet have yielded little. Once girded for war, like some African Quixote, he now feels he has been chasing shadows:

> The times when I sought distinctions
> Are far behind me now
> > A soldier
> > Whose wars are over
> > The soldier
> > Whose fight was never

The sombre mood persists to the close of the poem. He admits his sensitivity to critical claims that he is unoriginal, unvaried in theme and style, and too often a trader in the commonplace. Even his defence is half-hearted, involving a flaccid claim to kinship with Baudelaire, Villon, Rimbaud, Nietzsche, and de Gaulle. This whole piece is one of Taban's most intensely subjective works, at once more lyrical and more compelling than much else among his poems.

There are several curious features about *Another Nigger Dead* (1972), Taban's second book of verse.[25] The entire text is printed in lower case without punctuation, and every stanza is listed as a separate poem. The major point, however, concerns the verse itself, which has now moved firmly into the new tonal colour seen in 'The Throbbing of a Pregnant Cloud'. Clearly and steadily, it seems, Taban is now hearing 'the still sad music of humanity' and has responded by changing his own harmonies from major to minor keys. There is a sense of pause too, of puzzlement and stock-taking, as if the early adventures have left vast areas of human experience uncharted, so much of the mystery unsolved. Wherever the causes may lie, a simple truth is stated:

> ive clowned enough

The jester no longer finds the world funny. There is a new humility before life with prayers to God for help. He is focussing his light more, no longer whirling it about at random. It gleams more steadily, its rays are more concentrated. Hence the following exhortation (37):

> through the superficial
> learn the hidden meanings
> the map of eternity
> glitters in a glance

And again, in *The Uniformed Man*, his most recent work:

> In our jaded form, let us strut forth on the stage displaying every angle of our Harlequin uniform. And rather than attempt the impossible task of displaying all facets of our unfathomed make-up, more and more we should try to focus attention on the one facet at one time and call it a day.

Ironically, this looks like acceptance of the advice of a *TLS* reviewer of *The Last Word* who said that if only Taban would 'cool and sharpen his wit he may yet learn to cut deep'. (*TLS* 18 September 1970).

The note of personal growth and quest sounds stronger now, reflecting a slight shift from public and social concerns. As if recovering from a mid-career depression, there is cautious determination amidst surrounding gloom. Another start will be tried; past errors ensure a better present and future. Taban's growth, tinged now by a fuller awareness of the depth and range of human suffering, will not stop (38):

> evolution never helped amoeba fashion feet
> through trials and errors the tortoise learnt a lesson
> you create yourself.

Surrender would be cowardly (40);

> to give up and curse god
> is to despair too soon
> even the blind struggle to see
> have courage ablebodied.

*Developments in verse*

Tragedy is a key word here as perhaps the book's title suggests. The Ugandan bloodbaths, memories of Biafra, the massacres in Rwanda-Burundi, and endless coups provide the opening poem's setting; and Taban can squeeze comfort from it all only by suggesting, with Soyinka, that perhaps tragedy is what is needed for the new birth he is praying for. There is also a strong attack on evil (not insignificant in a writer who once hymned Satan), and even a defence of virtue and the spiritual life. The writer who once called himself a god confesses:

> my selfishness is boundless
> immersed in the self am i day and night
> grant me the hidden thread
> loving god

Increased knowledge has brought increased acquaintance with tragedy; and tragedy, a great teacher, has taught him much. As he puts it in the middle of this strongly gnomic piece (2):

> the tragic is that
>    which alters a peoples whole concept of good and evil
> and the tragic has many faces:
> it is tragedy
>    when you curse your god
> it is tragedy
>    when you question goodness in the world
> it is tragedy
>    when you are turned into a beast for other men to hunt

But tragedy is a crucible for new patterns, a purger of old evils, an instrument of renewal:

> can tragedy also be the fire
>    which burns the phoenix
> can tragedy also be the stage
>    in which proteus changes states
> can tragedy also be the death
>    according to hindu religion
> can tragedy also be the death
>    of christ on the cross
> may tragedy also save us

Tragedy is also the cure for pride:

132

but tragedy also
>teaches us that we are not the lords of this world
tragedy also
>makes us know our place in this world
... ... ...
tragedy also
>elevates us to grander
>>levels
tragedy also
>shows us the top of the mountains for the last time

Revealed now is the weakness of his old clowning posture, for:

Hidden from the comedians eyes are the secrets
>of the tragic
the cynic can never perceive of that which is
>tragic
a born optimist will never realize when the cloud
>is overcast

In a sense, then, *Another Nigger Dead* brings Taban more into line with his colleagues, unable to jest in the face of powerful evils. The more serious tone and gnomic style might also win back some of those disciples who once sat docile at Taban's feet only to find that the teacher spoke in riddles and contradictions, fooled with masks, and offered no vision for his society except something like a typing pool where all hammered daily at their own creative script. Africa, ancient and modern, will only allow its teachers a modicum of clowning.

In *Another Nigger Dead* Taban seems to be coming closer to shaping a coherent social vision, though, as with all else in Taban's work, not everyone would agree. Mauri Yambo rightly cites poems such as 'there goes my son' and 'the filed man laughed and said' to suggest that Taban is reflecting bourgeois ideas. But it seems rather extreme, after failing to allow a possible irony in all this, to state that the whole book puts Taban unashamedly on the side of the imperialists:

Another Nigger Dead is the latest proof that Taban has become, in East African literary circles, the loudest and funniest apostle, the champion *par excellence*, not so much of the African lumpen-bourgeoisie – whom he adores, envies, attacks (with his tongue in his cheek?) – but, indeed, of imperialism in its numerous

133

aspects and manifold "glories". In his writings he echoes, almost verbatim, bourgeois (even racist) prejudices and propaganda as the world has known them for decades. . . . His "thoughts". . . are polluted by a heavy dosage of Western decadence, which he sugar-coats with an impressive device – wit. . . Is Taban aware of his role as an indigenised bastion of an alien, predatory culture; as medium through which the bourgeois "spirit" haunts East Africa?                                       (*Ghala*, Dec. 1972)

Perhaps Chris Wanjala's view is more accurate. He would toss all Taban's work onto the table as evidence of a claim that the Ugandan's basic philosophy of life and art is 'cultural synthesis', and that this stands at the heart of what he calls the 'Tabanic Genre'. The debate will continue, but in the meantime none can deny the enormous impact Taban has made on the East African scene. One wonders if it is a sense of a completed task or private disillusion that has persuaded him to leave East Africa recently and follow Ulli Beier's footsteps to New Guinea. Does he give us a hint in his strongly gnomic saying from *Thirteen Offensives*: 'But if ignorance still encompasseth this world like a tornado, flee before its onslaught, and cool thy feet on plains that are safe'? Whatever his reasons, his departure is to be regretted, for he is urgently needed further south, in Botswana and Lesotho, Zambia and Rhodesia, Swaziland and South Africa.[26]

### Interlude III

If criticism does not always deal with writers who are well established, at least it deals with writers whose work is in print. It might be refreshing, therefore, to examine some Central African poets whose careers are still so nascent that, for the most part, their work is known only locally through the medium of typescript and the script duplicator. Starting later than their East or West African colleagues, they include, even so, men destined to earn the distinction of poets like Okigbo and Okot.

Though a substantial anthology will soon appear from Malawi (a slim volume, *Mau*, came from the Hetherwick Press in 1971), readers looking for Central African verse in familiar texts are likely to be disappointed. They will find nothing from Zambia or Rhodesia, and from Malawi only one poet, David Rubadiri. Moore and Beier's *Modern Poetry from Africa* includes his 'An African Thunderstorm' and Reed and Wake's *African Poetry* two better poems, 'Livingstone Meets

Mutesa' and 'A Negro Labourer in Liverpool'. This poetic famine, however, is now being cured – rapidly in Malawi, rather more slowly in Zambia and Rhodesia. New programmes in schools and universities, publishing ventures like Zambia's Neczam and Multimedia and the Montfort Press's Malawian Writers Series are providing outlets where once stood only small magazines, of which Malawi's *Odi* and *New Writing from Zambia* are examples.

Literary growth in Zambia, however, has given cause for concern. Although *New Writing* often carries promising work from such poets as Medard Kasese, Smith M'hango, M. B. Ng'andu, Munyinda Imasiku, and Malukula, an editorial in Volume 8, No. 3 (1972) asks: 'Why is it that every time we seem to be on the edge of a breakthrough in our literary development the situation slips back to mediocre normality?' It argues that while there should be at least four voices of potential distinction in the country, so far none has appeared. It might be tempting to reply with these lines from the same magazine, in which Jan Askelund says: 'old people know that it is better/to bake one loaf of bread/than to write two poems'. It is doubtful if the elders see artistic matters in quite this way; but it might be correct, and more significant, that young Zambians do.

Following the South African pattern, Rhodesia's emphasis falls heavily on vernacular writing: the two major literary conferences held there in the last decade or so (1964 and 1974, and both convened by Mr Ken Mew, the vigorous principal of Ranche House College) have been devoted entirely to work in local tongues. However, promising English verse by Chinodya, Marachera, Mubonya, Muchemwa, and Mucheri has appeared in *Two Tone* magazine and in McLoughlin's *New Writing in Rhodesia* (1976).

Malawi's position is much better, for among a large group of active poets several show potential for strong growth. A weekly vernacular workshop at the University run by the Chichewa scholars Sam Mchombo and Enoch Timpunza (both of whom are pursuing fundamental research into vernacular poetics) is matched by one for English language poets begun by David Kerr and now directed by Mupa Shumba and Jack Mapanje. Among the liveliest in Africa, meetings attract up to seventy students and writers, and general standards, of material and discussion, are high.

While there is no identifiable school of Malawian verse (writers tend to cherish privacy) the poets as a group do share a range of common features which set them apart from their colleagues elsewhere. Malawian verse, for example, prefers a quieter tone and a less public posture than its East African equivalent. It uses a more subtle and circumspect statement and is rich in irony and ambiguity. It seems often to lie at the opposite pole from East Africa's ear-splitting verse. No one roars 'To hell/With your Pumpkins/And your Old Home-steads' or 'We will arrest/All the village poets/Musicians and tribal dancers'. Such clamour would be entirely misplaced. Nor is the shifting openness of the Tabanic mode quite right either, though it is moder-ately admired. A quiet lyricism is preferred and there is little frontal assault even on easy targets like colonialism (these poets in any case have grown up in a post-colonial world and find their matter here). An early poem like Rubadiri's 'Stanley meets Mutesa', describing a momentous meeting between Africa and the West, is characterised by quiet distaste rather than strident fury. All is muted and courteous suspicion as the two men meet, with children peering from reed fences and no one drumming a welcome. The closing lines carry the re-strained tones found throughout:

> The gate of polished reed closes behind them
> And the West is let in.

Beginning late, Malawian verse in English has overleapt the colonial romanticism through which West Africa had to pass. There are no sweating Byrons hiding behind the baobab trees and no Words-worthian images doing service on Lake Malawi. Echoes, when they occur, are conscious and a widespread eclecticism comes more from independence than from immature flattery. Content and influences are mainly African – a trend accelerated by the repatriation of school and college syllabus – but poets here can still respond to Western voices, and Eliot in particular remains a potent source. Rubadiri himself, the country's first published poet, illustrates a national trend, for while his Stanley poem carries clear echoes of Eliot's 'The Magi'

> Such a time of it they had;
> The heat of the day
> The chill of the night
> And the mosquitoes that followed.
> Such was the time and
> They bound for a kingdom

the substance of 'A Negro Labourer in Liverpool' owes a modest debt to Diop's 'Nigger Tramp', though significantly this is a more restrained performance than the Senegalese poet's and less infused with mes-sianic zeal.

Discussing Malawi's poets in a paper called 'New Writing From Malawi' (1972), David Kerr and Lan White comment:

> The dead hand of Eng. Lit. is almost entirely absent. If English is their chosen medium, they are long past the temptations of fine writing, and well aware of the advantages of irony and understatement. If their interests tend towards the philosophical, there is little that is pretentious about their work, little attempt to force large meanings out of small confrontations.

This is fair comment, despite its odd allusion to 'fine writing', and the authors proceed with the further suggestion that among the new writers 'the clear superiority of their poetry over their short stories and radio plays has something to do with their isolation in the community as a whole'. Exception is taken to the omission of important issues such as racialism and unemployment (which has forced many Malawians into the drudgery of the South African mines); and one would not imagine, they say, that one quarter of the population was Moslem or that much of the country is surrounded by Mozambique.

It is not wholly true that the new writers are 'isolated in the community as a whole', for Malawi is an overwhelmingly agrarian society in which most writers retain a strong, if diminishing, link with the soil. Indeed village life is often a favoured topic, as it is in the multi-angled verse of Jack Mapanje. In 'Go Between', for instance, Mapanje (who writes copiously in the vernacular and is a keen student of oral tradition) has villagers scornfully addressing a town-girl via a third party:

> Tell her we still expose our bottoms
> Eat unseasoned nsima with bonongwe
> From a ladle our hands unscented;
> We still sleep in slums rolling
> In bird-droppings, friends of fleas

This is a poetic sequence in which Mapanje uses various voices to tease out some of the ironies of his generation's relationships with the past. Hence the girl's reply, sent from the depths of an urban forest, also gets care and sympathy:

> mother, it is a war here, a lonely war
> where you hack your own way single-handed
> to make anything up to the Chaka of
> the tribe!

137

Lupenga Mphande is another poet with a strong feeling for rural life. Though his work is of dramatically uneven quality, he is a prolific writer with a talent for blending landscape description with moral reflection. No one paints physical Malawi better than Mphande; no one is quite so sensitive to the scattered graces of its hills and waters. A rather solitary figure he is Central Africa's Okara, sharing the Nigerian's passion for experiment and persistence in the cultivation of his sensibility. A country teacher, he is still young enough to miss the University's critical milieu and his faults are precisely those of vocabulary, redundancy, and adjectival excess that receive weekly therapy in the Workshop. These are, however, outweighed by his skill at assonance, his variety of subject and strategy, his open-nerved sensitivity, and his modest manner of staying in the background as though to suggest that what he reflects of the external world is much more exciting than the poet's personality. Some of Mphande's strengths appear in 'Canopied Foliage':

> Strong stench of canopied foliage
> streamed all round us, reinforcing
> after-sunset humid tropical vapours
> as we made slowly through grey grass;
>
> The sky chimed as the slewing light
> came over distant hills across the plain
> striking the edge of white boulders –

and in these lines from 'Through the Thicket':

> Herds of cattle and goats move slowly across the hillside
> And pause to look like red and white blossoms on a village tree
> A cloud of shadows brings life to the far off hills....

The closing lines of this poem show Mphande fusing setting with reflection in some fine Okaran imagery:

> In youth the future is like a hazy hill in the dawn light of winter
> When fog in riverside deciduous trees propitiates glory in a
>     winter day

Chris Kamlongera, who, in addition to verse, has written plays for the BBC (*Graveyards*, his most recent play, was well received at Leeds in 1976), is at once a more introspective and academic poet than

138

Mphande, less concerned with the specifics of landscape and season and more exercised by the larger issues of the human predicament and Africa's performance in the post-colonial era. Influenced by Okigbo, Taban Lo Liyong, and the gloomier side of Soyinka, Kamlongera's is a diffident, unassertive voice, but capable of irony and ambiguity. The characteristic tone of his verse arises from the conflicting pressures of moral duty and local circumstance, of having much to say, yet, even from personal taste, not wishing to say it too baldly. Kamlongera's vision is sombre, and unusually so in a writer so young. Typical is this three-line miniature:

> Eggs hatch into chicks
> Sunrise gives way to sunset
> And babies grow to fit large coffins

where there is a sense not merely of a temporarily fallen world, which might be saved by human effort, but of the futility of life itself. Growth is a squalid lurching towards maturity where, far from catching a glimpse of life's riches, we only see its disasters more clearly. 'Maggots' makes his point:

> We are maggots
> Wriggling
> Within the glitter
> Of faeces
> That give us birth
> Only to slip back
> Where we began

In 'Our Sun' green-season growth is scorched by a heat that shrivels all; 'Sickness' is full of weevils, mucus, and disease; and an untitled piece beginning 'I am prologue to the future' is built round images of owls hooting doom from housetops, snakes whispering death in the grass, and stricken birds flapping helplessly in the dust.

Kamlongera likes the idea of the poet as seer (in both senses) and clings to a view that though the poet might in daily life appear unassertive and myopic – indeed though he might be forced into such a posture – he really sees and feels more than anyone else. Hence the twin figures in his verse of the blind prophet and the lofty satirist. A sequence called 'Teiresias' carries the lines: 'Soyinka has been/Up Idanre rocks/Seen it all.../Nigeria's witness/Teiresias.' Imagery, however, often lacks the tactual quality found in Mphande, probably because Kamlongera is concerned first with an idea and then with a physical object to embody it – whereas with Mphande the reverse seems true. Hence in 'Life Today' the lines

> High up a mountain
> The eagle soars
> Waiting
> The moment of break
> The time of anarchy

where we do not see the eagle clearly and get no sense of its size, shape, or movement; and this because, unlike Mphande (who with similar material once offered: 'Another shadow crosses the valley, whirls away, returns, pauses/Curiously seeking, hovers, for a long time, then makes a sudden/Sweep to take away a safely dead mouse'), Kamlongera isn't interested in the bird itself but only in its use as a symbol of doom.

The poet's gloom goes deep. Technological progress is a fraud, 'Our blindman's stick/On the way to our/Gravesides'; 'Tears for rain/Are cries for mud', and the poet's personal predicament could hardly be worse:

> I'm a cancer patient
> Another Bone Chewer
> Impotent in this ward
> Hospitalising my cancerous truth

Perhaps the most 'emotional' of Malawi's poets, Innocent Banda, also has a reputation as a radio playwright and an increasing amount of his energy goes into drama. Deeply sensitive, his concern and compassion were initially a poetic disadvantage, their intensity producing a verse that teetered on the brink of sentimentality. With Banda we move to the idea of the poet as a force for good and a champion of virtue, a man to cool conflict and pour oil, to heal the world's soul and make a merry heart. Banda's years with the University Workshop have slowly produced a tougher mode of statement in which his strengths are applied to varied, non-private topics. 'Like the Wind' shows his early phase, a period of bleeding hearts and flowing tears: 'Like the wind/that haunts/the world, I wish I could walk/Night and day/mourning for the unloved/Souls of the world'. But much stronger are these later lines from 'Bright Like the Sun', where strong reaction to an unspecified hurt is rendered in grand virile fashion:

Allow me
One more curse
Through this God-fearing mouth
For, trying to forgive
I choked close to death

The shift to a cooler mode of statement has also produced such
Okigboesque lines as: 'I will lean my head/against the old baobab/to
hear the echo of creation' and the simple religious beauty of:

For the kingdom is for children
Only those who meet God
In a raindrop
*Kyrie eleison*

Frank Chipasula is the only Malawian yet to have a verse collection
published. His *Visions and Reflections* (Neczam, Zambia, 1973), ranges
from juvenilia dealing with colonialism, negritude, and independence
to pieces that begin to cut quite deep. A compensation in the early
poems is their remembered scenes of colonial struggle seen through
the eyes of a child. Frank recalls the heady days of the early sixties,
when he threw stones at colonial police cars, helped with road blocks,
and shouted *Kwacha*! Happily, poems in the affectionate literal yield
to more figurative work as Chipasula develops a sense of the metaphoric. His most mature piece here is 'Suicide', whose triangular view
of a man's hanging provides the poem's basic virtue. The event
troubles the *persona*, yet to touch the corpse would be taboo and there
is some delicate counterpointing as the suicide's viewpoint is played
off against society's attitude and the private response of the *persona*.
As though suggesting an apt way to handle death and a taboo, the
entire poem is printed in lower case [50]:

i saw your face
  refracted
    through the window
pane
  hanging
    dangling
      at
      the end
      of
      a rope....

141

in your house
a crowd wailed you back
but
your eyes blankly stared
    up to your own heavens (not to return!)
we did not know
   you'd found peaceful solution
by creating problems
   for others and decided to go
      i accuse you not...
do not accuse me that i dare not touch you

Ken Lipenga and Anthony Namalomba persist with verse while
deciding whether to be poets, short story writers, or critics. Namalomba has the tortured nature of a Taban Lo Liyong (whose influence
he occasionally reflects), while Lipenga resembles Jared Angira in his
incisive manner and ability to strike off good work with little labour.
His seeming lightheartedness, however, can often mask an outlook
basically serious and while he revels in the creative excitement of the
new age, he is also aware of its hazards. In his 'Memorabilia' he admits
that he is 'but a riverside twig/caught in this wild torrent' and that
he is always at risk of being 'mercilessly tossed ashore'. But in the
meantime:

I gleefully flirt on
with the exotic torrent
lost, precarious, without myself

In 'You Used to be Nagama' (she's now called Priscilla), Lipenga mocks
in delicate erotic vein a villager who has assumed the style and name
of a modern town girl:

I've seen your face before I swear,
sweating beside an earthen pot,
with that long, long drawing gourd,
waiting patiently
for water to gather
at the bottom of the deep village well;
and you used to be Nagama.

Since you grew into a Priscilla
we men have not eaten life.

142

We can no longer deal in grasshoppers
nor brag about our mouse-traps,
nor even call you Nagama.

By contrast, Namalomba is more suffering, less detached, and not so lightly ironic. A typical poem called 'Self' is dense with plasmic swirl and gloomy introspection: 'Blood drips into the intestines,/Stale blood fills the bladder/Black blood flows stagnantly/Into the dark alleys of the Self'. One of Namalomba's best poems, 'I wept', grew out of having, within three days, a father die and a brother born. Brief excerpts show how the opposing emotions of mortal sorrow and natal joy create some strong poetic energy. The notions of golden joy and cold death are fused in the lines:

A nugget of ice carrying
My orphan status
Slid inside me.

And vivid physical imagery yokes private hurt to cosmic fracture to emphasise the events' magnitude:

My backbone was broken while
I was turning a somersault.
The earth cracked, the world
Slipped away...

A sense of drift, confusion, insignificance, and new vulnerability are expressed in one of Namalomba's most allusive images: 'I was plankton on lost waters/Of oceans and seas and/Weirdly meandering rivers'.

With the possible exception of E. Msuku, whose work, even in typescript, has been curiously neglected by Malawi's academic community, the country's two most developed poets are Felix Mnthali and Steve Chimombo, both lecturers at the University. Both belong in that group of poets called in recent critical debate 'prodigals', of whom Wole Soyinka, Christopher Okigbo, and Michael Echeruo are the best known representatives: men whose training makes them at once recipients of a local African heritage and of a universal tradition of art. In literary matters they are citizens of the world and cherish a freedom to express their identity as men shaped by more than a local culture. Currently under attack in the pages of *Ikeke*, they would all agree with Mnthali's style of defence: '...it is only human/to belong/not to two worlds/or even three/but to the world'.

*Developments in verse*

Besides commanding a broader cultural reference than his younger colleagues, Mnthali has a firmer grasp of technique. His clear scholarly style is precise and logical; he draws lines of poetic argument with the detailed care of an architect. His work's characteristic pace (which, regrettably, seldom varies) is a measured *andante*, its tones firm yet humble. The sense of ordered argument is so strong that a constructive or studied kind of creativity is suggested rather than an impulsive spontaneity. Typical is the opening of 'The Semi-detached Intellectual', a poem in which the *persona* hovers over the choice between personal comfort and social duty:

> I sought not
>> to precede my dreams
>> when the quest for contentment
>> outran the counsels of reason.

The formal tone does not mask the fact that the poet is engaged in a struggle to check passion with reason, to eschew escapism, to maintain and hold an inner balance, and above all to face and solve the problems posed by modernity. The poem continues:

> And now
>> though Cancer and Aquarius
>> though Virgo and Taurus
>> should line up in my favour
>> and though votive candles
>> should burn all night
>> and burn all day
>> and though indulgences
>> should swell the reservoir
>> to quench the fires
>> and thaw the chill
>> though divining bones
>> and healing herbs
>> should pronounce me saved.
> I shall
>> break the tablets
>> from a scented deity
>> and gulp the aroma
>> of petulant mortality
>> as I groan

144

at the stench of vials
and the whiff of
putrid corpuscles.

The statement is ordered, the rhythm smooth, and the poem proceeds along firm logical lines that emphasise a painful but necessary way forward. Once the road is accepted, one must never lose patience or good humour. One must cultivate the positive and never yield to despair. Sometimes the landscape will be harsh, as it is in 'A Critique of Pure Emotion':

I SAW
    the crevices of the earth
    yawn
I SAW THEM
    close and multiply
    into smaller tributaries

And at such times the trick of emotional survival will lie in acceptance.

'The Straws of the Fields' comments on the old question of what went wrong in Africa's past and particularly which key events led to the painful fragmentation of the present. Echoing Achebe, Okigbo, and, indirectly, Yeats, the poem seems to lay the loss of tradition at individual feet rather than with historic determinism, and penance incurred in the closing stanza involves pain and unrest:

And therefore
  there shall be no rest
    for the like of us
      there shall be no rest
        for those of us who have drunk
          from the troughs of the pigsty
        and laid our trunks
          in the gutters of the ghetto.

1972 was an auspicious year for it marked the return from Leeds of Steve Chimombo, who in four brief years has become Malawi's most versatile and prolific writer. His work is not confined to verse, for already he has written his country's first full-length drama, *The Rainmaker*, and its sequels, *The Harvest* and *The Locusts*, while among thick sheafs of prose stands some of the most original short story writing in Africa. Chimombo's is a modern sensibility discovering a tap-root

145

in a traditional culture from which he was almost cut off. Like Mnthali, he delights in an eclecticism that does not deny local values, and if his young voice lacks the deep-toned resonance which experience has given his older colleague, compensations abound in his bold approach to form and content and in his sheer creative energy. Chimombo is a morally serious artist, though an apparent flippancy can sometimes puzzle his readers. Deep currents, for example, flow beneath the frothy surface of 'Modern Advertising':

> The song gyrated across the mind
> Elbowing out reality
> Pirouetted onto the corners of the soul
> Bounced against the walls
> And curtsied through a chink to a crash of cymbals.
> It landed outside
> And parrot-like chanted to the world:
> Leonex! Leonex! Leonex!

Beneath the jingly tones a mind is being disturbed, a soul trampled, and reality flung through the window. The poet is attacking various forms of brainwashing and also the cheap exploitation of Africanness for sordid motives.

Different in style, though equally serious, is 'Chaosis'. Searching the modern world for an oasis, says the poet, what one normally finds is chaos. Alternatively, given peace, you try to preserve it within a wall, but outside horrors reliably threaten your ramparts. Two features here are of interest. One is a tendency towards verbal tumescence, a symptom of poetic youth, and the second, evident throughout the work, is a delight in water imagery, whether of stream, river, or whirlpool:

> fractured elongations of shadows
> ride the ripples of the whirlpool
> multiply in the ego-gnomic currents
> and emaciate on the periphery grubbing
> under the mossy banks of oblivion
>
> atomised reflections reveal skeletons
> smuggling skullfulls of teeth crawling
> nearer to gnaw at an insulated mind
> traversing the same bloodied pathways
> that led to the walls where watchdogs
> prowl and snap at betrayed shadows

Eliot ('I almost worship him') has been a major influence on Chimombo and a piece called 'Lament' is an Africanised *Prufrock* complete with Chichewa epigraph and a beggar mother and child replacing the original's seedy hero. (The modern reader might usefully note that this very transformation makes its own point about the difference between the world and concerns of the bourgeois American poet and those of a new African artist):

> *Njala, bwana,*
> *Tandipatseni wani tambala yokha*
> *Njala, bwana*
> *Njala*
>
> Let us go then, you and I
> (Again the sigh)
> When the offices, shops and restaurants
> Vomit their inmates onto the pavements
> Like the front doors
> Of busy dungholes
> Pavements that stare past you
> To lead you
> To the inevitable question...
> Oh, do not ask this afternoon:
> Are we going to get much from it?
> Let us go and make our visit.

The poem continues in the same vein and and though one might object to the register created for a beggar woman addressing her child, there are moments when the imitation strikes a note of deep pathos. Consider the following lines:

> Shall I say: I have walked the lonely street
> And heard the march of well-fed feet
> Truck loads chanting
> Bus loads of women singing?
> I do not think they will sing for me.

Sudden growth came with Chimombo's 'Napolo', a work that developed into a long poetic sequence, published in Canada's *Malahat Review* (1975). Designed within a framework of local myth and topography, 'Napolo' explores the problem of blessings' inevitable mixture with pain and grief, a notion familiar from Soyinka's *Idanre*, a work with which the Malawian poem has some loose affinities. Where,

147

in the Nigerian piece, Ogun visits a parched earth with rain and slaughter, here the rainmaker pours his life-giving water but is accompanied by Napolo and his bloody violence. The mountains of Zomba, Mulanje, and Nyika shake on Napolo's arrival and a distraught people reel in terror before him. The beginning, which is also the end, is all drought and heat:

> Seeds cracked in the sultry afternoon
> The dessicated undergrowth sizzled
> Stifling new life in its pods.
> Twigs snapped
> Wilting trees panted in the long drought.

The elders pray. There is a week's purification and sexual abstinence. Offerings of beer and flour are made, and the vigil begins. The storm announcing the heavenly visitation begins with a sigh and gentle stirring, but soon roars to a climax:

> With thunder and lightning
> Earth's mouth gaped wide.
> Trees, boulders, villages
> Were sucked into its entrails
> Ground and ejected
> Down river.
> Heads, arms, legs, chests
> Disembowelled earth
> Churned
> In the furious current.
> The earth bled
> Reeked of mud and mangled flesh
> Guts bubbled in the torrent
> Gubudu Gubudu
> Gubudu Gubudu
> Zomba detonated its boulders
> And blasted a pathway
> Down its slope.
> Mulungusi was born.
> Napolo had decreed it.

In 'The Aftermath' an ancestral prophecy that the mountain is falling (Mphirimo! Mphirimo!) and Napolo coming gets swiftly silenced by the deity's smothering power:

148

Mutende's tomb roared again:
"Mphirimo! Mphirimo! Mphirimo!"
The snarl of brakes strangled the sepulchral voice
Boots crunched the gravel
And the cold muzzles of machine guns
Confronted the dawn.
Napolo was here
To stay.
By the waters of Mulungusi I sat down and wept.

Shifting through time, the *persona* takes us to a period years later when the god's coming is still a story told in whispers. The impact of his visitation, it seems, will not be soon forgotten:

We are going to laugh together again
With empty mouths
Dead eyes
Grimaces echoing hollowed minds.

'Napolo' is Chimombo's most extended poetic performance and provides enough evidence to suggest that here is a young Malawian with the career of a major writer before him. His example is already inspiring the pens of an eager group of student poets, several of whom show a good measure of promise. These include Anthony Nazombe, Lance Ngulube, H. Chirwa, Leonard Nkosi, and George Kaliwo.

# 3

# Aspects of South African verse

In African affairs, South Africa has long been a special case, provoking a mixed response from writers and scholars in free Africa. When Ezekiel Mphahlele visited Paris in the Fifties, his negritudist colleagues were shocked that he could not identify himself fully with their aims, and that he saw South Africa's problems as radically different from those of West and East Africa. Most alarming was his inability to imagine a future South Africa without the presence of its large white population. In part, Mphahlele's point is that black South Africans faced up to, and in their own way long ago solved, problems which only began to stir Senghor and his disciples in the Thirties. Under attack by a black American, he defends his people in vigorous style:

> Anyone who imagines that we in South Africa are just helpless, grovelling and down-trodden creatures of two worlds who have been waiting for the 'messiah' of negritude, does not know a thing about what is going on in our country.[1]

Black South Africans, he argues, have already created a new urban culture, having integrated Africa and the West; they have completed a process scarcely begun, or being undergone with pain and confusion, elsewhere on the continent. Against this background and other aspects of South African history, the aims and substance of negritude appear in a most unusual light, sharply emphasising South Africa's exception to continent-wide patterns. Hence the irony of the following:

> The bits of what the white ruling class calls 'Bantu culture' that we are being told to 'return to' are being used by that class to oppress us, to justify the Transkei and other Bantustans.

Unlike West Africa, and immeasurably more than East Africa where only Kenya provides a real parallel, South Africa is a multi-racial society whose various communities all produce writing that reflects a bond with its soil and landscape. This is true whether the writing is conceived in English or Afrikaans, Xhosa, Sesotho, or Zulu, and Mphahlele's claim that 'the only cultural vitality there is is to be seen among the Africans' is less than convincing. Where 'alien' ethnic groups such as Europeans and Mid-East traders are mentioned in West African literature and where East African writing reflects at times the fact that White and Asian have grown attached to the land, in South Africa substantial quantities of writing have appeared from each of its racial communities. Though reflecting a broadly common geographical background, these are independent literatures built on diversely inherited traditions of language, race, and religion. Where countries such as Brazil and the United States have attempted a melting-pot approach to such diversity to produce new forms and shapes (and where, if Mphahlele is right, black South Africans have already done the same), white South Africans cling to their vision of a vertical mosaic, where, they claim, each fragment can shine in its allotted place, though with political cement preventing contact with other fragments in the pattern.

South Africa is also a major industrialised power on a continent overwhelmingly agrarian. It is not always realised that the industrial urban figures of West African writers like Ekwensi and Ousmane were considerably predated by the characters of Paton and Abrahams. But increasing industrialisation, with labour shortages, militates against the aesthetics of a mosaic social pattern. For black South African writers, the fact that they have not only been raised in an industrial society but have, many of them, been engaged actively in its business and processes, at once distinguishes them from their colleagues elsewhere in Africa where writers of Ousmane's background (years spent as a Marseilles docker) are a distinct rarity. They bring to their work an outlook recognisably 'modern', fraught with the stuff and pain of industrial society. For such men merely to rehearse the beauty of a traditional life they no longer know would be a hollow exercise performed at the expense of more vital concerns.

Apartheid, the blue-print for the vertical mosaic, is both a chance lost and a provocation to artists at every angle of its jagged outline. This, more than any other single fact, has meant that modern South African writing, almost unique in human history, is a literature of exile, written in the gardens of Nigeria, the waiting rooms of Europe, the libraries of America and England, or in planes high over the Atlantic

flying men to freedom. Oswald Mbuyiseni Mtshali sums it up in a
poem in his collection *Sounds From a Cowhide Drum* (24):

> Where have
> All the angry young men gone?
> Gone to the Island of Lament for Sharpeville
> Gone overseas on scholarship,
> Gone up North to milk and honeyed uhuru.
> Gone to the dogs with the drink of despair.[2]

Writing an obituary preface to Can Themba's *The Will to Die*, the South
African writer Lewis Nkosi says:

> Time, frustration and despair, with their attendant drugs –
> alcohol and suicide – are taking a toll on South African writers.
> Nat Nakasa. Ingrid Jonker. Now Can Themba...Their deaths
> are not simply natural deaths even when they are technically so;
> for even though they do not die at the end of a bullet, flattened
> against some executioner's wall, their anguish is in so many ways
> related to the anguish of the people of South Africa.[3]

This was written before the suicide of the poet Arthur Nortje, who,
writing in exile, produced his ironically titled 'Autopsy':

> In the towns I've acquired
> arrive the broken guerrillas, gaunt and cautious,
> exit visas in their rifled pockets
> and no more making like Marx
> for the British Museum...
>
>    The world receives
> them, Canada, England, now that the laager
> masters recline in a gold inertia
> behind the arsenal of sten guns.[4]

Presumably Nortje lost his belief in the artist's ability to break chains,
and survival itself became intolerable. Hence his lines:

> The luminous tongue in the black world
> has infinite possibilities no longer.

Mazisi Kunene, who has translated much from his own Zulu poems,
offers the following brief piece called 'Exile' (72):

Our lives were ruined
Among the leaves.
We decayed like pumpkins
In a mud field.[5]

The age and influence of apartheid are attested, among others, by
Arthur Keppel-Jones, an historian who predicted with great accuracy
how apartheid would develop after Smuts. 'It ramifies' he says, 'into
every corner of South African life, legislation, administration, custom,
and thought...its roots reach back at least to the roots of the hedge
planted by Van Riebeeck.'

Yet literature has flourished in the Republic, whether as physic for
sorrow or prop for racial triumphalism. The whites have a tradition
linking them with Hoft and Couperus, Coleridge and Burns; and black
writing as a modern phenomenon began earlier here than anywhere
in the continent. In their Introduction to *The Penguin Book of South
African Verse*, Cope and Krige write:

> Poetry is something of an obsession in South Africa, or perhaps
> it is a territory which for a variety of causes has always called from
> its often lonely inhabitants the response of song or verse-making.[6]

Of writing in Afrikaans, they comment:

> Pride in the Afrikaans language and its success in the production
> of a many-sided literature have helped place writers, and parti-
> cularly poets, in a relatively advantageous position. The estab-
> lished poets are honoured national figures showered...with
> prizes and public awards.

This appears to describe a state of poetry in a white community
livelier and more genuinely popular than poetry in any corner of the
white Commonwealth. It also describes a community which sees itself
continually under siege, needing always to assert and flaunt, to keep
its culture pure. It is linked, with evil irony, to a situation elsewhere
on the mosaic, where non-white writers are driven to suicide or exile,
have their works proscribed or publishing facilities denied them, a
situation summed up by Oswald Mbuyiseni Mtshali:

Black is the mole of the poet,
a mole burrowing from no entrance to no exit.

153

Equally impressive is the list of established English-speaking poets which white South Africa boasts, and the Penguin anthology proves this even in its judicious selectiveness. William Plomer, Roy Campbell, H. C. Bosman, Anthony Delius, Guy Butler, Roy Macnab, Laurence Lerner, and Sydney Clouts are all poets with much in print and reputations deservedly high.

Predictably *The Penguin Book of South African Verse* is thin on black poets, including only a scattering of work by men like Z. D. Mangoaela, N, M. Khaketla, S. E. K. Mqhayi, L. T. Manyase, and B. W. Vilakazi. This reflects in part the fact that a major effort has gone into vernacular writing, which the editors are modestly reluctant to translate, and also censorship laws which would prevent any anthology carrying the works of banned authors.

### Vilakazi

One of the few black poets included is B. W. Vilakazi, a Zulu who died in 1947 after a career as a lecturer at Witwatersrand. His work in places resembles the old protesting harmonies of early negritude verse from West Africa and the Caribbean. Typical is this stanza from his poem 'Because' (297):

> Just because I smile and smile
> And happiness is my coat
> And my song tuneful and strong
> Though you send me down below
> Into unbelievable regions
> Of the blue rocks of the earth –
> You think then I'm a gatepost
> Numb to the stab of pain.

His piece "Then I'll Believe", recounting the death of his father, shows a gift for pathos that is strong because undramatic (298):

> I'll believe then that you are dead
> Only when the hills and flickering rivers,
> The wind roaring from North and South-West,
> When the cutting winter frost and the dews
> That lay on the grass today and yesterday –
> When all these are swallowed and fade away.

Sometimes the pathos arises from reflecting on dead traditions he might have worked harder to save. The old songs failed in his youth to strike a sympathetic chord; but now they resonate deep within him as part of the turbulence of a soul filled with anguish, haunting him with echoes of an order that has passed away (299):

> At first when I heard the old song
> I listened bitter, ignorant,
> But now in a new light I make amends.
> When your voices murmur in your breasts
> Echoing from the depths of old passions,
> Carried from the Zulu hills out across the earth,
> They call back to me things that are no more,
> Faint almost beyond grope of memory
> And the long river of my tears.

The difficulties faced by black South African poets wishing to work in written forms, yet now influenced by Europe and weaned away from their own condemned poetic traditions, have been discussed by several commentators. In his Introduction to his own volume, *Zulu Poems* (1970), Mazisi Kunene writes:

> Modern Zulu poets like Vilakazi, Mthembu, Made, S. Dlamini, A. Kunene, when first attempting to put in writing what had been an oral tradition, faced immeasurable problems. First, because they had been brought up on a tradition of English poetry they found themselves confined to English literary forms and styles. This assumed such bizarre proportions that, for instance, though the Zulu language structure does not lend itself to rhymes, words were twisted to express this form. Some of the poems are hardly intelligible, because of their preoccupation with form. The second problem they faced was a psychological one. Since Zulu traditional poetry had expressed themes connected with actions of the community, they found it difficult to find new themes other than those dictated by English poetry... Most of the new Zulu poetry became an imitation of, in particular, nineteenth-century English poets like Keats, Shelley and Wordsworth.

Vilakazi's poem 'On the Gold Mines' gets its energy by opposing the cries of an exploited group seeking humanity and the steely silence of machinery of which it is a victim. This is not merely an African poet investing machinery with an organic life and capacity for response. The 'dialogue's' implications go deeper, suggesting that you might as well plead with machines as with the whites; that the whites now resemble the machines they have invented; that their civilisation is

steely cold and hard. Lines addressed to well-tooled steel and iron
become a manifold indictment of Vilakazi's white South African masters (304):

> Not so loud there, you machines;
> Though whiteman may be without pity
> Must you too, made of iron, treat me thus?

Firmly and skilfully the relationships are drawn between machinery,
Blacks, Whites, and the central questions of poverty, wealth, and
exploitation. Because the machines are also the servants and property
of the Whites the *persona* regards them as brothers, a term he noticeably
denies to the whites. Hence his remarks on the tragic loss of life in
the mines (301):

> For these men, your brothers, they rust too
> Caught and held fast by the mines.
> Their lungs crumble away diseased
> They cough, they sink down and they die.

The movement of the verse, its tired plodding rhythm, suggests the
anger of a mature soul. It is verse heavy with experience, as if it has
outgrown the shrill screaming of youth.

> And today I am going underground
> To drive a jumper drill into the rock.
> You too at the pithead, unaware of me,
> You'll see how well I work the jack-hammer
> Of the white men down below, and watch
> The frame trucks and the cocopans come up
> Loaded with white rock and blue ore.

The *persona's* place in this industrial pattern – one tiny link in a vast
chain – is pinpointed when he asks (303):

> If I should die down in the deep levels
> What matter? Just who am I anyway?
> Day after day, you poor sufferer,
> The men drop dead, they keel over while I watch.

The questions are all rhetorical. But notice that when Vilakazi writes
'Just who am I anyway?' this is no Sartrean enquiry (psychological
crises of identity are luxuries of a higher economic order); rather is

it the poet's parody of an oft-heard question designed to keep the
majority in their appointed place, to fix them low on the ladder of
significance.

Vilakazi's poem also touches on the devastation of family life which
the apartheid system has caused. After the *persona's* first experience
underground he was so appalled that he decided to return home at
once:

> But there ruins and bare fields struck me.
> I scratched my head, went into a hut
> And asked: Where is my wife, her parents?
> They said: The whiteman called them up to work.
> Then I was dumb, my mouth sewn up in silence.

The relationship of machines to economic exploitation and human
misery is reaffirmed at the end of the poem. The *persona* can hear the
engine's voice even when he is away on the location. Its sound conjures
tall chimneys and the

> Wealth and the wealthy whom I made rich,
> Climbing to the rooms of plenty, while I stay
> Squeezed of juice like flesh of a dead ox.

Mazisi Kunene, the Zulu poet, might have been echoing Vilakazi
in his piece 'The Gold-miners'. Indeed, Vilakazi's poetry was his first
model:

> Wealth piles on the mountains.
> But where are the people?
> We stand by watching the parades
> Walking the deserted halls...

### Dennis Brutus

So much of the poetry of Dennis Brutus, who does not appear in Cope
and Krige's anthology, is marked by modesty and reason. It is remarkable that a man who has suffered the worst inhumanities which white
men have inflicted on Africa, including forced labour and a bullet in
the back, should protest in so quiet a voice, in such measured tones,
in such unpretentious verse. Where violence or screaming despair
might be appropriate from an artist in Brutus' position, his characteristic response blends dignity with patience, and calmness with

reason, determined always that emotionalism must never triumph. Even when his oppressors are discomfited, we find modest joy rather than thumping triumphalism, joy that is almost embarrassed and self-conscious.

Brutus' natural statement is a short poem of perhaps twelve lines, ostensibly prosaic in its movement, organisation, and diction. His case, too urgent for hysteria, must be stated plainly, that is literally, without undue recourse to the figurative. Indeed, he often confines his word play to closing lines as if rationing for himself the poet's joy of luxuriating in the beauty of his own words; as if indeed the figurative represents escapism. Emotion is rarely overstrained and metaphor is subtly unobtrusive. Perhaps, too, Brutus believes that a coolly argued low-key approach is best suited to an oppressor who appears to scorn hysterics and claims above all that he is reasonable. Thus, like Kenyatta in the Thirties or Awolowo in the Forties, Brutus offers an extended exercise in forensic persuasion, though he has stated his broad aims in terms of morbid pathology. He will:

> ...pin down the raw experience
> tease the nerve of feeling and expose
> it in the general tissue we dissect;
> and then, below this, with attentive ear
> to hear the faint heartthrob –
> a flicker, pulse, mere vital hint
> which speaks of the stubborn will
> the grim assertion of some sense of worth
> in the teeth of the wind
> on a stony beach, or among rocks
> where the brute hammers fall unceasingly
> on the mind.[7]

But why has such unassuming verse been received so warmly, with *The Guardian* critic saying 'he has a grace and penetration unmatched even by Alexander Solzhenitsyn'? The answer lies partly in a skill with poetic logistics which normally underlies Brutus' verse. If complex metaphor, recondite allusion, and sensual imagery are played down, the struggle to persuade must be waged with other devices. If the fiery protest of a Diop and the pathos of a Vilakazi are ruled out, what remains? Like the Nigerian poet Okara, Brutus recognised how energy can be produced simply by pitting one force against another, as rubbed sticks create fire or two notes harmony. Also the exploitation of grammatical mood and syntax can achieve results as efficiently as devices of a more conventional variety. Hence the calmness of Brutus' statements often jars with the violence of the cruelty he is describing. The cool logic of his verses, making points with caution, is fruitfully at odds with the unreasoning nature of the system which oppresses him. His dogged clinging to the rocks of humanity energises the verse by its contrast to the bestiality sweeping about him. There is a concern to match attack with tactful and dignified retreat, introspection with objectivity. Stated another way, the tensions of Brutus' verse arise from the finest possible balance between the demands of reason and the claims of emotion. Brutus' verse as a result often resembles the best neo-classic work which succeeded most when emotional fire was forced through the channels of reason. The comparison can be pushed further, for like the best neo-classicists, like Pope especially, Brutus' style and structures are at one with his morality: the order and balance of his poetic art reflect witheringly on the disorder he sees around him. Like the Pope of the *Dunciad*, he is writing ever purer verse as the darkness closes around him.

A useful example of Brutus' poetic manner can be seen in this early poem from his 1963 Mbari collection (7):

> More terrible than any beast
> that can be tamed or bribed
> the iron monster of the world
> ingests me in its grinding maw:
>
> agile as ballet-dancer
> fragile as butterfly
> I eggdance with nimble wariness
> – stave off my fated splintering.

Notice here a trim plainness, unobtrusive figures, and counterpointing statement. It is monster versus butterfly. One seeks destruction, the other survival. The monster will win, but not yet, not while the poet can eggdance. Moral and physical survival are possible, despite the horrors of a police state (4):

> Somehow we survive
> and tenderness, frustrated, does not wither.
> Investigating searchlights rake
> our naked unprotected contours;
> over our heads the monolithic decalogue

of fascist prohibition glowers
and teeters for a catastrophic fall;
boots club the peeling door.
But somehow we survive
severence, deprivation, loss.
Patrols uncoil along the asphalt dark
hissing their menace to our lives,
most cruel, all our land is scarred with terror,
rendered unlovely and unlovable;
sundered are we and all our passionate surrender
but somehow tenderness survives.

Here, the solid violence loaded into 'boots club the peeling door', with
its visions of police bullying the weak, is answered by the calm repetition about the survival of tenderness. 'The Sybil', another early poem,
is on balance rather turgid; but it also demonstrates Brutus' basic
manner as he fights down a kindling anger, checks a rising flamboy-
ancy or an insistent vein of metaphor (6):

Her seer's eyes saw nothing that the birds did not,
her words were sharp and simple as their song;
that mutant winds had honed their teeth on ice
that sap ran viscous in the oaks and senile pines –
these things were common cause except to those
whose guilty fear had made them comatose:
who could not guess that red coagulate stains
would burst from summer's grossly swollen veins
or spell out from the leaves of opulent decadence
that autumn's austere nemesis would come to cleanse?

Details like the absence of a full point anywhere (which underpins an
idea of inevitability which the poet wants); the couplet rhyming 'stains'
and 'veins' which, with a delicate steadying of the rhythm, marks the
climax and ugly eruption of what all could have predicted – these
contribute to the poem's strength. Notice also how tactual provocative
words – words which by their nature and currency assault our senses
in a physical way – are balanced with those of a softer, less concrete
sort. Hence 'birds', 'sharp', 'simple', 'song', 'winds', 'teeth', 'ice',
'sap', 'oaks', 'pines', 'guilty', 'fear', 'red', 'veins', 'stains', 'leaves',
'autumn', and 'burst', balance 'mutant', 'honed', 'viscous', 'senile',
'comatose', 'coagulate', 'opulent', 'nemesis', 'austere'. Even the final
word 'cleanse' seems to have been chosen over its rougher relative

'clean' for its muffled impact, desired here as part of the overall poetic strategy.

'This sun on this rubble after rain' is the opening line of a poem in which Brutus describes the warmth of the sun shining on a mound of rubble after the grey coldness of rain. After a stanza worked in subdued tones (9)

> Bruised though we must be
> some easement we require
> unarguably, though we argue against desire

where in the third line Brutus hovers on the brink of word-play, we get the sense-assaulting violence of the following:

> Under jackboots our bones and spirits crunch
> forced into sweat-tear-sodden slush
> – now glow-lipped by this sudden touch:

By the time the poem closes with a repetition of the opening line, 'like this sun on this debris after the rain', Brutus has identified himself and his community with this rubbish. He and his people are the cast-offs of South African society, the garbage spilling from an opulent life-style.

A passionately protective love of the land, as well as its people, keeps Brutus' zeal for the cause constantly fuelled. The land is being scarred by the apostles of this hideous system and it is the land he is addressing in 'Nightsong: City', a piece whose subtle rhyme scheme and familiar balance of forces makes it one of Brutus' most perfectly realised early poems (18):

> Sleep well, my love, sleep well:
> the harbour lights glaze over restless docks,
> police cars cockroach through the tunnel streets;
>
> from the shanties creaking iron-sheets
> violence like a bug-infested rag is tossed
> and fear is immanent as sound in the wind-swung bell;
>
> The long day's anger pants from sand and rocks;
> but for this breathing night at least,
> my land, my love, sleep well.

Even finer is a companion piece to this poem on urban night sounds, a poem which provided a title for Brutus' first collection, *Sirens, Knuckles, Boots* (19):

161

The sounds begin again;
the siren in the night
the thunder at the door
the shriek of nerves in pain.

Then the keening crescendo
of faces split by pain
the wordless, endless wail
only the unfree know.

Importunate as rain
the wraiths exhale their woe
over the sirens, knuckles, boots;
my sounds begin again.

Three four-line stanzas, a fairly tight rhythm, and a rhyme scheme are basic elements in a deceptively simple poem. There is paradox even at the simple level of aim, for here is a poem, necessarily built out of words, trying to conjure a situation that is wordless, which consists only of sounds. Nobody here, except the listening poet, says anything: we hear siren sounds, a thunderous knocking at doors, terrified folk shrieking, and a sorrowful wailing. The people's plight has gone beyond words, and in the last stanza we listen to wraiths exhaling their woe, the dead of this night and others simply ghosting forth their sadness. Rhyme helps the poem's auditory nature and its related pathos, for the thin, piercing vowel in *again*, closing the first line, recurs in *pain* (twice), and in *wail* and *rain* in the remaining stanzas, creating a subdued effect of ceaseless wailing throughout the poem. Sound thus records a situation which is beyond words. Brutus closes his poem typically by repeating its opening line; but notice that his repetition involves a slight change of wording. 'The sounds begin again', with its suggestion of ceaseless pain, gets repeated as '*my* sounds begin again', where a mere possessive adjective effects a whole shift of posture. What was reported, as it were, from arm's length, apparently existing outside the poetic sensor, is suddenly pulled close, as the poet places himself in the midst of the sounds and agony that are his own as well as those of the nameless ones in the poem. The effect of introducing this close identification at the end rather than at the beginning is to add a sense of surprise and sharpened pity to the poem. We are left with the sorrow of a poet protectively mourning the suffering of a speechless people at the hands of a grim inhumanity.

Brutus' experience as a prisoner on Robben Island off Cape Town was a major landmark in his personal life and hence in his poetry too; it has become a focus for his thinking and reflection, a central point around which his career as poet and activist can be arranged. The early poems seem almost to have been a preparation for imprisonment, and verse written since Brutus' exile seems constantly to hark back to it. The result is that at the centre of the Brutus *oeuvre*, whether the poet intends it or not, stands a prison, and whether we take that prison to be Robben itself or the Republic as a whole does not matter. Robben Island has become a symbol of a whole people's incarceration.

The prison term itself has produced some of the finest poems Brutus has written, particularly those collected in *Letters to Martha*. Imprisonment not only pushed the poet to explore the deepest recesses of mind and soul, but also demanded, constantly and at their highest pitch, all those imaginative and spiritual resources necessary for his survival as a man of dignity and self-respect. Hindered, frustrated, and insulated in his daily life by the system he sets out to fight, the poet is now jailed by that system in conditions contrived to reduce men to beasts and drown them in a cesspool of perversion. Yet somehow (and here is where Brutus' verse gets its superb moral strength) by every stratagem that the reasoning mind can devise, by resort to prayer, memory, art, patience, acceptance, and faith, he survives, though spiritually hurt and scalded. All this is felt through verse which moves quietly on the surface in a plain, unstrident way, avoiding grandiose statement, sentimentality and hysteria because these would announce defeat and fail to produce the kind of art Brutus wants. It would weaken the faith he is anxious to keep alive in 'a land/whose rich years, unlike England's lie ahead'.

The poems collected under the general title *Letters to Martha*, together with their *Postscripts*, often reflect a clash of moods, a clash of grammar. The poet's personal response to prison is reflected deep in the verse as a struggle between two dominant moods, the subjunctive and indicative. The indicative reports what really did, and does, happen in the prison, the certainties of life there, while the subjunctive from the start is a grey cloud of uncertainty and doubt, of potential evil and event constantly threatening the poet's delicate balance. The indicative records what is physically experienced and therefore known; but the known, while appalling enough, is infinitely more bearable than the unknowns reflected in the subjunctives. As Brutus puts it in Letter 9:

> The not-knowing
> is perhaps the worst part of the agony

Letter 1 records the relief after the uncertainties of the trial, the fact that sentence has been passed and the prisoner will be going to Robben. The indicatives of the sentencing bring relief after a subjunctive period in which the prisoner has been guessing what might, perhaps, be his fate after the court procedures. But the indicative does not entirely dominate for the known sentence is still hedged by uncertainty on the possible horrors of prison conditions. And present too in this finely honest account are feelings of challenge and self-pity (54):

> After the sentence
> mingled feelings:
> sick relief,
> the load of the approaching days
> apprehension –
> the hints of brutality
> have a depth of personal meaning;
>
> Exultation –
> the sense of challenge
> of confrontation,
> vague heroism
> mixed with self-pity
> and tempered by the knowledge of those
> who endure much more
> and endure...

In the lines 'hints of brutality/have a depth of personal meaning' the grammar is saying that the intimations of possible brutality are given a sharper edge, a deeper horror, by an indicative which is the poet's experience already of the system's day-to-day brutality. The custodians of apartheid have already shot him in the back. Thus, because of his knowledge, he suffers a sharper sense of the horrific potentialities attending his sentence.

This basic tension between subjunctive and indicative is very clear in Letter 3. The poet is now in prison trying to understand the weird behaviour of his colleagues. From his new indicative situation an enormous growth of questions erupts. Trying to come to terms with its surroundings, the poet's mind reaches out into a jungle of subjunctives (55):

164

Suddenly one is tangled
in a mesh of possibilities:
notions cobweb around your head,
tendrils sprout from your guts in a hundred
    directions:

The rest of the poem becomes a series of unanswered questions:

why did this man stab this man for that man?
what was the nature of the emotion
and how did it grow?
was this the reason for a warder's unmotivated
    senseless brutality?
by what shrewdness was it instigated?

His approach to scenes of subhuman behaviour is no different from his approach to the system which is his main target. The calm sensibility goes to work, asking reasonable questions, fighting to make sense of all this falling from grace, seeking always to understand rather than condemn.

By letter 5, the fearful nature of the subjunctives' possibilities is now becoming clearer. Indeed the subjunctives are now threatening to become indicatives. They are beckoning from the depths of the poet himself. In a poem which can be read as both a statement of the Christian view that man is flawed by original sin, and as part of a related argument that man's nobility lies in fighting always to higher peaks, the poet describes some of the creatures that he and mankind are host to. It makes a perfect anti-romantic contrast to the joy-in-solitude effusions of Wordsworth (56).

In the greyness of isolated time
which shafts down into the echoing mind,
wraiths appear, and whispers of horrors
that people the labyrinth of self.

Coprophilism; necrophilism; fellatio;
penis-amputation;
and in this gibbering society
hooting for recognition as one's other selves
suicide, self-damnation, walks
if not a companionable ghost
then a familiar familiar,
a doppelgänger
not to be shaken off.

The tension between the grammatical moods grows complex here since the monsters that swim the deep pools of self are called 'wraiths', that is, creatures with only an abstract, intangible existence; and we are told that the poet only hears 'whispers' of them and the sound of a threatening approach from within. In a sense, then, they are still chained in the pens of the subjunctive. Yet their existence, the fact that they are *real*, is insisted on by the remark that these are horrors 'that people the labyrinth of self', a statement in the simple indicative. The point is clinched in the reference to a 'doppelgänger', for this describes a situation in which the indicative self has a subjunctive correlative.

Surrounding the indicative realities, then, are those areas of the unknown, of doubt, which we call the subjunctive. These also include the areas of fantasy, dream, and insanity. Brutus feels drawn into these regions and here several inmates actually flee for escape when indicative horrors grow too oppressive. Letter 6 offers an example. Two men are faced with an impossible situation: the overwhelming pressures 'to enforce sodomy'. A 'tense thought lay at the bottom of each'. Their reactions differ but both take an escape route to fantasy (7):

> One simply gave up smoking
> knowing he could be bribed
> and hedged his mind with romantic fantasies
> of beautiful marriageable daughters:
>
> The other sought escape
> in fainting fits and asthmas
> and finally fled into insanity:

One way of cushioning the mind is to leap to prayer (as Brutus notes in Letter 4 where he says that it is not uncommon in 'the grey silence of the empty afternoons' to find oneself talking to God), or to music with remembered bars of Mozart or Bach, or to literature with its refreshment and reassurance in such ironic snatches as 'At daybreak for the isle', 'Look your last on all things lovely' and 'Nothing of him doth change/but doth suffer a sea change'. A Wordsworthian recourse to the external world of nature can also help with glimpses of clouds, stars, sea, and sun. But this can sometimes be disappointing as we note in Postcript 3, where white gentle seagulls serve only to emphasise a grim truth about man himself, rather than illustrate what his nobler side might let him grow to be. Religious allusions such as 'full of grace'

166

and 'redeem' suggest the poet's depression at the thought of man being locked into a generally fallen nature (24):

> The seagulls, feathery delicate
> and full of grace when flying
> might have done much to redeem things;
>
> but their raucous greed and bickering
> over a superflux of offal –
> a predatory stupidity
>
> dug in the heart with iron-hard beak
> some lesson of the nature of nature:
> man's ineradicable cruelty?

Physical and spiritual vulnerability are constants in these poems. The hangman's rope, for example, threatens the prisoner only physically. But the ever-present temptation to suicide, a mortal sin, can destroy him on both counts. 'How easily I might be damned', he writes. The suspense at the heart of so many of the poems is felt to be a delicate centre that is somehow holding against physical destruction and spiritual chaos.

And behind all lies Brutus' faith, his belief that tomorrow will be better, that change is possible and probable, that 'peace will come' and 'men will go home'. Faith and patience are strong in him and the voice that cries 'Destroy, Destroy' or 'Let them die in thousands!' is condemned as the voice of unwisdom. He is thankful that he has been spared exposure to rhetoric, though a few 'immature' prisoners resorted to it. For rhetoric would 'have falsified/a simple experience;/living grimly,/grimly enduring'. It is true that Brutus does allow himself an occasional flush of mischievous delight at having pained a society that makes a God of sport, and it is true that he whips this society for its 'bared ferocity of teeth', its 'chest thumping challenge and defiance', and its prayers to 'a deity made in the image of their prejudice'; but even here he can assert that all this evil merely reflects the predicament of his own people, who, though today's victims, are as open to the temptations of power and inhumanity as those currently oppressing them.

# 4

# Prose

If the quality of the prose written in East, Central, and Southen Africa does not uniformly match the poetry, it has compensations in quantity and variety. Nor does it have hanging over it the ominous questions of direction and commitment that face modern verse. At every level, an expanding reading public is thirsty for prose and the writers coming forward to provide it increase daily. The reverence accorded not just to books but to the printed word generally is one of the central facts of modern African life.

Newspapers and journals, society's most common encounter with the printed word, and therefore most potent sources of influence, have been enriched by the work of men like Ochieng, Ngweno, and Ojuka in East Africa, who are professional journalists of energy and skill, and also by men who have developed into creative writers of substance such as Uganda's Oculi and South Africa's La Guma. At the same popular level, albeit mainly in the vernacular, a group of market writers resembling West Africa's Onitsha school, and producing on hand presses the same pamphlet-size books of advice and entertainment, has appeared at Karatina, near the Kenyan town of Nyeri. In Kenya too the prolific young writer David Maillu runs his own publishing house, Comb Books, and turns out mini novels like *After 4.30 Troubles, Unfit for Human Consumption*, and *No*, plays bearing such alluring titles as *The Flesh: A True Nasty Monologue of a Prostitute in the Pen Name, Jasinta Mote*, and poems like *My Dear Bottle*, written in the style of Okot p'Bitek.

On a loftier level, scholars such as Alan Ogot, Gideon Were, and Ali Mazrui are making strong contributions in the fields of history, politics, and sociology, Kenyatta's *Facing Mount Kenya* remains a classic document in anthropology, and criticism, though still small in quantity, has so far been characterised by originality and a strong questioning

168

posture. In East Africa, this has come from the pens of Taban Lo Liyong, Mazrui, Ngugi wa Thiong'o, Chris Wanjala, Peter Nazareth, and Gideon Mutiso. As yet no book of criticism has appeared from Central Africa, but Ezekiel Mphahlele's output in South Africa has been of major significance. His *African Image* and *Voices in the Whirlwind* have been as much landmarks of criticism in the South as Taban's pioneering *The Last Word* was in the East. Also in the Republic C.L.S. Nyembezi has written a *Review of Zulu Literature* (1961), and Lewis Nkosi *Home and Exile* (1965), while in Lesotho, S. M. Guma has produced *The Form Content and Technique of Literature in Southern Sotho* (1967), and D. P. Kunene *The Works of Thomas Mofolo* (1967), and *Heroic Poetry of the Basotho* (1971). Other active critics of perceptiveness and persuasion include Albert Ojuka, R. C. Ntiru (both in Kenya), Felix Mnthali, Ken Lipenga, and Paul Zeleza from Malawi.

Autobiographies from Kenyatta and Kaunda have been matched by work of a similar kind from those who have also played (or are still playing) a part in the historic struggles of the continent. Mugo Gatheru's *Child of Two Worlds* (1964), Josiah Mwangi Kariuki's *Mau Mau Detainee* (1960), the life of the Mau Mau leader General China, and Charity Waciuma's *Daughter of Mumbi* are paralleled to the south by Alfred Hutchinson's *Road to Ghana* (1960), Noni Jabavu's *Drawn in Colour* and *The Ochre People* (both 1963), and Legson Kayira's *I will Try* (1965). Other writing in the same general area includes Oginga Odinga's *Not Yet Uhuru* (1967), Tom Mboya's *Freedom and After* (1963), Nyerere's *Uhuru na Ujamaa* (1968), Ndabaningi Sithole's *African Nationalism* (1968), Nelson Mandela's *No Easy Walk to Freedom* (1965), Luthuli's *Let My People Go* (1962), Mphahlele's *Down Second Avenue* (1956), and Todd Matshikiza's *Chocolates for My Wife* (1961).

If contributors to children's literature are still thinly scattered (Pamela Ogot, Miriam Were, and Barbara Kimenye are the most notable), the list of short story writers is impressive for both its quality and its quantity. It includes Ngugi, Kibera, Kahiga, Ogot, Seruma, and Palangyo, from East Africa, Lipenga, Chimombo, Mungoshi, Zeleza, Namalomba, Mulikita, and Ngombe from Central Africa, and La Guma, Mphahlele, Hutchinson, Matthews, Motsitsi, Themba, and Rive from South Africa. Among these the finest at the moment are probably Kibera and La Guma, who have both done for the short story in the East and South what Abioseh Nicol did for it in the West.

Novelists include, from East Africa, Ngugi, Palangyo, Bukenya,

*Prose*

Mangua, Mwangi, Asalache, Ruhumbika, and Seruma; from Central
Africa Kachingwe, Rubadiri, Kayira, and Mulaisho; and in South
Africa La Guma, Abrahams, Mphahlele, and Bessie Head. Taken as
a whole, the quality of their fiction compares very favourably with
that found in West Africa, but so far only a handful have produced
work in any substantial quantity. In East Africa the best known is
Ngugi Wa Thiong'o.

### Ngugi Wa Thiong'o

I grew up in a small village. My father with his four wives had
no land. They lived as tenants-at-will on somebody else's land.
Harvests were often poor. Sweetened tea with milk at any time
of day was a luxury. We had one meal a day – late in the
evening...

One day I heard a song. I remember the scene so vividly: the
women who sang it are now before me – their sad faces and their
plaintive melody. I was then ten or eleven. They were being
forcibly ejected from the land they occupied and sent to another
part of the country so barren that people called it the land of
black rocks. This was the gist of their song:

[......]
And you our children
Tighten belts around your waist
So you will one day drive away from this land
The race of white people
For truly, Kenya is a black man's country.

They were in a convoy of lorries, caged, but they had one voice.
They sang of a common loss and hope and I felt their voice rock
the earth where I stood literally unable to move.

(*Homecoming*, p. 48)[1]

The contents and concerns of Ngugu Wa Thiong'o's fiction might
be easily understood even without this revealing piece of autobiography. Born of landless peasants in a colony where the white presence
was greater than anywhere north of Pretoria and Salisbury; born into
the Agikuyu, at once the most dispossessed and most deeply land-
centred people of all Africa; born into Kenya's most thoroughly
missionised region where a highly Calvinistic strain of Christianity
predominated; born at a time when childhood memories would

contain echoes of a World War vital as a catalyst in the Independence struggle; and growing through impressionable youth at precisely the time when Mau Mau erupted. The stuff of the fiction should come as no surprise.

There is then an abiding concern with the soil and man's relationship to it, not as some Lawrentian dream of giving industrial man an anchor for his sanity, but as the central factor in an equation guaranteeing the economic, social, psychological, and spiritual survival of a people. Urban-dwelling strangers must not underestimate this point about land. Ngugi might not have explored it, might indeed have written a different kind of fiction, if colonialists had not taken his land and post-colonialists not failed justly to redistribute it. The soil is also portrayed in its extra-economic aspects, in its aesthetic and artistic role as landscape and background, as a milieu of hills, valleys, and ridges in which Ngugi's characters are born and live their lives. Other African writers have a feeling for landscape and paint it well: Palangyo, Kayira, and La Guma are familiar examples. But one's sense of a land-scape's beauty and its meaning for an author and his people are vitally more present in Ngugi than in most. Where often it is simply a felt background or backcloth to a narrative, as it is in, say, Achebe or in the Malawian novelist Kayira, here it is a palpable shaping influence on the physical and spiritual lives of the characters. It is, in a sense, a part of character. And it is a reflection of both a different colonial history and a different artistic outlook that while we worry with Achebe's people whether they will harvest their yams as Ezeula plays his religio-political power games, we get little feeling that it is only by courtesy of the soil that there are any yams to harvest at all and no sense of alarm that next year the Umuaro people might be dispossessed of their land altogether.

Religion too is never far from Ngugi's mind. As everywhere else in African writing, Christianity is identified as a deeply potent element in the encounter between local society and the West. But its treat-ment here transcends the superficial levels found too often elsewhere and becomes deep sensitive investigation. Ngugi's work is the best account yet of how Christianity not only gnawed away at tribal values (the standard charge against it), but how it actually resonated with deep elements in the hearts of the people. All too often the genuine appeal of Christianity is ignored. The gospels were received with enthusiasm in Gikuyuland and not only by the weaker brethren. The Scottish missionaries, dour, tough, and thrifty, accustomed to wresting

171

a meagre living from a lovely capricious landscape, were not unlike the Gikuyu peasants they came among and admired the hard work and self-reliance for which the Gikuyu people were already reputed. The gospels they brought lauded self-sacrifice, humility, subservience to the common cause, and, crucially for this moment in Kenya's history, the glory of martyrdom. Christ on Calvary did not seem to threaten Ngai on Kerinyaga. The gospel words sank deep, and there is more than casual significance in the fact that Kihika, the purest of revolutionaries in *A Grain of Wheat*, carries not Marx but a Bible he knows as intimately as the land he is fighting for.

Ngugi's work bears the marks of surprise and disappointment that the world is not as he once thought, that the goodness he perhaps sees in his own nature does not predominate in the affairs of men. It records the response of a sensitive Christian soul who discovers, sadly, that he has been serving an unsatisfactory cause. But the power of that cause has struck very deep and hence those lines from *The River Between* (114):

> After all [Waiyaki] loved some Christian teaching. The element of love and sacrifice agreed with his own temperament. The suffering of Christ in the Garden of Gethsemane and His agony on the tree had always moved him.[2]

Hence too, in *Weep Not, Child*, Ngugi's comment that the 'Bible was Njoroge's favourite book. He liked especially the Book of Job and the Sermon on the Mount', words followed at once by a statement that Njoroge's mother's stories had reinforced all this. Finally there is that extraordinary passage in *The River Between*, where Christianity and Gikuyu tradition are pulled together as close as they possibly could be. It is a statement that might be hung up in mission houses and seminaries everywhere (117):

> Muthoni said she had seen Jesus. She had done so by going back to the tribe, by marrying the rituals of the tribe with Christ.

A trinity of themes is achieved with 'education', or more exactly schooling in a western mode. This is important, for Ngugi's main characters (those whose consciousness we get close to) are men who see beyond their own milieu, who understand the forces at work on a world rather than tribal scale, and have an awareness of comparative justice, economic fairness, and grand political intrigue. Their mode of training, which Ngugi consistently calls 'education' (ignoring Kenyatta's caveat and inviting the suggestion that traditional Gikuyu education does not merit the name), is seen as a catalyst to development, the moulder of new leaders who will guide the clans through the complexities of the modern world, a way of achieving the possibles of political theory. Like Christianity, however, it has also the side effect of creating class divisions, of disrupting tribal unity and alienating individuals from their peers and families. Hence the agonising position of Njoroge in *Weep Not, Child*, and John in the short story 'A Meeting in the Dark'.

If these are main themes in Ngugi's writing, what holds them together? What constitutes the shaping vision behind them? Politics is an obvious answer, and more specifically the doctrines of Marxism. If ever the point was in doubt, Ngugi's *Homecoming* records how deeply his world view has been influenced by Marx. The niceties of land disputes, cultural vertigo, and spiritual chaos are well enough; but behind and beneath them all, as if in explanation of them, lies the framework of ideas which are the parameters of Marxism.

While some may doubt the importance of the relationship between a writer and his beliefs, Ngugi gives his own views in very plain terms. The boundaries of a writer's imagination, he says, are limited by his 'beliefs, interests, and experiences in life, by where in fact he stands in the world of social relations'. Furthermore:

> Literature does not grow or develop in a vacuum: it is given impetus, shape, direction and even area of concern by social, political and economic forces in a particular society. The relationship between creative literature and these other forces cannot be ignored, especially in Africa, where modern literature has grown against the gory background of European imperialism and its changing manifestations: slavery, colonialism and neo-colonialism... There is no area of our lives which has not been affected by the social, political and expansionist needs of European capitalism... Yet the sad truth is that instead of breaking from an economic system whose life-blood is the wholesale exploitation of our continent and the murder of our people, most of our countries have adopted the same system... There has been no basic land reform; the settler owning 600 acres of land is replaced by a single African owning the same 600 acres... There has been no socialization of the middle commercial sector; the Asian dukawallah goes away, to be replaced by a single African dukawallah.[3]

173

Thus Ngugi's political outlook. It might not, on the face of it, appear promising background for creative writing, though it would be good testimony to the zeal of a social reformer. A little later, however, an all-important comment appears, tacked on to a sentence about his travels abroad:

> Nobody who has passed through the major cities of Europe and America, where capitalism is in full bloom, can ever wish the same fate on Africa – as far as human relationships are concerned.

This final clause is a saving grace, for what novelist can hope to produce good art who is not, ultimately, concerned about human relationships? Ngugi's creative work clearly shows that for all his sensitivity to political and social issues, human relations are what he cares about most passionately. His vision includes a horror at what has been done, and is being done, to human relationships in Africa, political convictions about why this is happening, and a dream of 'a true communal home for all Africans'.

Ngugi is regularly compared with Achebe (to whom he modestly professes inferiority), and Conrad's influence is also rightly canvassed. But his general growth as a writer, and especially his espousal of 'political art', brings him closer to Orwell than to either of these. Ngugi and Orwell are both shy, burningly honest men, provoked by injustice; defenders of the weak, public figures through circumstances rather than inclination. After reading Ngugi's lines from *Homecoming*, it is useful to glance at Orwell's essay 'Why I Write'. Listing the four main reasons why men write as egoism, aesthetic enthusiasm, historical impulse, and political purpose, Orwell says:

> By nature – taking your 'nature' to be the state you have attained when you are first adult – I am a person in whom the first three motives would outweigh the fourth. In a peaceful age I might have written ornate or merely descriptive books, and might have remained almost unaware of my political loyalties...The Spanish war and other events in 1936–37 turned the scale and thereafter I knew where I stood. Every line of serious work that I have written, has been written, directly or indirectly, *against* totalitarianism and *for* democratic Socialism, as I understand it. It seems to me nonsense, in a period like our own, to think that one can avoid writing of such subjects...And the more one is conscious of one's political bias, the more chance one has of acting

politically without sacrificing one's aesthetic and intellectual integrity...[4]

The parallels are striking enough. Coming from Ngugi's novels, with their care about love and human relationships, their concern for 'the surface of the earth', it is easy to conclude that he too is an artist who, in a less revolutionary age, would have written differently; or at least that his work would have been the result of a slightly modified equation of egoism, aesthetics, and the rest. If Mau Mau had never happened, if Kenya had won its freedom in peace, if independence had been marked by political virtue with the peasant gaining from land reform, Ngugi would have had to work with different material. Meanwhile, like Orwell, he is not a propagandist in the crude sense, but a committed literary artist, concerned about aesthetics, anxious to reflect beauty in the external world and in human experience through well-built prose. In any era Ngugi would have been a literary artist; but the present age has given him a shaping principle that has strong political roots. While deriving an artist's pleasure from recording his impressions of human life, he is fired also with an urge, in Orwell's phrase, 'to push the world in a certain direction, to alter other people's idea of the kind of society that they should strive after'. That the political theory only clarified slowly is implicit in the writing itself. A sort of injured innocence blows slowly off the prose like smoke from a burnt-out village. The writer is shocked, but will grow wiser through it. Despite this disappointment, and the political commitment he believes will cure it, Ngugi neither plumbs the depths of an abject pessimism like Armah in *The Beautyful Ones*, nor seeks the escapist frivolity of an amoral literature as Mangua does in *Son of Woman*. Ngugi espouses politics, the science of the possible, because he believes that change can occur: he remains, therefore, a hurt optimist rather than a defeated Jeremiah.

But neither politics nor large issues guarantees successful fiction; and while critics argue (as they did at the 1974 Makerere Conference) whether Ngugi qualifies for such exalted titles as Genuine Socialist Novelist, the question whether he possesses the basic skills of his craft seems too infrequently raised. Fortunately, he is strong in all those necessary areas of scene-setting, plot, structure, characterisation, and firmness of prose without which his books would be either unreadable or mere political ephemera.

*The River Between*'s hero is described as having eyes that are 'delicately tragic'. A happy phrase, it evokes a pervading quality in Ngugi's vision and in his prose. Neither heavily proverbial like Achebe's nor crisply economic like Oyono's, Ngugi's prose is unpretentious, neither over-refined nor casually rough-hewn. It is free of the excesses associated with rhetoric, for despite a slow hardening of tone, Ngugi seems to agree with Dennis Brutus that rhetoric tends to falsify experience. Hence his quiet-voiced prose, one-speed and steady, never racing out of control, and possessing a clarity that keeps event and character always plainly visible. An honest, sensitive style, it neither cavorts nor strikes attitudes; nor will it court the vanities of over-dressing. Its measured pace allows for silences, giving Ngugi's writing a reflective quality, as if the consciousness producing it is still, as it articulates, puzzling over human experience, trying honestly to interpret it aright, wanting to understand and record it all exactly, and thus needing pauses, a stillness, to do it properly.

Some of these qualities occur in a passage from *The River Between*, where Muthoni, daughter of a Christian cleric, confesses to her sister Nyambura that she wants to be circumcised and become 'a real woman, knowing all the ways of the hills and ridges' (28):

> For a second Nyambura sat as if her thoughts, her feelings, her very being had been paralysed. She could not speak. The announcement was too sudden and too stupefying. How could she believe what she had heard come from Muthoni's mouth? She looked at the river, at the slightly swaying bulrushes lining the banks, and then beyond. Nothing moved on the huge cattle road that wound through the forest towards Kameno. The yellowish streaks of morning light diffused through the forest, producing long shadows on the cattle path. The insects in the forest kept up an incessant sound which mingled with the noise of falling water farther down the valley. They helped to intensify the silence, created by Muthoni's statement.
> 'Circumcised?' At last Nyambura found her voice.
> 'Yes'.

The news' impact, received deep in Nyambura's living centres, at first numbs her then slowly pushes her attention out onto the landscape about her, whose stillness and indifferent sounds heighten both the personal shock and the momentousness of news which will produce a radical effect on the movement of the plot. Much care and skill have been lavished on this passage, though it could be described neither as precious nor purple. It possesses minute yet significant details. Muthoni's announcement is heard by 'the river' which neatly divides the landscape and the human community of the book. Its name means 'cure' or 'bring-back-to-life', it never dries up and seems to 'possess a strong will to live'. Ngugi calls it 'the soul of Kameno and Makuyu'. The ridges on either bank divide in their rival espousals of tradition and modernity, yet, with all the flora and fauna of the area, are 'united by this life-stream'. Even 'the slightly swaying bulrushes' have their place in this scene, repeating a reed-in-the-tide image which J. P. Clark popularised as a symbol of cultural hesitation. Muthoni so far has been weak like this plant; but now by the waters of Honia she has made a decision which will restore her to strength.

The pervading elegaic tones of Ngugi's prose can be felt in an extract from *Weep Not, Child,* where the domestic joys of simple togetherness and story-telling are overshadowed by the haunting presence of Boro, who has been a tragic spirit ever since he fought in the War for the British and saw his brother Mwangi die (24):

> Boro, who had been to the war, did not know many tribal stories. He drank a lot and he was always sad and withdrawn. He never talked much about his war experiences except when he was drunk or when he was in a mood of resentment against the Government and settlers.
>
> 'We fought for them, we fought to save them from the hands of their white brothers...'
>
> Then on such occasions, he might talk just a little about the actual fighting. But he very rarely alluded to Mwangi's death. It was common knowledge that they had loved each other very much.[5]

We share the sense of treachery carried in Boro's statement beginning 'We fought for them', which trails off into a void because his sense of disbelief and the enormity of the injustice leave him incapable of finding words that are adequate.

Clearly felt in the river scene is the organic relationship between Ngugi's figures and the Gikuyu milieu. The author's rendering of the shape, colour, and texture of the landscape is important on two special counts. First it marks him as a true Gikuyu who has not entirely lost his own bond with the soil. Secondly its deep sensitivity confounds all those scholars, black and white, who, despite massive literary evidence to the contrary, argue that African people have no feeling for landscape, ignore its beauty, see it only as so much soil to hoe. The affectionate pictures of Gikuyuland are also a sign of how Ngugi, though an African novelist in the broadest sense of being a spokesman for the whole continent (and even for the black race) is basically working as a regional novelist, like Achebe and Beti, or Laye and Hardy. Though universal in appeal, he portrays a particular people in a particular locale. His canvas is restricted to Kenya's Central Province. It is not the open Maasai plains sweeping down to Tanzania nor the arid semi-desert of the Samburu and Turkana. Neither is it the fertile lakeshore of the Luo reflected in the writings of Grace Ogot. Only the upland ridges and valleys of Gikuyuland are chosen for evocation.

The bond between character and land is especially strong in *The River Between*, where Waiyaki, soon after his second birth, goes with his father to visit one of the clan's sacred places. Making their way through the countryside, Chege discusses the herbs and juices of the forest, displaying a medicinal knowledge that has come from ancient intimacy and traffic with the environment. Especially significant during this pilgrimage through the land (and in a literature where sons are perpetually at odds with their fathers) is the fact that 'Waiyaki felt close to his father as he had never felt before.' He felt 'a glow rising inside him'. In his own mind he was maturing. 'The hidden things of the hills were being revealed to him.' The landscape, the forests and hills, are conspiring to unite father and son as they have united the Gikuyu nation for generations. We cannot understand the individual, social, and spiritual significance of either character outside their relation to the landscape. Chege's whole life has been moulded by the land. His maturity, his fulness as a human being, are owed to it. Only when Waiyaki too has been initiated into a full understanding of the land, reborn into a full relationship with it, will he in turn become a mature member of his people. It is the Confirmation necessary after Baptism – a comparison that is not overstrained. The bond is established now in this dawn journey to one of the holy shrines of Gikuyuland. An Easter-like scene, uncovered as the sun lifts a veil of darkness off the countryside, revealing for Waiyaki the full extent of his people's land and the great lifting peaks of Mt Kenya whence came the gift of land itself – this is an inset of remarkable force and beauty. Its sense of renewal, of fresh life, of eternal dawns, of the ritual unveiling of secrets, is matched by the strong sense of an author at one with his creations in the subtle web of soil, spirit, and history.

Father and son arrive at an ancient Mugumo tree, towering over the hill and watching over the whole country (19):

> It looked holy and awesome, dominating Waiyaki's soul so that he felt very small and in the presence of a mighty power. This was a sacred tree. It was the tree of Murungu. Waiyaki, now on top of the hill, on the other side of the tree, surveyed the land. And he felt as if his heart would stop beating so overcome was he by the immensity of the land. The ridges were all flat below his small feet. To the east, the sun had already risen. It could now be seen clearly, a huge red ball of smouldering colours. Strands of yellowish-red thinned outwards from the glowing centre, diffusing into the thick grey that joined the land to the clouds. Far beyond, its tip hanging in the grey clouds, was Kerinyaga. Its snow-capped top glimmered slightly, revealing the seat of Murungu.

The passage has its faults. The sentences 'This was a sacred tree. It was the tree of Murungu' strike a faintly dead note, the note of superfluous material that spells out what we have already learnt from previous detail. Nor are the two sentences following quite perfect and the allusion to Waiyaki's 'small feet' is unnecessary, for the immensity of the scene and its overwhelming impact on Waiyaki as viewer are felt strongly enough without this minor detail. But as a portrait of Gikuyu man, linked through all his living centres with the landscape that has produced him, this scene could hardly be better. There is no Romantic harking back to the land in all this. It does not smell like some half-baked scene cooked up in Bloomsbury or Los Angeles. The tough peasant world Ngugi speaks for is much too real for that. Ngugi's is one of the few genuine voices of the land in English-language writing anywhere; and he is spokesman for a people whose sacred bond with the soil caused them to undertake a bloody uprising against the colonial power.

Ngotho, in *Weep Not, Child,* is in the same position as Ngugi's own father, working Gikuyu soil for a settler. The settler is Howlands, a man who also loves the soil of Kenya. But however deep a white settler's love for it – and Ngugi frankly states that it was often very deep indeed – it cannot match the blood-and-soul complexity of the bond it has for a people whose total survival depends on it. We see Ngotho not so much against a backcloth of the land he tills for Howlands, but as an organic breathing part of his ancestral home temporarily in the hands of a stranger, though still available for his care and sustenance (31):

> Ngotho loved the rainy seasons when everything was green and the crops in flower, and the morning dew hung on the leaves. But the track where he had disturbed the plants and made the water run off made him feel as if, through his own fault, he had lost something. There was one time when he had felt a desire to touch the dew-drops or open one and see what it held hidden inside.

Ngotho awaits the fulfilment of a prophecy by Mugo Wa Kibera that the white man will one day go as suddenly as he came. In his stoic strength Ngotho embodies the patience and wisdom of a whole people and the elegaic cadence of his words on the land question carry the soul of the entire Gikuyu nation, waiting, like him, praying and watching (29):

> The war ended. We were all tired. We came home worn out but very ready for whatever the British might give us as a reward. But, more than this, we wanted to go back to the soil and court it to yield, to create, not to destroy. But Ng'o! The land was gone. My father and many others had been moved from our ancestral lands. He died, lonely, a poor man waiting for the white man to go. Mugo had said this would come to be.

Three colonial products which Ngugi frequently identifies are loneliness, class divisions, and guilt. Loneliness is common in all three novels, and in the short stories. We are meant to see this, I think, not as reflecting a modern existentialist infection but as a palpable result of the fracture of an old order by the engines of capitalism, the Puritan ethic, and the progress myth. When Okello Oculi argues that men were basically alone even in the most gregarious traditional communities, he is making a philosophical point rather than stating a feeling which ordinary folk might have. Ngugi's men and women are lonely, and feel lonely, in a new way; and it is clearly, from textual evidence, a result of their encounter with Europe. A simple exercise is to read Kenyatta's *Facing Mount Kenya* before approaching the fiction of Ngugi. The change worked on the Gikuyu people since Kenyatta wrote in the Thirties is astonishing. The first is a picture of tight cohesion where men and women acknowledge a common cause in a highly democratic society. The second is a picture resembling Picasso's Guernica (a significant favourite among African writers), where all is fragmentation and anxiety as members of the same group cut throats and betray friends, all in a chaotic fight for selfish enrichment.

Hence the sight of so many lonely figures scattered against the landscape of Gikuyuland. When Ngugi opens Chapter Four of *The River Between* with 'Soon Waiyaki joined again in the daily rhythm of life in the village', he is spelling out a loneliness we have felt about Waiyaki from the start. He is a child apart, a special case, living on the fringes of his community. Those passages where Waiyaki and Nyambura watch each other walking singly through the landscape also emphasise the nature of a real loneliness. They are frequently 'lost in their own thoughts', and 'whenever they met they were like strangers'. Nyambura feels distant from her father (in a manner usually reserved by Ngugi for his heroes), and her sister's death has also left her feeling desolate (86):

> Nyambura still feared her father. She knew that if he saw her standing there he would be angry. She was often lonely. The death of Muthoni had deprived her of the only companion she had ever had. So now she went to the river alone. She went to church alone...So the river, especially on Sundays, was her companion. She had her own place where she often went.

These people are lonely because their community has been split by Christianity into rival camps. On one ridge stands Nyambura's father with his cold, prejudice-ridden version of the Christian gospel, while from the other waves the flag of tradition as Waiyaki and his father Chege cultivate the old ways. It is a deeply divided community and the loneliness, the distance physically and spiritually between the characters, stems from this. The religious element is given ironic colour by having characters on both sides turn to the land for consolation and by having them do this habitually on the Christian Sunday.

One of these consolatory visits, the riverside meeting where Waiyaki finally declares his love for Nyambura, draws much of its poignancy from the very isolation which both these people feel. (The delicacy with which the encounter is handled deserves comment too, if only because relationships between the sexes in African literature tend to be shallowly drawn, and Ngugi is very exceptional in this regard.) The conversation begins with a reference to Nyambura's sister, Muthoni,

181

who had rebelled against her Christian father and become circumcised, finding, as Waiyaki feels, 'something that filled her soul and
made her endure everything', even her own death, in which, inciden-
tally, Ngugi has her achieving a triumphant fusion between Jesus and
Ngai, as though he means it as a sign for his people of how divisions
can be healed and rival traditions coexist (120–121):

> 'My sister was initiated there', she said abruptly. She made him
> feel guilty.
> 'You still remember her –'.
> 'How can I forget her? I loved her'.
> 'Were you only two in your family?'
> 'Yes; now I am alone'.
> 'I am also alone in my family. All my sisters are married. The
> youngest, whom I loved most, died a long time ago. I was then
> young – !

In *Weep Not, Child,* loneliness is like a disease endemic in the land.
The sad Boro, in one of his rare trenchant comments, strikes a
keynote for the whole book when he laments, 'All white people stick
together. But we black people are very divided.' War strengthens and
accelerates the forces at work in *The River Between* as the Mau Mau
rebellion begins. Njoroge and Mwihaki, young lovers whose innocent
relationship is drawn with a care reserved in African writing usually
for mother–son relationships, drift apart in the same manner as
Waiyaki and Nyambura and go wandering round the landscape of the
book failing to meet and growing unbearably lonely. Kamau, Mwihaki,
Njoroge, Ngotho, Boro – they are all desolate figures in the landscape
of *Weep Not, Child.* Indeed a meeting here between Mwihaki and
Njoroge is virtually a carbon copy of that between Waiyaki and
Nyambura. Two lonely souls are coming together after a long absence;
there is strain and awkwardness, yet great tenderness. The hero too
has the same sensitive decent soul we saw in Waiyaki (98):

> Again he felt embarrassed. While he had for years been deli-
> berately avoiding a meeting with her, she had at last taken the
> initiative to seek him out.
> 'It's a long time since we last met', he said.
> 'Yes. And much has happened in between – much more than
> you and I could ever have dreamed of.'
> 'Much has happened...' he echoed her words. Then he asked,
> 'How's boarding school?'

'Nice. There you are in a kind of cloister.'

'And the country?'

'Bad. Like here.'

He thought he would change the subject.

'Well, I hope you'll enjoy your holidays', he said, preparing to go. 'I must go now. I must not delay you.' She did not answer. Njoroge looked up at her.

'I'm so lonely here', she at last said, with a frank, almost childishly hurt voice. 'Everyone avoids me.'

The hesitation, the shyness, the desire in Njoroge not to finger old wounds, the initial loss for words, the general hovering quality of the encounter – all these give the incident the stamp of a real life encounter as well as emphasising the element of solitude. The whole scene is rendered with that exactness, delicacy, and underlying sense of sadness that are a hallmark of Ngugi's writing.

Both the fragmentation of Gikuyu society and the loneliness it breeds reach their highest pitch in *A Grain of Wheat*, whose picture of isolated guerrillas operating in a hit-or-miss way in scattered areas, with little sense of a home base and frequently slaughtering their own people, is the most poignant evidence for the fracture and isolation that haunt Ngugi's imagination. Figures like Mugo, an only son anxious for solitude and prepared to betray the tribe to achieve it; figures like Gatu and Gikonyo; and Kihika, the Messianic figure so loved by his people, a man essentially alone in his special level of spiritual and military involvement – they are all victims of a condition Ngugi laments.

A predictable result of Westernism and its accompanying new economic order is the growth of social class in what Kenyatta once described as an extraordinarily egalitarian society. As the new order fosters individualism, offering excessive rewards to those who can get trained, social competition begins. Men get ahead of their fellows, build their own fortress and drop the portcullis – raising it only for their own children to sally forth to gain the same privileges and the same rewards. Men are set against men, groups emerge with special interests whose solidarity is based on money and the command of strategic areas of the economy.

Gaps are already seen opening up in *The River Between*. Joshua is a leading convert to Christianity. His house is no rich man's villa, but it is architecturally different and physically set apart from his neighbours'. The building marks off the owner. He is separate, in a category of his own and the physical manifestation of his world view – which is what the house is meant to be – reinforces this. Where the Makuyu houses are normally 'round thatched huts standing in groups of three or four', Joshua's is 'a tin-roofed rectangular building standing quite distinctly by itself on the ridge'. This building, Ngugi says, stands apart 'distinctly and defiantly', and the 'little scraps of sacking that covered' the leaking parts of the roof tell their own chapter of the tale. They show an absurd refusal to use even traditional methods of water-proofing, and they also give off a whiff of the sordid that the author associates with the new class Joshua represents.

The process has gone much further in *Weep Not, Child*. Class is now a furrow Ngugi seems determined to plough – as though its presence and significance in the total pattern of his awareness has suddenly become clear. Early in the book class follows racial lines. The Whites dominate; the Asians are nervous in the middle; and the Africans are at the bottom. This would correspond roughly to the classic model of upper, middle, and working classes of European experience. Some of these distinctions are even reflected in the landscape. 'You could tell', says Ngugi, 'the land of Black People because it was red, rough, and sickly, while the land of the white settlers was green and was not lacerated into small strips.'

But the pattern is not quite so tidy as this, for already, as Ngugi saw in his previous novel, class divisions are opening up in Gikuyu society itself. Njoroge, who dreams of a schooling that will let him work wonders for his people, has been born into a society where already a sense of social class impinges on daily life and attitudes. Hence his reflections as he walks home from school with the tiny Mwihaki and dallies with her on a hill-top (17):

> It was sweet to play with a girl and especially if that girl came from a family higher up the social scale than one's own. She looked more precious because rare.

And again (55):

> Education for him...held the key to the future. As he could not find companionship with Jacobo's children (except Mwihaki), for these belonged to the middle class that was rising and beginning to be conscious of itself as such, he turned to reading.

This childhood sense of social division is echoed when Njoroge's mother appears and angrily watches him throwing stones with Mwihaki. 'She did not want her son to associate with a family of the rich because it would not be healthy for him.' Notice the phrase 'a family of the rich', suggesting that Nyokabi already recognises that there are now at least two classes in Gikuyuland – her own which is poor and another which is not. To read even this brief comment is to hear, softly yet unmistakably, a note of radical social change; change as momentous as Achebe's arrival of the Missionaries, the prophecy of Mugo Wa Kibero, or the arrival of the railway in the Kenyan Highlands. To hear it is to learn that something profound has occurred in Gikuyuland: the hatred, the fear, the envy, and the class lines of Europe are suddenly glimpsed in an African setting. When Njoroge visits Mwihaki's house, he is like some poor child peeping through the hedge of a palace (29):

> The houses were hidden by a big hedge of growing fir trees that surrounded the household. You could see the corrugated iron roof and the wooden walls of the imposing building through an opening or two in the hedge. Njoroge had been there, out in the courtyard, a number of times when he and others went to collect money for picking pyrethrum flowers for Jacobo. The place looked like a European's house and Njoroge was always over-awed by the atmosphere around the whole compound. He had never been in the big building...

Much is said and much implied. Jacobo is part of the new elite, employing others to work for him, a mini-capitalist whose home is a world apart from Njoroge's. Where under the old dispensation Jacobo and Njoroge would have been equal brothers, there is now only the much less humane bond of employer and employed, with all the potential conflict which this implies. Jacobo's interests are no longer those of the class Njoroge belongs to; and this explains the nature of the conflict that erupts when Jacobo sides with the Europeans during Mau Mau. To balance the equation, Ngugi remarks that Mwihaki's mother, for her part, 'never likes her children to associate with primitive homes. Njoroge sensed that the way he had been brought up was being criticised.' Relations between the Jacobos of Gikuyuland and the peasant mass can never again be what they were in Kenyatta's *Facing Mount Kenya*.

Even in fairly traditional pursuits like carpentry the seeds of class divisions are sown. Kamau is apprenticed to Nganga, who in his own way is another Jacobo, a businessman insensitive to the traditional values and codes governing the division of labour. Hence, Kamau at work must mind Nganga's baby as if he were an ayah and Nganga's wife a European. When Kamau airs his bitterness to Njoroge, the child's astonished reply comes straight from the norms of the old order. 'But why does he treat you like that'? he asks. 'He is a black man?' We are meant to feel that the child is speaking from a perfectly reasonable set of assumptions about tribal and racial solidarity. Kamau's reply shows how deep the new thinking has cut into the tissue of inherited ideas from which the child's comment has sprung (24):

> 'Blackness is not all that makes a man', Kamau said bitterly. 'There are some people, be they black or white, who don't want others to rise above them. They want to be the source of all knowledge and share it piecemeal to others less endowed...It is the same with rich people. A rich man does not want others to get rich because he wants to be the only man with wealth...

*A Grain of Wheat*, remarkable for its tough handling of virtually every character except Kihika (and, as usual, the women), offers the sad career of Gikonyo.[6] Gikonyo is basically a good man; but like so many of Ngugi's characters he is haunted by feelings of guilt and inadequacy. He has confessed the Mau Mau oath to return to his beloved Mumbi, though after an extraordinary display of stoic courage. Ngugi does not deride him – at least there is no textual evidence to suggest this – yet Gikonyo grows prosperous after Uhuru as a rather sordid businessman. He is the prototype of a class Ngugi has grown to detest. He has learnt the tricks of his former masters, coolly playing the market and exploiting the thriftlessness of his weaker brethren. It is an implied thrust against the post-Uhuru world that, far from official ire falling on such behaviour, it is widely admired and held aloft for emulation. Gikonyo's is a story of how even a good man can be corrupted by a bad system. The new élite applaud his thrift and business sense and preach his example. Ngugi's quietly maintained posture is clear: that black should exploit black is not what Uhuru was won for. The maggoty results for society as a whole are implied with nice irony when Gikonyo's exploitation of the peasants is mentioned in the same chapter that recounts his own experience of being cheated out of Burton's farm by an M.P. channelling government loans into his own pocket. Such is the pattern of creeping corruption. Such is a kind of decay in the East which Achebe, Soyinka, and Armah attack in the West. The new system and its corroding effects on human relationships are described with simple clarity (67):

> God helps those who help themselves, it is said with fingers pointing at a self-made man who has attained wealth and position, forgetting that thousands of others labour and starve, day in, day out, without ever improving their material lot. This moral so readily administered, seemed true for Gikonyo. People in Thabai said: detention camps have taught him to rule himself.

For the Gikonyos of Kenya the new order works miracles. His rags-to-riches story is in the best Samuel Smiles tradition. Frugal and enterprising, he denies himself today so that tomorrow might be prosperous (68):

> Instead of buying clothes for himself or his family, Gikonyo did what Indian traders used to do. He bought maize and beans cheaply during the harvests, put them in bags, and hoarded them in his mother's smoky hut. That's where he and Mumbi also lived...At the right time, he poured what he had hoarded onto the market at a high price...At first other men derided him for doing a woman's job. Brushing sides with women's skirts. But when his fortunes changed, they started respecting him. Some even tried to follow his example with varying degrees of success.
>
> The story of Gikonyo's rise to wealth, although on a small scale, carried a moral every mother in Thabai pointed out to her children.
>
> 'His wife and his aged mother need no longer go rub skirts with other women in the market.'

As the monkish Gikonyo mortifies his flesh to break into the monied class the deep impression his money makes on the people around him is clear to see. A man already respected, his newfound respect is based mainly on money, a commodity with miraculous power to change. Old attitudes about women's work are broken under its spell. Even the bonds of everyday social living are threatened when ordinary folk see that with money you don't even have to mix with other people any more! It is not important that Gikonyo traffics in black market goods; it is immaterial that he's quite prepared to bribe traffic and market policemen; it matters even less that he builds his prosperity on a cynical calculation of other people's weaknesses. The fact is that he has money and in the new Gikuyu society this is what counts. Thus the lament rises as with sickening accuracy Ngugi records the development of class divisions among his people. The old values of Gikuyu-land have been perverted along the lines of Orwell's version of I Corinthians:

> Though I speak with the tongues of men and of angels, and have not money, I am become as a sounding brass, or a tinkling cymbal.[7]

A factor which compounds the hardships of land deprivation and social fragmentation is the enormous guilt load Ngugi's people seem doomed to carry. Whether this is a general truth about the Presbyterian impact on Gikuyu society or a generalisation of Ngugi's personal experience (the artist imagining that others must feel the world in the same manner as himself) one does not know. Yet the amount of guilt gnawing away at the minds of Ngugi's characters in all three novels and in such short stories as 'A Meeting in the Dark' is extraordinary. Waiyaki in *The River Between* is his mother's only son and 'felt guilty that he did not spend more time with her', a sentiment revealing once more that classic African mother–son relationship. Guilt also festers in Waiyaki's response to his special social position, caught between the traditionalists and Joshua's Christians. Listening to Joshua's sermon on conversion and a new life, he felt the preacher's words 'touching a chord in the dark corner of his soul so that he was afraid' (99):

> Again Waiyaki felt guilty. Guilty of what? Perhaps of something to do with the light or something to do with being unfaithful to his father's voice of long ago – 'be true to the tribe and the ancient rites'. Yet here he was in Joshua's church.

While the guilt here arises from Waiyaki's cultural ambivalence, elsewhere it has a different source. At the close of *Weep Not, Child*, Njoroge, once a passionate believer in education, religion, wealth, and love as instruments of social change, has now so completely lost faith that he considers suicide. He is pulled from the brink, but the book ends with him suffused with feelings of inadequacy and guilt. He returns home meekly with Nyokabi his mother (153):

> He followed her, saying nothing. He was only conscious that he had failed her and the last word of his father, when he had told

188

him to look after the women. He had failed the voice of Mwihaki that had asked him to wait for a new day. They met Njeri who too had followed Nyokabi in search of a son in spite of the curfew laws. Again Njoroge did not speak to Njeri but felt only guilt, the guilt of a man who had avoided his responsibility for which he had prepared himself since childhood.

But as they came near home and what had happened to him came to mind, the voice again came and spoke accusing him: *You are a coward. You have always been a coward. Why didn't you do it?*

The mountain of guilt in *A Grain of Wheat* is enormous, though this is not surprising given its concern with conflict and betrayal. The lonely Mugo is guilt personified. The betrayer of Kihika, he is, if reluctantly, the ultimate wolf in sheep's clothing. The villagers' insistence on hymning him ever more fervently serves only to fuel his guilt more effectively. How ironic then (and Ngugi has a fine skill in irony) that Gikonyo, also guilt-laden, should unburden himself before Mugo as though before a loftier spirit. Gikonyo is recounting his feelings at returning from Yala Camp and finding that Mumbi, for whom he has confessed the oath, has borne another man's child. He describes the shock of it and his determination to lose himself in work, never again to sleep with Mumbi, and never to mention the child. Mugo is impassive, like a god in a shrine (141):

> And still Mugo did not say anything. Gikonyo felt vaguely disappointed. The weight had been lifted. But guilt of another kind was creeping in. He had laid himself bare, naked, before Mugo. Mugo must be judging him. Gikonyo felt the discomfort of a man standing before a puritan priest. Suddenly he wanted to go, get away from Mugo, and cry his shame to the dark...

Ngugi's strengths have been acknowledged widely. It is argued, with little contradiction, that his skill at structure and characterisation increases throughout the three novels; and while some might argue, as undergraduates do, that *A Grain of Wheat* has too complex a structure, none denies that this is an advance on the symmetrical apprentice-work structures of the first two books. Ngugi has also achieved the difficult task of fusing the 'artistic' with the 'political' so that we have here creative literature and not simply a propaganda sheet. One suspects, however, that he began his career simply reporting life as he found it, portraying his society as it really was, and then

189

later discovered that Marxist theory crystallised his thoughts, confirming his own hunches and providing a theory about why matters were the way he saw them. This schedule would explain why the tone of *Homecoming*, especially the 'Author's Note', is palpably at odds with the restrained, patient prose of the novels. This sounds like a new Ngugi, strangely bitter, like the Achebe of *A Man of the People*, losing his patience but finding a cause.

Ngugi's special achievement is partly to have analysed sharply a people's agony at a particular moment in their history and also to have given us a powerfully honest reading of human nature. His moral honesty guarantees that, like Soyinka and Achebe, he simply will not romanticise his people. That he should draw fully-rounded people early in his career when the temptation was strong to canonise them is a sign of artistic honesty and toughness. While the folk-machines that turn men into gods whirred at Uhuru, Ngugi was quietly drawing a people full of hopes and fears, often inadequate, guilt-ridden, inconsistent, roughly noble as a group, yet selling themselves individually to the new gods of money.

The result of this honesty is that Ngugi's level of character portrayal is second to none in Africa. There is a constant prodding beneath the skin of his figures, a picking over the entrails of emotion, fear, and motive: and these he relates to the great backcloth of historic circumstance, the movement in time of a whole society and its world view. Why did Gikonyo confess the oath? Why did Mugo betray Kihika? Why did Mumbi yield to Karanja? Why did Koinandu rape Dr Lynd? Why did Waiyaki and Nyambura drift apart? Why was Ngotho content to work for Howlands? Why did Thompson behave the way he did? That questions like these are raised without being given simple answers reflects the complex nature of life as Ngugi sees it.

Finally, what has developed over the three novels is not simply Ngugi's ability to draw character but to handle, over a distance, the careers of a range of different figures. *A Grain of Wheat* is particularly important for this. But ultimately what counts is the vision of the author himself. Here is a reflective, moral artist whose outlook and prose tone are summed up in that phrase he himself chose for one of his characters: 'a tragic delicacy'.

*Leonard Kibera*

The Gikuyu novelist and short story writer Leonard Kibera has been much overshadowed by Ngugi wa Thiong'o, with whom he shares some basic characteristics. His canvas for the most part resembles Ngugi's: Kenya's Central Province with its ridges and hills, fertile soil, cool upland air, and seasonal drought. His rural scenes are played out in villages which, like Ngugi's, are only a bus ride from the capital. It is the same heavily Christianised area, where author and people know their Bible and the gospels cause more trouble than they were meant to. Kibera also shares Ngugi's sense of man's relationship to the soil, with the landscape a living force as it is in the older writer's novels. Even Kibera's brand of satire resembles Ngugi's, whether it is directed against common targets such as the new bourgeoisie, or headmen and home guards who seduced lonely wives during Mau Mau. Kibera possesses too Ngugi's concern about human relationships, and there is the same close sympathy with his characters, as though he is writing among them, sharing a common humanity that is sometimes strong and often weak. Kibera's are a suffering people whose hardships and failures he registers with unfailing energy, sympathy, and precision.

It would be unnatural if Kibera had not been influenced by Ngugi for as an undergraduate at the University of Nairobi he was literally Ngugi's pupil. But while it was worth noting that here is further evidence that African Literature has its own dynamic, its own inter-actions and cross-currents, it must also be emphasised that Kibera is an independent writer with his own vision, and that in some respects (compare, for instance *Voices in the Dark* and *A Grain of Wheat*) he takes off where Ngugi ends. The differences between these writers are indeed of more concern than their likeness, because they help to define the precise nature of Kibera's art. Closing the eyes to view Ngugi's world what emerges is an *oeuvre*, a wholeness of which all the novels and stories are a part. A trinity rather than a trilogy, the novels portray the same scene glimpsed from separate vantage points. The landscape and figures of *The River Between* merge with those of *Weep Not, Child*; and when all reappear in *A Grain of Wheat* little, physically, has changed except the sunlight, now veiled by a prevailing shadowy cloud. It is true that from this third view *more* folk are seen, pursued further and with inner lives subjected to closer scrutiny. This is to say that Ngugi is a more accomplished artist when he writes his third novel. But essentially, and admirably, these figures are part of the same

191

world, and if students find it hard to recall which book Mwihaki is in and which Mugo, this merely confirms what the imagination's eye reports.

The remembered picture of Kibera's world is quite different. It lacks the unity of Ngugi's work, partly because Kibera's energies have so far been channelled into the short story with its demand for varied setting, theme, and voice; partly also because of a personal preference for a 'caravanserei' view of the world. There is a firmer preoccupation with city life than in Ngugi whose vocation is avowedly to be spokesman for the peasants. And villages, when they occur, seem closer to Nairobi than Ngugi's, so that even in the rural depths there is always a sense that Nairobi is in the background, over the hill, or visible round the next bend on a dusty road. Nairobi exerts a strong pull on Kibera, and its melting-pot culture and variegated scenes provide him with a good deal of inspiration and material. While Ngugi still sees himself as part of a rural world, Kibera has really packed his loads and moved to the city. Ngugi's sense of community founded in his concern with rural life gives way to a fascination with the individual, the rebel, the urban adventurer.

Ngugi's feel for social structures has given his work a pattern, a symmetry, a direction. Once the core is put in, all else falls into place like iron-filings round a magnet. The structure of both novels and short stories repeatedly exhibits this. His vision is basically patterned, and while allowing for the complexities of life, with its caprice and eccentricities, at base his writing has an order. To the extent that Kibera so far has not fixed on a central theory to explain his scene (though *Voices in the Dark* suggests he is approaching one) he evinces a greater sense of life's complexity and puzzlement; his work more often recoils with doubt, with curiosity, with bewilderment. It cannot tidy away life's paraphernalia into neat boxes. Granted that art involves a shaping of experience, Kibera seems anxious not to over-shape, as if to do so would involve not only taking sides but closing off sources of truth and insight.

If Kibera's vision is less tidy than Ngugi's, it possesses as much moral heart and a set of sympathies amounting to a point of view. From *Potent Ash* to *Voices in the Dark* the writing displays a passion for justice, anger at self-seeking, fury at hypocrisy, and profound sympathy with the victims of the modern world. The agonies of Gerald, for example, hero of *Voices in the Dark*, are clearly felt in the bone of Kibera himself.

'Letter to the Haunting Post', printed at the end of *Potent Ash*, is in the nature of an artistic manifesto. Ghostly visitors are addressed who point accusing fingers and suggest, like echoes from Soyinka's *Dance of the Forests*, that the past has been betrayed by the present. The author agrees as he sits in his modern city flat and even feels some nostalgia for antiquity. But in turn he accuses the past of yielding too easily, of selling itself 'for a pinch of salt and a touch of calico'. He was never in any case a real part of the old order. 'I never knew you', he says, 'never met you. Awake, I now find the ancestral herald so distant.' Yet for all that, a slim bond remains:

> Between us, between my nostalgia for you and the reality of the moment, between the incantation of the witchdoctor's magic wand and the bible, between your arrow and my pen, swirls, yet in the contrast the thick lifeblood; so that you and I revolve in a tied history.[8]

But it is impossible to go back. Instead the author has pledged himself to mix a new product in his mortar, blending the local and the exotic. City youth, he admits, is currently wasting its substance on escapist dreams of neon lights and harlots. Politicians too are a scandal. But beneath it all there is 'a reservoir of good craving for an outlet, a direction'. His task lies here. The grains of hope lying in his mortar are too precious to discard; they contain the promise of the future and are part of the author himself. 'Here shall I stay', he says, 'and strive to yield shape to this transitory embryo.'

If a characteristic figure in Ngugi is a wide-eyed, sad-looking youth seen against a background of ridges and fields, the Kibera equivalent is a rebel of some sort, a misfit, alienated by historic forces, left now to grapple with life alone and seek his own path to salvation. The opening story of *Potent Ash*, 'Silent Song', offers one example. Mbane is a young cripple, dying. He has been living, if that is the word, on Nairobi's thoroughfares. More precisely, he has begged beneath the windows of a brothel, amidst scenes of galloping opulence as hotels rise and tourists pour in for the sun. Mbane's brother, Ezekiel, and his sister-in-law, Sarah, have decided to rescue him from the streets and ensure a decent death, meaning one that will not leave them tainted in the eyes of their friends. Mbane must be brought home to the village and baptised. Rooted in cant and self-righteousness, a bizarre haggle erupts over the dying remains of this poor wretch. Neglected in life, in death he must be made respectable. His relatives are prepared to acknowledge him now, even 'help' him, if only he can be baptised and save them from disgrace. But will he accept Christ? Will he believe in God? These pharisees believe he is cherishing a traditional deity, presumably Ngai, High God of the Gikuyu; but in fact he has long sung his own 'Silent Song', a personal vaguely agnostic refrain, half hopeful because a teleology is psychologically comforting, half despairing because he wonders how God could so use a man. He dies smiling and the holy pair believe they have won.

The story is put together with a good deal of skill. The relatives' arrival is carefully controlled, for the substance of Mbane's life must predominate to show their intrusion for what it is: absurd, misguided, and evil. Kibera deftly evokes Mbane's twilight world of cold, hunger and sorrow, of public scorn, blighted hope, gnawing despair, and only half-human fulfilment. This heavy world of pain, borne so stoically, makes the rescue operation all the more collossally brutal and insensitive. The prose is heavy with anguish and defeat (9–10):

> In the gloom of his eternal night, such things as time, day, or beauty, had no meaning. Flat and almost imperceptible, they were for him impossible and lay beyond the bitter limits of darkness...For it seemed to Mbane now as he slumped his youth in horror under the weight of closing death, that his short life had been one of retreat. Crawling away on his lameness, he tackled the world around him negatively and never hit back.

The story is partly about hypocrisy, but mainly about failure. Kibera depicts a life which by any mundane standards must be counted a hopeless failure. Nothing has gone right for Mbane. Nothing. Cut off from normal life, he has even fallen through the safety net of the extended family. He has failed miserably to fit into his mother's vision of what life is about (12):

> She used to say that all men were one stream, one flow through the rocks of life. Twisting and turning the pebbles, they would get dirty in the muddy earth. They cried in the falls and whirlpools of life, laughed and sang when the flow was smooth and undisturbed. And while some cried and whirled in the pot-holes of life's valley, others laughed triumph elsewhere. But it seemed to Mbane that he was not only crying. He was not even a part of that stream whose waters branched out into the narrow valley towards the heavenly pool...

194

A close-up study of human misery, this is also an opening salvo in
Kibera's attack on a society that will cynically countenance such trage-
dies. In a sense he is expanding an area mapped out by Ngugi. 'Was
independence fought for this?' he seems to ask. 'Where now are the
claims of family togetherness?' Such questions rise naturally from a
story which has a narrow focus yet broad reverberations.

'It's a Dog's Share in Our Kinshasa' is an even more direct commentary on African society. A public execution is held on a Saturday
morning and attended by a broad cross-section of the capital city's
population. The victim is allegedly a national traitor and the story plays
skilfully on the mixed motives and shifting response of people who
come to watch. Mass hysteria, nationalism, the individual and the state,
sadism, ghoulishness, herd instincts that sweep us into a submerged
identity with the crowd, collective guilt and private innocence, the
curious trivia that can prompt a reassertion of our individuality – they
are all present in this tight-woven tale.

The narrator is an honest, frank participant, the ordinary man in
the street perhaps. He goes to watch this shooting swearing that he is
not really sadistic, yet admitting that something inside him, which he is
quite prepared to call evil, got him out of bed earlier than usual. These
are the mixed feelings of a real individual who wants to think and
behave rightly yet recognises that his impulses are not always holy. The
swirling responses recorded from the narrator's consciousness testify
to the complex reaction which life provokes in Kibera; they also
suggest that even in the herd individual conscience in never quite dead.

The *persona* on this particular morning would have preferred to stay
in bed and hide what he 'might perhaps be capable of'. But he went
anyway, asking, 'What was wrong with joining in the spirit of the
State?' and 'Did not the damned man deserve death?' The prisoner is
shot and the people get what they came for: 'smoke at one end, blood
and dust at the other'. But around this piece of disgusting business
curious happenings occur in human hearts, and Kibera pulls us close
in to examine them.

It is a holiday, fraught at first with that fresh, games-and-fun atmosphere peculiar to Saturday. Everyone is there: 'Black, white, brown,
humanity breakfasting in unison and all pushing forward, necks
craned with a strange passion.' The limits of the short story form soon
force Kibera to pinpoint individuals. The masses are represented by
a bloodthirsty, unshaven man who turns to the narrator and, assuming

a common response, says, 'Great sight, eh! Hang all traitors!' When the narrator fails to respond, he calls him a 'sentimental bitch'. The crowd patiently wait five hours for the sight of slaughter, and meanwhile there is ice cream and Coca Cola. Thieves enjoy a bonanza. Then, just when the firing squad is ready, a little girl runs forward to lay flowers at the prisoner's feet. A fixed smile he had been wearing melts, his head droops, and he weeps. The child's action, at one stroke, changes the whole mood of the day. From the arena centre waves of human decency flow into the hearts of everyone present. The impact of the child's gesture is such that when the guns finally roar, the representative of the mob clutches the narrator in a grip of horror and remorse.

Care is taken over the smallest detail. The ragged man has yellow teeth which he seems to bare at the victim, suggesting the predatory nature of ordinary people in this particular mood. Though the sky is clear, there is a sliver of moon, and the narrator reflects that to his forefathers a certain lunar shape spelt madness. That morning, 'the dawn sun crept its claws through [his] bedroom curtain' and its usually healthy warmth was felt to be 'sinister'. The sky is over-shadowed from time to time by clouds. Or, as he puts it, 'A clear African sunrise is no guarantee of a cloudless day', a remark which might be interpreted as a simple comment on the weather, an exercise in pathetic fallacy, or as a suggestion that this grisly incident is evidence for what has been called Africa's false dawn.

Inevitably, the whole event takes on spiritual and ritual overtones. The prisoner is a sacrificial lamb or scapegoat carrying away the evil of a society which smugly shouts derision and bares its teeth. With no crime specified we feel both an innocence about the man and the inevitability of his fate. The affair is at once a commonplace bloody event and also an African Calvary releasing forces of spiritual change. The event has drawn people together: policemen and soldiers become friends for the first time; the *persona* and the ragged man share an ice-cream in sadness and embrace each other. The victim's innocence is embodied in the girl whose childish impulse is a shattering challenge to the values of this crowd and the society it represents. Is she a symbol of future hope? Do the crowd represent what she, as an adult, might become? Is she simply the crowd's conscience reminding them of the waters of sympathy bubbling deep under their hardened hearts? The answer is not clear. But what we bring from the story is not so much the horror of the execution as this tiny human's act of love, a gesture of towering moral beauty. It is, once more, the act of a rebel soul, like Mbane's, still free enough to assert itself (20):

> All I can say is that as the little girl wept her way back again, a knowledge of something sacred betrayed to public emotion seemed to have touched our hearts and weighed there heavily, like the day of judgment...Women drew out their handkerchiefs. We, the brave men, seemed to drop our heads down in chorus and pressed together.

A rebel who preserves his moral integrity is also the subject of 'The Stranger', one of the longer stories in *Potent Ash*. An eccentric figure appears in a village during the Emergency, plies his cobbling trade, and ultimately, after a good deal of friction, disappears. This simple story displays several qualities in Kibera's writing. First, it differs sharply in setting and theme from its companion pieces. Secondly, it is a more ambitious exercise verging on the long story. And thirdly it is clothed in a thin veil of fantasy while sticking close to the raw realities of life during Mau Mau.

At a time of strict control on people's movements, of constant surveillance by the colonial Government, of precise door numbers and identity cards; at a time when families are riven by suspicion, when villagers are acutely aware of one another as possible traitors, this strange cobbler arrives and defies it all (30):

> He just happened. None of us knew where he came from, how long he would stay and – if he would after all carry his suspect self away – where he was bound. He just happened... This is how we had to dismiss this man whom we could not pin down to a label, either of tribe or origin; this arrogant piece of work which carried no identity card – and got away with it.

Kibera's cobbler ranks as one of the most curious figures in all African writing. He is at once unique and yet an embodiment of a whole tradition of similar figures. He is part Wandering Jew or minstrel, part Gikuyu Nazarene, Pied Piper, Hans Andersen, and Arastafarayan. He echoes figures like Eman, Murano, and Professor in the writings of Soyinka or Okolo in *The Voice*. A timeless figure, he simply cannot be pinned down to a date, a period, or a style. Once again, Kibera leaves us with a knot of teasing questions. What kind of man is this who, amidst the 'Emergency' tearing the heart out of society, can preserve his dignity and values, his identity as an honest man? Who is this man who will put a cross on his door instead of the required number? Is he a resurrected embodiment of the African past with its freedom and human togetherness? A madman fixed in virtue, doomed to be misunderstood by a wicked age? A tool created simply to provide a moral core for a story really designed to satirise the mercenary cleric who appears here? Is he, like the girl in the previous piece, an agent for shaming society all round him?

In a story attacking every corner of village society, only the cobbler escapes censure. The *persona* (not the author) attacks him for being arrogant, but even then in a manner which suggests that the mote is really in his own eye. The stranger is driven off the land of the village preacher, who owns the local shop, and who, like Ngugi's Gikonyo, is exploiting the villagers in a way that allows the author to hint at a link between Christianity and imported materialism. In part, the preacher symbolises the corruption of precisely those values the cobbler represents. If the official shepherd is so weak, what chance is there for the sheep? With nice irony, this monied man of God drives out a dumb holy man, a Christlike figure – not from the door of his temple, but from his shop, his real place of worship. Unable to preach by words, the cobbler's actions and smiles, his willingness to help others, speak for him. He suffers in silence, eschews money, and gets on quietly with mending the world's soul, which is what his mission seems to be (58):

> Perhaps it is a heavy boot or a light shoe, black, brown or a lady's white but the story will be the same. There is something the matter with it and what is wrong is that it needs mending.

Woven into the story, to comment on the sickness of Gikuyu society during the Emergency, is the theme of discourtesy. Where the village world prides itself on elaborate rules of hospitality, the cobbler here is not only fiercely resented but manhandled and delivered to the police. Kibera is not simply arguing an anti-negritudist point of the sort Soyinka made in the *Swamp Dwellers*. He is making the broader comment that in times of prolonged social crisis, when the dawn seems never to glimmer, a people will find a scapegoat on whom they can vent their frustration. A stranger is an easy choice, no matter how remote he is from guilt. What matters is relief of some kind, albeit brief or inhuman (43):

> We were all suspected of harbouring strangers. In turn, among ourselves, we suspected one another of giving cover to the terrorists, blaming our suffering on anyone beyond our immediate family.
>
> [......]
>
> Only when we could all turn our eyes on a stranger did we, in a generous spirit of common sadism and triumphant revenge, feel free to come together again and jointly hand the trespasser to the headman. He never thanked us. But it would be too good to last; the stranger would be locked up out of sight. The object of our collectiveness thus gone, we would break paths again to our isolated and lonely huts where we washed the dust off our feet, perhaps now individually feeling that the whole thing was a dirty conspiracy that we did not want to associate with after all.

Apart from exploring the scapegoat idea, this reveals that same curiosity about the conflict between group response and individual conscience, group convenience and private remorse, which Kibera examined in the execution story. Herd behaviour is easy and a reaching for security; but for the reflective man it will always stir misgivings in the loneliness of his heart.

The cobbler has a hard time of it. Terrorists steal his shoes; others beat him and make off with his nails; he is attacked by a white soldier for refusing to clean his boots. But he never complains. Nor is he a simpering character in whom Christianity has crushed all manliness, for he retaliates viciously when the headman initially tries to arrest him.

The stranger has retreated into his own private world. Amidst hardships tearing at the texture of Gikuyu society, when suspicion, feuding, and every variety of treachery erupt, when children grow used to seeing corpses on paths and blood on their desks, a man must leave the centre and norm for a twilight zone where he can build his own world and hope to survive spiritually intact. Like a snail's shell, this is the world the cobbler carries with him through the 'real' world he will serve but not address. His energies are directed totally towards mending the world, and the strength to persevere is drawn from his private world of the spirit. But others in Kibera's story have their private worlds too, though of a different kind. The celluloid world of

Tarzan, Charlie Chaplin, and cowboys is seen by village youngsters as another safe escape from reality. This is a more synthetic world than the cobbler's but the reason for its choice are little different. Of Manyua Kibera writes (52):

> In effect he had retreated into his own world which assessed any situation on two uncompromising lines like a railway engine, there being, for him, only good and bad cowboys.

'The Tailor', a brief, tightly organised piece, emphasises situation and idea and recounts one crucial event in the lives of its two main characters. A simple incident occurs against a background of historic, national, and racial forces. Njogu is a Gikuyu boy, orphaned by the Emergency. Homeless, jobless, he vainly seeks employment down Nairobi's busy streets, faced with the ubiquitous *Hakuna Kazi – No Vacancies* – signs that a whole generation of East Africans have come to detest. With Gikuyu society fragmented by war, Njogu cannot look to the security of the extended family. In his own country he has neither money nor work. Colonial Kenya does not allow him even second-class citizenship; he is firmly confined to shelf three, for between him and the ruling Whites stand the Asian community running the country's commerce. The Asians have known colonialism too and the aim of this story is partly to bring together two victims of colonialism and see if they recognise a common bond of suffering.

The two oppressed communities meet, symbolically, in Mr Shah's tailoring shop, where Njogu asks for work. But there is no flicker of sympathy, no understanding, no recognition of past hardships, not the slightest evidence of bonds forged in the fire of suffering. Instead there is hardness of heart, and a fawning desire on Shah's part to please the white authorities. Njogu wants a job and Shah tries to hand him to the police as a suspected terrorist, only to get himself killed by a car in the process.

Educated up to Standard Six, Njogu is prepared to tackle 'any kind of job'. But Shah's answer is brutally dismissive: 'No job. No job at all for your qualifications.' As Kibera puts it, 'He never reflected on those early days to identify his plight then with that of the numerous haggard faces brown or black who called to ask, or more often than not beg, him to take them in.' The irony is that when Shah first arrived in Kenya, at Njogu's age but without any education, he was given a job as a Health Inspector. Here is a son of the soil, with a decent schooling, who can get nothing, not even sympathy.

Yet when Shah chases him from the shop and dies crossing the street, Njogu feels sorry for him. Shah's cold lack of sympathy is not matched in the youth he wants to arrest. We are taken into the consciousness of Njogu as he stands on the pavement, arrested by the police because his sorrow prevented his escape (120):

> He found it hard to believe the reality, the actual being of a man only a while ago, a man who had looked so powerfully intimidating as he chased him, shouting, blowing his whistle. He was now helpless; perhaps dying, at best maimed. An island of loneliness, he lay only encircled by a group of people with hard, urban faces which registered more curiosity than emotion. And it might well be, Njogu thought sadly, that in that rough hour of unexpected pain, Mr Shah did after all need him, did need someone, anyone.

This final comment strikes a slightly false note, the sound of an author trying too hard for a good ending. But it doesn't quite hit the reef, for perhaps the sight of a suddenly dead man is enough to bring tears to a youthful face even when that same man has coldly rejected him in the midst of adversity.

Reading Kibera's novel *Voices in the Dark* (1970) after more orthodox African fiction is to be reminded that the novel in Africa, in line with the pioneering work of Okara, is steadily being moulded into new shapes, as Dr J. E. Stewart in a 1968 *Busara* essay, and more recently Achebe at the 1974 Kampala Conference, said it would.[9] Part plain fiction, part drama, part impressionistic poetic prose, and part pastiche, this book resembles a ghastly mosaic built from the fragments of human suffering. To shift metaphor, reading *Voices in the Dark* is like looking at the sun over a prison wall crowned with smashed bottles jaggedly set in concrete with all their lurid colours glinting weirdly in the sunlight. The effects are striking and deliberate. Kibera has opened himself to a myriad modes and styles encountered in his training and let them pour into a work which is a statement of his complex response to modern life. Yet despite the book's derivative aspects, there are qualities of intimacy and spontaneity in its style.

This is the story of yet another only son, Gerald (already one can see how the only son or orphan has become a classic figure in African writing), who, like Kibera and Ngugi, had a tough upbringing during the Emergency. His father was a freedom fighter in the forests, always away, leaving the boy under the influence of his mother, who is tough

201

as leather and traditional in her world view. Gerald's father was killed in the forest. Now, still young enough to recall his mother's plight and his own childhood feelings about a golden era that would rise from the bloodshed, Gerald is full of political commitment and racial bitterness because the new era has not dawned. More particularly, he sympathises with Mau Mau's casualties, the human debris that still haunt Nairobi's streets, with wooden legs or no legs: men with a brave past and no future.

In a sense, this is not new; it is the familiar post-colonial disenchantment felt across the continent. But there is more to the book than this, for, in a special way, *Voices in the Dark* joins the debate about the artist and his society raised first in West Africa by Okara and Soyinka. Those voicing the groundswell of discontent about post-colonial life, the writers and artists, deserve praise. But more sharply than anyone, Kibera is questioning the artist's own health and record of achievement. To what extent have their elegies and lamentations been effective?

This is Gerald's problem. Filled with righteous indignation against the new bourgeoisie, he realises, to his horror, that he not only belongs in the same group, but that this is recognised by the poor he champions – who have failed evidently to hear the sociologists' dogmas about the classlessness of the artist. This is where *Voices in the Dark* begins to differ from other anti-bourgeois fiction. What was begun when Achebe ironised Odili in *A Man of the People*, revealing a common human weakness in attacker and attacked, is further refined in this curious pastiche from Kenya.

Gerald, a reformist zealot, knows that his position is ultimately futile. The plays he writes seem to him revolutionary dynamite, until the truth strikes home that they change nothing, alleviate the agony of the poor not a jot. It is a fate the African artist shares with expatriate lecturers who preach to students on the joys of village life or with those monied Marxists who genuinely sympathise with 'the worker' as they sip sherry in Senior Common Rooms or relax by their swimming pools in Sussex or Berkeley. Gerald comes from peasant stock and retains a strong and recent link with the land; but the beggars who haunt the alleys of Nairobi, whose voices in the dark play the theme music of the book, inhabit a different world from his, and tell him so.

In this situation, what can an artist achieve? Gerald's problem is the more urgent because it is Kibera's own position and one he shares with all committed writers in Africa. Thus it is not just the Odilis who are ironised but even their creators. Kibera is questioning the whole orthodoxy of African writing, its nature and function. It is fine, he seems to say, for Achebe to teach his people, for Soyinka to satirise, and for Okara to be a voice of vision; splendid that Ngugi and La Guma should write to get fair shares for the poor. But what really do they achieve? Did they stop the Nigerian War? Prevent the massacres in Rwanda–Burundi? Was Ghana after *The Beautyful Ones* one germ less corrupt than it was before? Have Ngugi and p'Bitek yet managed to persuade Kenyan society about the plight of the post-independence peasant? Will Kibera's own work make any difference? As Wilna constantly reminds Gerald:

> As long as writers just write they will do nothing only praise one another at literary conferences and mutual admiration groups. A good line done for the day and you are off to celebrate. Like the rest of them...you do too little and live by sheer anger and righteous tears.

The questions Gerald's situation provokes are central and timely, and his despair over the artist's calling pours irony over his own creator and over the book itself. Gerald's ultimate message is that novels like *Voices in the Dark* are a waste of time. They make no difference to the victims they champion, though initially they make a difference to the author, allowing him the luxury of a regularly eased conscience. From the idea of art to change the world we are reduced to art as private therapy, art as penance and absolution. Thus an assumption instinct in most African writing – that literature can change men's hearts and hence the course of social history – gets some very sceptical treatment. We are left with beggars in the darkness of their alley hooting with laughter while they ask if they too should write plays. We hear also the gritty voice of Mama Njira, Gerald's tough old Gikuyu mother, growling that the only book worth writing is one on food and politics.

Gerald's position becomes impossible. Failure in his revolutionary writing, failure in his love affair with Wilna – it is all too much. The outcome is perhaps too easily tacked on as murder (with a touch of comic brilliance, Kibera has the hero shot in brackets) but it seems the logical, if slightly contrived, conclusion to Gerald's experience, no matter how much the reader might feel about the importance of the artist and his capacity genuinely to help transform the world.

Gerald's career is one element that holds the book together; at a more contextual and symbolic level the rain motif is another. This echoes an idea running through the short story *1954*, an apparent trial run for this novel, where, in a paragraph reminiscent of a mode of repetition found in Okara's *The Voice* we find (101):

> Rain. Rain all over the beggar's pavement, rain seeking pools in gutters, rain rushing rivulets. Rain upon the pedestrian ladies and gentlemen who brushed aside the weather report...

The idea is not idly repeated for in *Voices in the Dark* the rain never comes. The book is a long futile waiting for it. It is what everyone across the social spectrum says they are praying for. Gikuyu pastors, expatriate bishops, politicians, the rich, the beggars – rain is on everyone's lips. The land is in drought, a season of hunger and despair, and the rain, a useful symbol, holds the promise of halcyon days when justice and plenty will come, when the poor and maimed will get their rewards, and when radical protestors like Gerald will have nothing to complain about. The rain is what people *say* they want; but the tone of the book is heavy with cynicism. Kibera himself would probably settle for the modest dreams his people nurtured before Independence: a land of justice and fair rewards, without selfish groups modelling themselves on their former masters. But the cold dry night of his book promises nothing for those beyond the warmth and plenty of Etisarap Road. There will be no rain and no dawn. One of the closing passages of the book, a dialogue between the two beggars Irungu and Kabura, and which carries overtones of J. P. Clark's *The Raft*, is typically gloomy (171):

> Why must you disturb your neighbour and only ask stupid questions? Look at the clouds and tell me if you can see any water this coming sunrise. – It is too dark. I can hardly see you neighbour and you are my only friend. It is frightening when you cannot see your only friend because of the night and all you hear is his voice rising out of the night like a bad echo to say that it will not rain.

Though fond of devices associated with Absurd Theatre, *Voices in the Dark* contains a strong vein of reportage. At times hopelessly oblique, with scene and event hidden in mists of impressionism, the clouds will suddenly lift to unveil a mundane item of modern history. Kibera wants to speak to the times his readers are living through. Hence his allusion to the assassination of Tom Mboya; the student

unrest of 1969; Kenyatta's dictum 'Suffer your neighbour without bitterness'; the government's detention policy; the Africanised syllabus
at the University; Barnard's heart transplants; Enoch Powell; Rhodesia; Anguilla; the Pope's Uganda visit; Britain's Asian problem; and
Northern Ireland. An archbishop's statement in a Nairobi paper that
the human debris hovering round his cathedral begging for alms
have fat bank accounts at home is included undisguised; so too the
anachronism of the Donovan Maule, East Africa's own Restoration
Theatre in the Tropics, decorating an opulent corner of national
life untouched by African culture. *Voices in the Dark* will ultimately
resemble an historic satire, potent in its day, but requiring all the
footnote-machinery of an American scholarly edition.

In every sense the love affair between Gerald and Wilna is a failure.
Wilna herself is a flat character. She has no depth, no distinctive voice,
no physical presence that stays in the mind when the book is closed:
she is merely words on paper. Her relationship with Gerald looks
hopeless from the start; but how, in any case, could an intelligent girl
so deliver herself to the appalling Gerald, a bloodless garrulous non-
entity who admits that his heart has gone sour? Nasty, abrasive, and
prejudiced, he is a selfish fool, though perhaps a sad victim of historic
circumstance. Morally small, and much smaller than the cause he has
battened onto, it is little wonder his plays fail: he is too self-centred
to make the imaginative leap necessary for good theatre or for any
of the literary arts. He resembles Comstock, Orwell's anti-hero of *Keep
the Aspidistra Flying*, messing about in a no-man's land between art and
materialism. For all his ideals, Gerald is mere bluster, a speaker of
many words. Yes, he did once assault an expatriate at a pineapple firm
(evidently an agent of international capitalism), he does write reformist
plays, and once gave a shilling to a beggar. But for the most part, he
is mere rhetoric which the reader, like the beggars, is glad to be rid of.

The love scenes are reliably bad. The exchanges between Gerald and
Wilna lack freshness and vitality. When their affair coldly shivers to
a crisis, we feel no sympathy but merely question Wilna's sanity for
suffering him so long. We feel neither interest nor concern by this stage
of the story. It is the same with Gerald's literary career. When he says,
'I am tired of writing plays', the reader yawns and replies, 'thank God
for that'. The Wilna–Gerald relationship is bad enough for us to
believe that Kibera planned it, perhaps as a hideous satire on modern
love.

More interesting are the beggar scenes, where Kibera's involvement is at a visceral level, and Mama Njira's gospel, which brings tough peasant sanity into this silly middle-class menage. Gerald's mother preaches a peasant Marxism, though her outlook is deeply spiritual too. As Gerald puts it, she was 'the only man left in the village after the men went to the forest'. When Independence looms and she has finished her fighting work in the countryside, she sets off with her son for Nairobi to 'clear the English out of those stone houses which they think they built'. During this journey the bus they are on becomes, like J. P. Clark's raft, a symbol for the world and a forum for debate. Mama's philosophy is a potent brew of terrier-like determination, buffalo power, and leopard ferocity. And she has a passionate desire, alas unfulfilled, that Gerald should become a true son of hers (132):

> Where are you sitting now – first class, with Mama Njeri. After Uhuru we will all go first class, everybody. See the way they all look at us these white people...Son, look carefully and you will see only two kinds of people in this or any other silly bus: the oppressed and the oppressors. And even if things were different I wouldn't waste time wondering whether the oppressors were black or red, Kikuyus or Luos, I'd always say it loud and clear. What's more I'd fight them...You know, son, your father used to say that the world was like one bad bus with everybody trying to be the conductor and take the money.

Kibera reserves large stores of anger and ingenuity for a description of Etisarap Road, which he uses as the address of each and every post-independence evil he wants to attack. It reads like a fusion of a Swiftian vice list and Dylan Thomas describing the contents of his Christmas stocking (152):

> Etisarap Road is a road that accommodates all points of view. It also accommodates cheese and jam and BENZES and safari boots and white liberals and élite schools and houseboys and love for the poor and butter and insults and moist toilettes...and mean people and generous souls and lost souls according to the Archbishop and disillusioned peace corps and professors and bellbottoms and pineapple juice and regular regulated columns and greed and convocations and provocations and short sight and cigars and good editors and good-for-nothing advisers and loyal citizens and white secretaries and VSOs and two-year contracts and law-suits and imported judges with local victims and happy

marriages with bad divorces but good alimony and imported
peanut butter and makers of history and black history mutilated
over white coffee and the koran and the white man's bible and
garbage cans and sleeping pills...

While Kibera has an excellent ear, he is sometimes tempted into
verbal patterns that fail because they overreach or sound contrived,
in too smart a way. But the development of a smoother prose is
inevitable in a writer of Kibera's skill and commitment. In the meantime he has much to say, draws on very wide reading, can judiciously
learn from the stylistic strengths of others, and has a moral commitment
which will guarantee further work of power and significance.


*Palangyo*

The grindingly poor do not as a rule write books: their circumstances
preclude it. Those who have temporarily fallen on bad times might
write, but the permanently poor find their voice in others more
fortunate: an aristocratic Tolstoy with a conscience, a middle-class
Orwell destitute for the experience, a watchful Zola looking down from
his study. Descriptions of poverty, therefore, no matter how faithfully
reported, risk sounding second-hand or merely superficial. Alternatively, the reader who knows the author's background refuses to suspend disbelief and constantly raises doubts and objections. We rarely
get a cry *from the midst of poverty*, from the hearth of a Bolivian shack
or the slums of Delhi.

African writers, as a group, are better placed in this regard than
most. By and large, they are the first generation of the rural poor to
get a schooling and become spokesmen for their people, though even
here we have seen the beginnings of a gap suggested by Gerald's career
in *Voices in the Dark* and the beggars' view of him: 'How can he
possibly understand us?' But there is no shortage of writers who take
us close to the harrowing poverty of Africa. We smell squalor in Ghana
with Armah, feel the gnawing hunger of Gikuyu peasants with Ngugi,
and see the fearful indignities of South Africa's poor with La Guma.
Tanzania's Peter Palangyo, however, has probably succeeded more
than most in rendering the authentic feel of grinding poverty with its
shattering effects on the total being of its victims. Why he has done
this better than his colleagues is hard to say. His training at home and
in America, in Science and in Arts, has not been especially unusual;

as far as we know, his upbringing was no poorer than Ngugi's or Armah's or Achebe's. But his *Dying in the Sun* is by far the most powerful account of rural poverty yet to appear.[10] The vision is obsessive and intense. The world evoked, even in a third-person narrative, throbs with pain and despair. The onslaught on our senses is relentless; the details of darkness are repeated *ad nauseam*; the shadow of death is rarely absent from the landscape. Man here is not seen striding across his landscape head held high as in Ngugi's world, taming the soil and signing his name on hill and valley. Instead he is glimpsed lying on the earth or crawling painfully across its face, groaning sick and hungry on its bosom, trying to build happiness against all the odds before sinking into a dusty grave waiting ominously beneath the floor of his own hut. There is a more tragic relationship with the soil here than in Ngugi; doubtless because Palangyo's Tanzania is more arid than the well-watered uplands of Kenya. It also looks as if Palangyo's vision, less political than Ngugi's, is basically more tragic too. In other words, he is more fatalisic about life than the Kenyan novelist who believes that if you get your politics right life more abundant is really possible. The human condition for Palangyo seems less susceptible of change. Man here is victim, for the most part, a passive recipient of nature's parsimony and whim; and this despite the upsurge of optimism at the end of the book.

From the evidence of *Dying in the Sun*, Palangyo's strength seems to lie essentially in his tragic vision. Nothing makes him write so well as the tragedy of life. The first half of his book, where everyone is either sick or dying, and the whole natural order in a state of impending disaster, is better than the happier second half quite simply because it has engaged him more fully and profoundly. Death, and man's struggle against it, draws out Palangyo's strengths, especially his pity, anger, and astonishing powers of empathy. The intensity of the writing is enhanced partly by this empathy and partly by the strategy of focusing on the misery of one family and a couple of outsiders.

The plot of *Dying in the Sun* is of a piece with the literature of alienation and loneliness. Ntanya's mother is dead, killed by his father; his father is dying too and this takes up a large portion of the book. The boy's relationship with his parents is classically anti-father and pro-mother; but the boy wants to die too, for he is a misfit, a sacrificial goat born to suffer; an ugly duckling, delivered deformed into the world. He remembers his mother saying (2):

There are some people who just don't belong, some people who are marked off from birth and isolated to carry a bigger and bitter cross of suffering.

As a child he was 'bow-legged and clumsy', was slow to learn, lacked the fleetness of foot which is a magic possession in childhood, was jeered at and called 'clam, snail, and barrel head', and suffered that worst of all conditions: a little boy who has to play with the girls. Grossly unlucky, indeed feeling cursed, he struck out one day at his beloved sister, wounding her fatally with a stone. Remorse floods in . How can his people understand that despite all this he loves his sister more than life? He tries suicide (stretching our credulity a bit), and is found unconscious and bleeding. But even this cannot protect him from family blame heaped on him for the girl's death. Life accelerates downhill and eventually Ntanya goes away to work in a distant town. He walks home on hearing that his father is dying.

But everyone around the father seems to be dying too. Having caused his wife's death by inflicting upon her 'the corroding sorrow of the spirit', the wretched fellow now seems to have infected everyone else. The whole of Kachawanga village, glimpsed in a cruel arid landscape, has been blighted by his evil touch. Everyone in the village bears the marks of his ferocity, either physically or mentally, and this shows even at his funeral. Kachawanga has become a village of death, a symbol of how one soul can rot the entire social fabric. There is no sentimental reverence for Ntanya's father. The feeling is that he must die, must be killed even, before the disease he carries is removed from the land, before a new era can begin. The soil won't put forth new dress; crops won't grow; human relationships won't mend.

What exactly ails the father, and whether Ntanya is simply inheriting a curse, is unclear. Ntanya's grandmother, who seems to hint at a curse, puts the father's case into humane perspective:

> Some strange spirit caught him. I've seen him cry, in between his drunkenness, trying desperately to wrench this strange weight off his soul. He is a sad unfortunate child and he is only hitting at this, this thing in him, when he drinks and becomes cruel. The day he killed your mother...he had told me with sweat on his brows that something heavy had stood on his chest the night before, so heavy that be couldn't breathe, my son...My son, she repeated in pain, 'by the time you are as old as I am,' here

209

she spat blessings in the rising sun, 'you will understand and forgive...

Was her son cursed, as the old order would probably believe, or was his drunken violence the universal response to hopeless poverty? Was it, on the other hand, an early symptom of the new order's malaise, what the nineteenth-century called 'This strange disease of modern life'? This elemental passage with its dialogue between womb, earth, and heart, the burning honesty of the old woman as she reflects on her own tragic cycle of birth and reproduction against this hostile landscape, give her pronouncements the power of holy writ. It is enough to know that we live, suffer, and finally understand.

Meanwhile Ntyana drifts to a local bar-cum-brothel, another symptom of a diseased social fabric. It is an oasis for other wrecks like himself and he meets Teresa here, an orphan also badly mauled by life. Like most ladies in African fiction, however, she is a fountain of energy and wisdom: the ideal partner for the introverted Ntanya.

With Teresa's involvement in Ntanya's family, change begins to occur; and eventually, as the promise implied in the father's death is fulfilled, there is a steady resurgence of new life and optimism. The landscape itself turns a fertile green, on outward sign of the inner changes taking place in the individuals and village society generally. Blocked life streams are flowing again, there is an insistent note of promise, and the book ends (oddly after its grim start) with Ntanya and Teresa married, the parents of a child, and embracing a much richer life. In Carlyle's phrase, the main figures have woken up to a 'new Heaven and a new Earth', though in truth it is the same old earth, seen differently.

The book's structure is interesting largely because the final outcome is so euphoric. Palangyo's message might be that life is not, or need not be, ultimately tragic, no matter how grim one's conditions; that there can always be a rebirth, no matter how delayed or painful. The whole picture possesses that seedy transitional gloom of Soyinka's *The Road,* and perhaps something of that play's message: old orders must die before new ones can grow and the dying might be long and squalid. On the other hand, some readers insist that *Dying in the Sun* ends in only qualified optimism, and argue that the text, if continued, would inevitably reveal another advent of drought, famine, and despair.

This might be true, but it is certainly a part of Palangyo's strategy to preach a shift of attitude towards adversity. Instead of collapsing totally before its onslaught, he seems to say, it might be wise to accept it calmly, yet still assert life with boldness and joy; to be thankful that at least you have life itself. This is what James, Ntanya's bourgeois friend, develops as his personal philosophy. It contains an old lesson that a modern generation might have to re-learn (122):

> I have just met on my tax-collecting rounds today an old woman, a widow with her legs swollen with elephantiasis and her one eye completely blind. She invited me to share her maize in ground-nuts for lunch. You know I've never seen more life before. She was bubbling with happiness about how simply grand it was to be living, and she could not even move. She opened my eyes to the life and joy in me which has been wasted so much...Why she has really saved me. There is so much, so much to live for.

The book charts a classic Carlylean course. The Dark Night of the Soul is followed by a Centre of Indifference, and then by a joyous Everlasting Yea. Palangyo's own view, voiced through James, might be that the emphasis during the past decade has weighed too heavily on material promise, that life has been foolishly mortgaged to some future golden time, causing inevitable frustration and delusion. The old lady prefers to embrace life now, no matter how inadequate; she will cherish it in the present, rather than fret herself over a promised utopia. The old order personified, her human strengths are a wither-ing censure of a feeble elite that curses the present and lives neuroti-cally for the future. There is nothing new in her posture: she has inherited it from the constant interaction down the centuries between soil, flesh, and heart. It is moral rather than political and represents in powerful form one response to an abiding human problem. It neither denies the claims of a transformed economy nor contests the need for better human justice. But it transcends all these by containing within itself a higher truth: that when a better politics and economics have improved and redistributed land, produced more food, cured the old lady's elephantiasis, placed her in a luxury villa, and guaranteed her an extra twenty years of life, the basic problem of how she can be happy remains. Circumstances change, but the most fundamental human problems do not. A glimpse of this kind of truth gives Palan-gyo's vision its special attraction. He will not merely write a rationale for Ujamaa, attractive though that programme is.

Once again landscape is a living element in Palangyo's novel. It is stronger than the folk who wander over its surface, striving, but never really succeeding, to scratch an adequate life from its soil. There is a strong sense that Palangyo's people are but dust, the creations of their landscape, doomed to be the victims of its parsimony and caprice. The landscape is greater than the people, who have not yet conquered it; and by virtue of its decrees, people are born into hunger and must learn to struggle on, nursing in their hearts a poignant optimism that one day, for a truth – perhaps as a reward for patience and goodness – life will improve and loads grow lighter. Palangyo has more than an intimate acquaintance with the landscape: he is himself its creation; its character and contours have moulded him. There is, therefore, the closest possible relationship between author, environment, and characters. Tanzania's scenery effortlessly reflects the text's thematic concerns. The author, a product of this land and at grips with its shaping pressures, uses it to give the novel its necessary background and for constantly refuelling his own brooding reflectiveness.

Something of the close identification of character and environment can be seen in comments such as the following (27):

> I have gone around the world like a lame ostrich picking seeds on a dry brushland. The seeds that I have picked have been bitter at the kernel, but I have limped on quietly and alone with only the grave knowledge of my curse and a hope. A hope of one day understanding the cause of my lameness and what made my brushland dry.

The landscape, while external in the sense of being background, is internalised here so that it becomes Ntanya's inner landscape too. Later Palangyo writes (49):

> Ntanya's mind started soaring high above the ground of his past life. Like an eagle flying over a burnt grassland, he had many spots to look at, many places on which to come down...He was looking for something, a lost seed on a wilderness of burnt grass.

Death and darkness are a fixed part of the scene. Despite Ntanya's mother's belief that when God beats you he always wipes your tears, the scales usually tilt on the side of pessimism. 'Living', Mama Ntanya says 'is very little more than the knitting of a necklace of scars.' Nor do Palangyo's figures face death with a smile; it is rare, even among the older folk, to meet that joyful attitude to death found in so much

oral literature. Mama Ntanya claims that she and Ntanya's father will
die 'the old way'; but this turns out to be a pretty joyless affair.
'We die', she says, 'to relieve ourselves of both the joys and scars of
life.' She fears that in death all will be cold and uncomfortable,
without the warmth of the sun. Ntanya himself, more modern, has
a horror of death too. 'Deep down in the darkness', he says, 'when
we are alone we are afraid of death.' Hence too the gloom that sunsets
always bring, reflected here by Teresa (41):

> She was probably just afraid of the setting sun, as many people
> are. Maybe she was afraid that it might not come up again, and
> even if it did, the interim of darkness might frighten here... The
> heart of a human being is a dark universe.

Palangyo's prose is poetic in flavour. He has resisted the temptation
to rely on proverb, but has pursued a figurative vein that gives his
writing depth and tightness. That it sometimes fails in detail, however,
is shown by one of the brothel scenes. Teresa, an orphan experiencing
this deathly 'illusion of relief', is the favourite of an old man doomed
to live out his last days here, unwanted or disowned by his family (34):

> Like an old man polishing and caressing a spear he had used
> during his successful youthful warrior days, this old man spoiled
> and doted on the young girl, wetting his mouth in desire that
> was now calcified once and for all in his mind; he claimed
> complete monopoly of the girl, and strangely she in turn clung
> to him like a crab clinging to a dead shell.

This is well-carpentered prose exploring devices like assonance and
alliteration, and employing images chosen with care. Aptly sexual
allusion surrounds the spear idea; the process of calcification suggests
old bones and ageing; and crabs clinging to dead shells is vivid and
haunting. Yet subject and image do not harmonise perfectly. Slightly
blurred and overworked, the figures tend to dissipate our attention
instead of focussing it. While the spear idea is good (except that the girl
can hardly be seen as a weapon), Teresa is surely too young and pretty
to be a crab, a creature conjuring whole lists of unpleasant and
unflattering associations of which *old, ugly, sour, tetchy, sulky, uncivil,
obscure, difficult, unintelligible, devious,* are just a few. None of these fits
the humane, sadly beautiful Teresa. The old man as 'a dead shell' is
excellent. We are meant to see him as sexually dead, and therefore
no threat to Teresa. But it is not quite perfect, for the image suggests
the stillness and finality of death, whereas the old man is not dry bones

yet and is forever fondling Teresa. Furthermore, 'calcified', with its scientific ring, disturbs the tone of the passage. While revealing Palangyo's background in science, it does not belong in the world of Ntanya, Teresa, and the old man. Reminiscent of the 'rheumatoid and peristalsis' prose of Lenrie Peters' *The Second Round*, it is only a slight blemish, but it is not an isolated case. Soon afterwards, Palangyo recounts how Kachawanga people believed everyone shelters a snake, a sort of 'pith of life at the anatomical centre of his body'. He then says: 'it could have been that Muga's pith was wriggling itself silly in all its *liquid tensility*'. This lurch into a scientific register again spoils otherwise good writing, partly because it is at odds with the rest of the prose, and partly because it would be unintelligile to the average reader.

The lure of the figurative sends Palangyo sprawling on other occasions too. When the text says, 'He continued to turn himself round and round on the dissection table of his mind', the point about Ntanya's obsessive introversion is well taken; but the image conjured of surgical merrygorounds is somehow less than right. These minor faults occur often enough to spoil the overall effect of Palangyo's prose, even while demonstrating its boldly adventuring strengths. At its best, it offers a passage like the following, where Ntanya has left school after his mother's burial and feels he can never go back again. It is a moving moment of departure, a tragic second birth, realised with soily imagery of the most palpable kind (52):

> Ntanya had walked straight from the school to his mother's grave. It was still fresh and wet and not a seed had grown. He sat down on the mud with his hands resting on the raised mound and cried...He knew that he could never go back to that school again. He could never learn roots now after crying at his mother's grave. It was as if sitting on the grave had washed him clean of boyhood ...What did anything really matter if his mother was living deep in the ground with her mouth full of mud?

As a first novel, *Dying in the Sun*, though badly edited, augurs well for Palangyo's growth. With its moral intensity, its feeling for the ebb and flow of human suffering, its concern over basic matters of survival, it casts, more than any African novel I know, a withering glance at the whole critical exercise. The minutiae of analysis seem to pale into absurd irrelevance before the overwhelming human problems raised by the text.

# 5

# Central and Southern African prose

Central Africa has not yet produced a large body of prose, and though several writers are developing strongly (they include Dominic Mulaisho, Fwanyanga Mulikita, Steve Chimombo, Paul Zeleza, Antony Namalomba, James Ngombe, Ken Lipenga, and Charles Mungoshi), they are known only for single works or as contributors to small magazines. There has been the usual autobiographic work, of which Kaunda's *Zambia Shall Be Free*, Kachingwe's *No Easy Task*, and Kayira's *I Will Try* are the best known, but the amount of published fiction either in the novel or short story form remains small. David Rubadiri's *No Bride Price* was an early attempt at the novel which he has not followed up. Dominic Mulaisho's *Tongue of the Dumb* was published in 1972, and Fwanyanga Mulikita's collection of short stories, *A Point of No Return*, appeared in 1968. Meanwhile the Malawian Writers Series has recently published *Night of Darkness*, a book of short stories by Paul Zeleza.

Legson Kayira remains the most productive novelist, though his Malawian readers argue that his long stay abroad has resulted in a loss of contact with the home scene. Certainly Kayira's wanderings (he set off walking 2000 miles to Khartoum carrying a Bible and *Pilgrim's Progress*), while heralding both staying power and a facility in English have produced, inevitably, a detachment which is a hallmark of his writing. This detachment is born of long separation (longer, for instance, than Laye's from Guinea), of seeing home from a distance and constantly with the eye of memory. While the prose takes us close enough to scenes and characters, this is writing that suggests light engagement and minimal involvement. Malawian students are apt to say that Kayira can capture the flavour but not the authentic detail of modern village life. Until the appearance of *The Detainee*, his most recent work, amused detachment slowly yielding to concern best

215

described Kayira's posture. Seen against the broad background of African literature this was a refreshing change; but it implied a light brand of fiction, non-political, and orchestrated in major keys. Charles Larsen rightly called it pastoral. Generally comic, any satire arising tends towards the Horatian, dealing gently with characters, laughing at foibles rather than revealing tragic depths. At this point, the mantles of teacher, negritudist firebrand, oracle, prophet or reformer were not for Kayira. Instead he would simply look at the homeland, mirror the beauty of its hills, cloudscapes, and bubbling streams, record the laughter of his people and the pretentiousness of those caught up with either village politics or modernity. But narrative technique, point of view, and the prose flavour suggest in a way that Kayira is no longer part of this life: he can sit quietly overseas and spin it round playfully with his finger. At this stage, the debates about post-colonial society fail to interest him; the shattering social harm caused, for example, by migrations to the mines of South Africa only begins to get reflected in *The Civil Servant*, his third novel.

Kayira's first work, *The Looming Shadow*, published in 1967, reveals his early posture and style.[1] Its title quite at odds with its content, it is an unpretentious book, and modestly successful within its limits, for Kayira does not set out to build a Gothic Cathedral and produce a prefab. Its lightheartedness betrays an ironic and comic view of life that keeps him from either the depths or the heights of human experience. He is at this point a man of the broad middle ground, where life proceeds in a pragmatic cheerful way. It is the same middle ground that attracted Fielding, Leacock, Smollett, and Chesterton, where there is smiling incredulity over smug philosophy and rollicking laughter at either misanthropic satirists or dreary-faced redeemers. Writing here celebrates people more than ideas, actual rather than potential life, average man rather than saint or demon. The comic spirit thrives in this middle ground because its essence lies in the community. In Dobrée's words, it 'expresses the general feeling of the community...it supports the happy mean, the comfortable life'. It not only shuns excess, but firmly tries to cure it. It tends 'to repress eccentricity, exaggeration, any deviation from the normal'.[2]

To understand the comic spirit is to see that Kayira's vision is at one with it; and hence there should be no surprise over the absence of strong negritude echoes, sustained anti-colonial protest or sermons on post-colonial disenchantment. A writer must be free to reflect his own vision and if Kayira's early viewpoint excludes the Gordian knot of African hunger, bloodshed, and cultural vertigo who would deny that he reflects an authentic response of a people smiling amidst adversity? Indeed it would be churlish not to applaud Kayira for placing within the broad stream of African writing texts which reflect a spirit everywhere manifest yet seldom given literary shape. A literature always grave and angry is hardly a reliable record, no matter what the age or society it rises in.

While indulging his comic sense, however, Kayira in his first three novels knows that comedy demands contrast, the sounding board of a social morality. 'Where everything is ridiculous, nothing can be ridiculed', as Chesterton once put it. And again, 'just as there is no fun in it when everything is serious, so there is no fun in it when everything is funny'.

*The Looming Shadow*'s plot is slight. Set in colonial times it concerns an argument between a village doctor and headman over the suspected betwitching of a man who dies, a very common theme in Malawian writing. The minutiae of the struggle provide some mild entertainment, for Kayira is good at portraits of men whose love of power makes them ridiculous. The struggle seems to be ending in the headman's favour (the power levers are firmly in his grasp) when the central government steps in with police, pricks the balloon of epic conflict, and deflates the struggle to a distinctly parish pump level.

What is the point of it all? Presumably it is the humour Kayira wants to exploit in this village power game. As an author who long ago left the village for world travels, Kayira derives great fun from old men who strut and posture as though the limits of the globe are co-extensive with the limits of their village kingdoms. Such figures are comic because their self-view, their conception of their power and importance, is at ironic odds with a broader reality that Kayira and his readers can see. Village politics amuse outsiders for reasons of scale, for reasons which made Gulliver laugh at the Lilliputians. This is as true of Kayira's world as it is of Gogol's and Leacock's.

There is the further point that Malawi's political structures have, with independence, undergone radical change – not yet realised by the elders. The power diagram has changed with a myriad petty village principalities now subject to the Party and Central Government. This is all symbolised by the police arm of central government who break in upon the village scene with a seriousness which declares they are the real power in the land and the village elders only performing a charade. The results of this are both mirth and sadness; for the old men, acting out their harmless scenes are pretty roughly stripped of their dignity.

217

This exploration of the comic rather than tragic energy in the two worlds clash sometimes includes more orthodox reflection. The following passage, which shows the clarity and care of Kayira's prose, is a case in point:

> An eclipse of the sun was always an occasion that was greeted with mixed feelings by the population of Kavuvuku Village, still caught between the light of modernity, flickering as from a distant candle, and the looming shadow of darkness left from antiquity, a reminder of their past and dictator of their present. To the young ones not yet graduated from the school of the cicada and mantis, still to master the great art of predicting the coming of the rainy season by the first spawnings of mushrooms, or the return of centipedes from their hibernation, still to understand the reasons behind the surrendering of the first harvests to the cemetery of the great ancestors, the eclipse of the sun was wonderful, exciting, and nothing more. But to the old ones, tempered by tradition, weak to challenge its occasional fallacy, nothing in their universe could be dismissed with a shrug of the shoulders...

Kayira can see both orders objectively but there is no doubt which he prefers and his writing often suggests that there are many aspects of the traditional order which he dismisses with both a shrug and a supercilious smile.

One of Kayira's better pieces of description, a skill sharpened in his subsequent novels, is this account of a sunset scene (104):

> At the sunset hour of the evening there is always a gentle wind coming down from the mountain in that village, whistling and whispering so softly that you would think the mountain itself was breathing. But wait till midnight. The wind will have gathered momentum and it will no longer whistle but roar. The mountain will seem to have opened itself, sending out such merciless gusts of wind as to threaten the grass-thatched roofs on all the houses. The ghosts, they say, are then awake, are mobile, propelling themselves from one place to another by the might of the wind.

This is not great prose, and the familiar tone of an outsider emerges in a comment like 'The ghosts, *they say*, are then awake'; but it has atmosphere, moves smoothly, and reflects Kayira's sensitivity to both landscape and traditional belief. This response to the local terrain is heard again when he writes (118):

Except for the funeral, the day was perfectly beautiful. Everything was still and calm. It was the sort of day one would like to wander in the forests, rub shoulders with bats or lie down under the trees and meditate or sleep; the sort of day when one feels happy for no reason except the thought of being alive and able to appreciate one's surroundings.

*Jingala* is a better book than *The Looming Shadow*, the result of a sharpened skill in dialogue, characterisation, description, and conflict.[3] Kayira is better able now to tease out fully the comic possibilities of his situations. Jingala is a widower and retired tax collector, proud of an only son who, alas, like the hero of *Blade Among the Boys*, wants to waste his education on the Catholic priesthood instead of coming home as a living monument to his father's distinction. The persistent strategems by which Jingala opposes Gregory's plans (they include marching on the seminary dressed in loin cloth and carrying an axe) are broadly the substance of the book, but the tremendous focus on the old man really brings him to life. Gregory finally wins a Pyrrhic victory and Jingala a two-fold defeat. For while trying to talk Gregory out of celibacy, he has been living a celibate life himself, waiting eight years to marry the young Liza, only to see her elope with a man loaded with cash and cockiness from the mines of South Africa. In one closing sentence (Kayira's endings are uniformly weak) comedy is darkened by tragic shadows as Jingala dies of a broken heart, unable to survive a trick which, ironically, is part of an old tradition of elopement.

Jingala himself is a successful portrait. More than most African comic figures he rejoices in that complex balance of strengths and weaknesses that constitute real human beings. He blends wisdom and foolishness, tenderness and arrogance, respect and scorn, caution and headstrong lunacy. He wins our sympathy even when proudly absurd – as when he makes the long journey to Gregory's school and moves through the grounds like a hunter dressed in loin cloth and wielding an axe before storming the Principal's office. He looks a fool to the pupils who, in their Christian charity, despise him for his 'bush' appearance, and also to his son, who is ashamed of him. But Jingala is only showing in his own way his rightful pride as a father and his support for a tradition showing no precedent for successful sons spending their lives in a celibate priesthood. Kayira appears to side with Jingala here for he works in a strong sense of a local citizen trespassing in the grounds of a foreign embassy, or a peasant asserting

219

his rights on common land. It makes therefore a point about the two worlds as well as generating sympathy for the old man. For Jingala tradition is a serious matter, but though he has an informed scepticism about the new order, he is not prepared to be extreme about it. His arguments are strong and simple: among his people, a son inherits all. For his only son to become the Rev. Father Gregory the family line must be doomed, with all this implies in terms of traditional status and attention due to ancestors.

Physically small, Jingala resembles the Charlie Chaplin kind of comic hero who has a small man's dreams of grandeur. He seeks significance as an elder, a father, and an individual, and he achieves it even when we laugh at him. The mind's eye sees this funny little man clearly for Kayira's portraiture is vivid (1):

> He was 55, small but very strong for his age. He had a high forehead, a pair of shrewd little eyes, a more than average size nose, and a very fine set of tribal marks on his cheeks which were now lightly covered by a short, thin grey beard. He laughed easily, often throwing his head back and showing the complete absence of his front teeth....
>
> He wore a black cloth tied round his waist and kept secure by means of an old Scout belt. From one of the two rings attached to the belt hung a bunch of keys which he had collected on various occasions in the course of his life, but whose sole function was now decorative. He had on a black waistcoat with a silver chain, now grey with age, dangling at a slant across the front, and attached to one end of the chain was a small travelling clock which had long since ceased to function. He wore no shirt, and no one could remember ever having seen him in one.

Like the bunch of keys he carries on his belt, Jingala and his whole generation appear in the modern world to be merely 'decorative'. The stopped clock makes the point most poignantly. Herein lies their charm and his; herein lies their humour; and herein lies a hint, an autumnal breath, of sadness.

Jingala is an extrovert, lively as the streams bubbling from the mountains around him. Honest, brave, sociable and quaint, he is an excellent father and husband, sufficiently concerned about tradition, decently responsive to modernity, rather too fearful of failure, but all in all a thoroughly likeable fellow. His honesty neither sinks into naivete, nor precludes sharp cunning when needed. He is disciplined yet given to capricious outbursts. He can plan for tomorrow yet act with sparkling spontaneity.

Gregory is a less sympathetic and less satisfactory portrait. We are not meant to believe that he is good priestly material, despite his claim that he wants 'to work for God', his uninterest in the sad-eyed Belita, and his sacrificing school holidays to learn Latin. He appears initially as a thoroughly unpleasant youth – sneeringly disobedient, arrogantly scornful of village life, niggling and lazy, and reluctant to dirty his hands in the fields. He is supercilious about tradition and feels superior to his own age-set, with whom, significantly, he was not initiated. He scorns those youths who have returned from South African mines, asserting (in a telling example of how African class divisions are opening up) that he has nothing in common with them. Yet Gregory changes with experience. Youthful arrogance yields slowly to some-thing more humane. He repents of his insolence, weeps over Belita's beautifully useless vigil, and musters a show of respect even for the village chief he finds so absurd. As a further sign that he has not rejected roots entirely, we see him amidst idyllic rural scenes chasing the honey birds up the mountains to seek out the dripping honeycombs of the bees.

The combination of a comic vision with a willingness to contrive events produces fiction of a rather low voltage. But even so there are passages of real strength and skill and these are not all purely descrip-tive. In *Jingala*, for instance, the central encounters between Gregory, his father, and the chief are of a high order. The early exchanges about Gregory's future are long, relaxed, subtle, and easy – masterpieces of careful planning and diplomacy. The learned Gregory with his Latin and Western snobbery is but clay in the hands of Jingala, a novice in the art of devious debate and subtle manoeuvre. Such exchanges seem all the more spontaneous for being punctuated by acts of domestic trivia; the poking of a fire, the washing of a dish, the glance at a watch. The old order's flavour and style are firmly registered in Jingala's easy verbal swordplay and his mature nimble-footed diplomacy with this sullen representative of modernity. There is a quiet, almost apologetic, logic in Jingala's way of laying down the cornerstones of his argument: 'You see, my dear boy, you are no longer a child'...'you should in fact be looking after me'...'you will soon be looking for a wife'...'if you don't have a house of your own, where are you going to put her?' ...'And if you don't have a garden, how are you going to feed her?' It is all so easy and painless, yet tension arises from our feeling

221

Gregory's inner response as one traditional assumption after another drops onto the table. And long before the meeting ends it grows clear, if it was ever in doubt, that Jingala has prepared it all in advance: suggestions for a wife, a plot to build on, a garden for crops, all that spells out Gregory's need to return home. But the exercise must be approached with care and delicacy. It must not be rushed.

A similar charade is staged when Gregory pays his long-delayed visit to the headman, Jingala's partner in persuasion. This shrewd old boy, dressed in rags and also carrying a dead watch, keeps suggesting that he is really very busy, has no time to stay, must be off to his garden. A high comic moment is reached when both old men peer at their dead watches (95):

> The chief swung his left arm around and looked at his watch as though it was functioning, and even said something to the effect that it was getting late. As if it was some sort of ritual, Jingala also pulled his clock from the breast pocket of his waist-coat, took an examining look at it, then shook it once and looked again. It was getting late, he agreed with the chief's pronouncement, then put it back in the pocket.

The effect of this and similar passages is to reinforce the comic view of tradition: the representatives of village government are being painted as fools. This is perhaps innocent enough, and neither elder is entirely stripped of his dignity; but a succession of scenes like this leaves the reader feeling eventually that Malawian elders have become as easy a comic target for Kayira as, say, celibate priests are for writers in East Africa. The humour, admittedly, is on occasion softened and even shadowed by notes such as the message behind the dead watches; but we are left with a feeling that Kayira broadly shares Gregory's view, and this despite an exceptional passage such as the following (97):

> Neither your father nor Devera nor myself can read. In your eyes we are therefore not educated; but we do know how to live with other people, how to raise our children, how to appease our ancestors, and how to bury our dead. Now, is that not education?

We do not need to consult Ivan Illich to provide an answer.

It has been claimed, wrongly, that Kayira does not touch Malawi's immediate problems. More correctly, he uses them initially as background material but gradually shows a deepening sense of their importance. One example is the exodus to the mines of South Africa which causes severe disruption in family life. In *Jingala*, Kayira uses this fact of national life only to provide comic potential not as a human problem crying out for attention. Gregory scorns the boastful young miners who return home richer far than their fellow villagers, and their awareness of his scorn opens up briefly the beginnings of a possible rift between a recognisable working class and the new bourgeoisie. But as with Ekwensi's picture of the unemployed staring at Jagua Nana's legs in Lagos, a classic moment is missed because shallower aims predominate. One of the youths, Muchona, is going to elope with Liz, the girl Jingala has been waiting eight years to marry, and this is the major concern just now. Muchona's accounts of life in South Africa, a Malawian echo of Lakunle's phony hymns to Sidi, concern Kayira more than the threat of basic trouble that he represents (105–6):

> 'In the town', he began again. 'In the town – that's where I live – water is brought right into my house and what a house it is! I would say it's about four times as big as the chief's . . . No, I would never allow my wife to carry a pot on her head. Why, that's unheard of in the towns. Firewood? My wife going to fight with snakes in the forest for firewood? Never! I have a cook and he uses a stove. Do you know what a stove is? . . . In the town, I ride my bicycle to and from my office every day . . . I go to the cinema every evening.'

*The Civil Servant*, Kayira's third novel, has a distinctly urban rather than rural setting.[4] His characters also, George Chipewa and his clerk Demero, are modern, western-trained employees of the central government. And though they both have strong and active connexions with the village world their scene is essentially the city of Banya and its leafy, stream-threaded suburbs.

There is also a slight but significant shift in Kayira's vision. It remains basically comic, and his shrewd eye for the ridiculous has not deserted him – witness the pictures of Chipewa fleeing half-clothed in the night; but the comic vision has been darkened as the real problems of African life break through in something more than a decorative way. Rural poverty is compared with city life when Isabella, upon George's first adulterous arrival at her village home, says (49): 'We are very poor here as you may have guessed already. We eat no bread and drink no tea. We eat sima and beans or spinach.' Less obvious, because the plot disguises the fact, is the plight of Isabella herself. She dies tragically in childbirth, bearing Chipewa's child after walking to the city, leaving behind her a family thoroughly devastated, and an orphan whose fate is uncertain. Her husband has died in the mines (the result, local belief would argue, of her infidelity.) While in one sense the entry of Chipewa on the scene is the immediate cause of this tragedy, it stems fundamentally from the fact that economic conditions have driven Isabella's husband off to the South African mines, leaving her with his parents, but obviously a prey to seduction and exploitation. Isabella is a lonely, frustrated woman, a tragic victim of economic circumstance.

Isabella's plight is matched by that of two other figures the comic vision finds hard to accommodate. First there is Vera, Chipewa's hapless wife, a stranger in Malawi and mother of many dead children. There is also the plight of Enid, the girl whom Demero's parents have chosen to be his wife. Enid is honest and humble, convinced she is not good enough for Demero. She is traditional society's ideal woman, yet her fate is to be kept vainly waiting up-country to be called to the city for marriage. She writes letters to Demero, but rarely gets an answer. Demero instead falls in love with Vivien, a badly-drawn white girl, and marries her. We are made to feel that the fate of all three women is not entirely uncommon. Enid's letters are especially touching. She suspects, early on, that Demero will not marry her (30):

> I am afraid that I am only living in a dream, that you will not marry me or, if you do, that you will always regret it. I know that I am not beautiful and not well-educated. I am only a simple girl.

Her letter touches a chord of poignant tragi-comedy when she writes:

> I know – and all the girls here have been telling me the same thing though not in so many words – that you are ashamed of me because of my hare-lip...

A world of sadness erupts with this *cri de cœur*, this final statement of what has been gnawing her heart for so long, the deformity which everybody sees but nobody mentions. Her fate is to have Demero marry a white girl while she must assume responsibility for her home when her mother dies suddenly in one of those contrived events Kayira resorts to overmuch.

Kayira's descriptive strengths do not desert him here. His evocation of the Malawian environment is done with increased attention to detail, so that a whole cycle of seasons moves with the events of the plot. His characters constantly show sensitivity to their environment, often seeking solace in the countryside from the hubbub of the city, as though feeling drawn to a former life pattern.

The appearance of *The Detainee*, however, shows that Kayira has traded pastoralism for satire and a mood of deep disillusion.

### South African Prose

Like their poet colleagues, South Africa's prose writers are largely a group in exile, producing texts banned from distribution in the Republic. Ezekiel Mphahlele has become a legend in his own time, drifting like a medieval scholar to campuses scattered through Africa and North America, and calling his first novel, significantly, *The Wanderers*. Alex La Guma lives in London; Abrahams long ago left for the Caribbean; Can Themba died an exile in Swaziland; Bessie Head writes and dreams in Botswana.

These writers' common experience has produced in them (Bessie Head excepted) a marked identity of posture, not always evident at the level of detail but consistently true in terms of basic aims and strategy. Faced with a common problem of appearance and reality in South Africa's image to the world, the constant objective, crystallised and most vigorously pursued in La Guma's *In the Fog of the Seasons' End*, is to paint, if necessary in the gaudiest of colours, the grim reality behind the facade erected by the Nationalist Government. This will often involve the temptation to indulge in mere reportage, to bring in the cameras, microphones, and shorthand pads of the journalist; to focus also on a narrow cluster of themes that centre in apartheid and racism generally. In other words, the imaginative area of literary activity risks starvation for the sake of the basic cause. And this presumably was in part Lewis Nkosi's complaint when he chose to remark that South Africa had nothing to compare with 'the imaginative power of Chinua Achebe's *Things Fall Apart* or the placid grace of its style', and even went on to ask whether it might not be prudent to renouce literature temporarily and solve the political problem first. At the same time (his comments were made in 1966), he saw twin difficulties facing the growth of good South African fiction in an 'over-melodramatic' political situation and the 'the barrenness and

225

infertile nature of tradition'. Before singling out for special praise
both Mphahlele and La Guma, he made the following attack on South
African fiction in general (110):

> What we do get from South Africa therefore – and what we get
> most frequently – is the journalistic fact parading outrageously
> as imaginative literature. We find here a type of fiction which
> exploits the ready-made plots of racial violence, social apartheid,
> interracial love affairs which are doomed from the beginning,
> without any attempt to transcend or transmute these given 'social
> facts' into artistically persuasive works of fiction.[5]

But surely the point must be made here that, given the basic aim
the majority of his fellow writers from the Republic share – to show
and tell the world the horrors of life in an apartheid society – it is as
natural as the sun rising in the East for a strongly journalistic form
of writing to emerge, writing that lives close to daily street-level
reality, exploiting every technique that might make a reader see, hear,
feel, and smell what it is like for non-whites to live in the Republic.
Granted this basic rhetorical aim, is the *cinéma-vérité* technique which
Nkosi attacks so bad after all? Is it even possible to avoid it? None would
deny that there is room within the South African canon for a *Hobbit*,
a *Drinkard*, or a *Jingala*, but a writer might be forgiven for feeling
irresponsible for attempting to write one. As Mphahlele has eloquently
testified, the South African writer's burden has not always been understood with the greatest of kindness by his colleagues in other parts
of the continent.

Thus, like children bullied at school facing parents asking why they
absconded, men like La Guma, Rive, and Mphahlele recount experiences they know their audience cannot duplicate and will find
hard to credit. While the official voice of the Republic, in polished
prose or decent middle-class idiom, assures the world that all is well,
parading its symbols of material muscle and sporting prowess, insisting
that the heart of the system is all sweetness and millenial concern, that
the whole country in fact is one huge happy state of sun-drenched
recreation and economic security, we now hear the voice it reserves
for its non-white citizens; the voice reserved for the banned, the
muzzled, the exiled, the proscribed, the detained, the majority in fact
of its people: 'We'll make you piss blood, you baboon...' 'Tell me
what I want to know, or I'll have your balls out...' 'Lord, all you
*bliksems* look the blerry same...' 'Listen, you baboon, this pass book

226

is no good, you should have been out of this city a long time ago...'
'We don't want any educated hottentots in our town...I will shoot
whatever hotnot or kaffir I desire, and see me get into trouble over
it. I demand respect from these donders.' We hear the voice of the
oppressed themselves: 'A man must *mos* fight for his brother, don't
I say?'...'We all got our burden to carry. Ja, only a man *mos* get to
reckon and think, who works out how much weight each person got
to carry'...'Christ, we all got hanged long ago.'...'Awright, I say. But
we all get kicked in the arse the same...' 'A family of three was
found stiff and cold yesterday morning...Dead as my father who
lies in Bantule cemetery.' We get cold hard statistics, such as these
from Can Themba: 'Child: Sekgametse Daphne Lorraine Mabiletsa,
Maria's child, age 3 years. Father undertermined. Free clinic atten-
dance. Medical report: Advanced Kwashiakor.' Or these from La
Guma: 'When we sit down to write a book, I or any of my colleagues
around me, we are, as writers, faced with the reality that 80 % of the
population lives below the bread-line standard; we are faced with the
reality that the average daily population of prisoners in South African
prisons amounts to 70,000 persons. We are faced with the reality that
half the non-white people who died last year were below the age of
five years.' Where government handouts show a beach-and-cocktail
paradise inhabited, it would appear, entirely by whites, the Republic's
writers show a different scene. We see the police in the locations
beating down the doors of the poor and stripping covers brutally from
marriage beds. We see an old man dead by a road gang's site; an old
woman amidst the heaped junk of her possessions sitting on the
pavement after her eviction, with nowhere to go but with a 'fierce
dignity' still burning in her eyes. We see parched landscapes and
desolate roads where black men trudge in single file, 'looking ahead
into some unknown future, wrapped in tattered, dusty blankets'. And
finally, that true voice of feeling again, addressing a tired Asian lady
seeking a mere cup of coffee in a cafe: 'Coolies, kaffirs, and Hottnots
outside. Don't you bloody well know?' It is as if, mindful of recent
German precedent, South African writers are ensuring that the outside world will never be able to say again, 'But we didn't know. If only
someone had told us.'

The endless tracery of the system's brutality revealed in the writing
makes the problems reflected in free Africa's literature – developing
class structures, post-colonial gloom, corruption – almost pale into
trivia. Urban squalor and rural penury, pass-laws, ubiquitous segrega-

227

tion, family-breaking residence laws, endless police raids, molestation, sadism, starvation wages, violence, drunkenness, some of the highest murder rates in the world, a subtle divide-and-rule game whereby whites sit back and watch hatred sown among other races erupt into violence, racial theories closer to Nazism than western commentators dare admit – all these, glimpsed against the usual squalor of an industrial state, comprise a scene almost too appalling to believe. The laments of Achebe, Armah, Ngugi, or Okot p'Bitek echo like academic exercises after the piercing stridency of South African writing. Whatever the problem or abuse raised in African literature, the effect of South African writing is to make them seem infinitely worse in the Republic than anywhere else.

The problem of imagination in South African writing that Lewis Nkosi mentions is illustrated by the career of Ezekiel Mphahlele, scholar, teacher, lucid provocative critic, wanderer, and creative writer, a man whose experience in a rough world (badly treated even in independent Africa) has turned a deeply compassionate view of humanity into a conviction that only guns and violence can cure the cancer of apartheid in Vorster's Republic. It is not that Mphahlele lacks imagination. Far from it. Various collections of short stories such as *In Corner B* and *Let Live*, and *The Living & the Dead*, and a substantial though highly autobiographical novel *The Wanderers* (1971), are evidence enough of an imaginative gift. Nor were the strengths of his first major critical book, *The African Image*, which added a wholly new dimension to African critical debates especially as they concerned negritude, underestimated, to say nothing of his most recent work, *Voices in the Whirlwind* (1973). It is simply that he feels that his autobiography *Down Second Avenue* (1959) is the best book, presumably the most important book he has yet written; as if, in other words, the workaday South African scene is too fraught with pain and urgency for mere fiction, no matter how clever, to take precedence over the naked truth hauled up from the well of memory and set forth with care in an autobiography.[6] Even his description of how the creative process worked in him while still at home makes a similar point about how close to daily reality the short stories are. Written in almost immediate response to sudden provocation, they have, on his own evidence, enjoyed little time for a slow steady fictive reworking of raw material where the fancy and imagination lift mundane stuff into the realms of literary art. Mphahlele strikes no poses, sees himself in the role of

neither prophet nor messiah, and the following remarks are as revealing of his humility as they are of the general difficulties facing the artist
as a black South African (xxi):

> I am clearly not a novelist in the special sense in which a man
> like Chinua Achebe can be said to be. I am just a writer: I have
> turned my hand to the critical essay, to reportage, to versifying,
> to fiction, wherever the mood has taken me. Now I don't have
> the impulse left to write a short story any more. The waves of
> something thrashing about inside me are too fierce and noisy to
> be contained by the short sharp precise statement that is the short
> story. I am now more confirmed than ever before in my belief
> that I wrote short fiction in South Africa because the distance
> between the ever-present stimulus and anger was so short, the
> anger screamed for an outlet with such a burning urgency, that
> I had to find a prose medium that would get me to the focal point
> with only a few eloquent movements. The short story was such
> a medium. Indeed it came to one as a reflex. Outside South
> Africa, in the bigger world of bigger ideas and in situations that
> demand a larger variety of emotional responses, one's reflexes
> take on a different quality, a greater complexity.

As individual pieces, the short stories are not always distinguished.
Sometimes it is stretches of slack prose that reduce their impact;
sometimes the standards of a professional teacher break through and
impose a correctness and a propriety where 'fluency' should rule.
Sometimes it is the very struggle between correctness and the desire
to run free and capture the registers and dialect of the people that
becomes obvious and therefore a weakness. But Mphahlele's stories
as a group, a body, a collection, are excellent. From 'Man Must Live',
where a whole life span is squeezed into the strait-jacket tightness of
the short story form, to 'A Point of Identity', which explores the
tragi-comic complexities of the colour bar, to 'Mrs Plum' and 'The
Living and the Dead', which play very deftly on the workings of the
white South African mind, liberal or otherwise, the evidence accumu-
lates that no other writer, with the exception of La Guma, can record
with such delicacy the slow tragic harmonies that lie beneath the trivia,
the unpolished surface of poor lives. The sad division among the
various non-white groups which is subtly fostered by the white
community is often reflected together with a plea for the kind of
solidarity needed to unite all the oppressed groups against a common

enemy. Hence the message of 'A Point of Identity', where Karel
Almeidea, a coloured, chooses to live among blacks (64):

> But Hotnotte, Boesmans and Kaffirs and coolies are all frying
> in the same pan, boy, and we're going to sink or swim together,
> you watch.[7]

The *persona's* wife in the same story reflects (71):

> I wonder how much longer it is going to be for us Africans to
> keep making allowances and to give way to the next man to turn
> things round in our head, to do the explaining and to think of
> others' comfort.

The same note of needful solidarity and grim endurance rings through
'In Corner B', one of Mphahlele's finest stories. Talita suspects her
hard-working husband of having an affair, despite a long period of
stable married life that the author describes as surviving against the
odds of a harsh environment (110):

> They had lived through nineteen years of married life that
> yielded three children and countless bright and cloudy days. It
> was blissful generally, in spite of the physical and mental violence
> around them; the privation; police raids; political strikes and
> attendant clashes between the police and boycotters; death; ten
> years of low wages during which she experienced a long spell of
> ill health. But like everybody else Talita and her man stuck it
> through... In the midst of all these living conditions, at once in
> spite and because of them, the people of Corner B alternately
> clung together desperately and fell away from the centre; like
> birds that scatter when the tree on which they have gathered is
> shaken.

Death is one relief from a pain that seems endless. A people's sorrow
breaks forth most pathetically at funerals. 'Here my children', says an
old man uncorking whisky at a burial, 'kill the heart and as the
Englishman says, *drown de sorry.*' Hymns are sung, speaking of hope
and release, a surrender to death once it has been unleashed. But as
the author puts it, 'Underlying the poetry of this surrender is the one
long and huge irony of endurance'. The supposed rival who is really
no rival at all, but only a girl the man knew in his youth, writes to Talita
an illiterate letter that again captures the pathos of ordinary people
(125):

now he is gonn i feel i want to rite with al my ten fingas becos
i have too muche to say aboute your sorriness and my sorriness
i will help you to kry you help me to kry and leev that man in
peas with his gods.

What the stories reveal constantly is the response to a brutal system
of a mind fundamentally humane, free itself of brutality, and free too
of racist blinkers. With the portrait of Stoffel Visser in 'The Living
and the Dead' there is even briefly canvassed the belief in white
conversion; and despite the swelling bitterness of recent years, despite
the fact that he now believes traditional African humanism cannot
alone succeed, asserting that when freedom is finally won 'the black
man will have no mercy, and rightly so' and that the only useful help
is that which at some point will 'promote guerilla activity in southern
Africa' – despite all this, Mphahlele's career is redolent with the signs
of a soul that has laboured hard, nailing courage and hope to the mast
of human decency and affirming the value of sacrifice. Even more, the
most eloquent testimony of Mphahlele's writing is their author's basic
and passionate concern not with himself but with other people, those
he knew in his youth and childhood, whose difficulties and aspirations
he shares and understands. This quality infuses all Mphahlele's writing and makes *Down Second Avenue* (1959) perhaps the least ego-centric
autobiography ever written. This is a remarkable if uneven work,
epigraphed with that Yeats comment so deeply felt in the modern
world:

The best lack all conviction, while the worst
Are full of passionate intensity.

The book has had a chequered history, for though it is now widely
read in the United States and appears on many a college syllabus, it
was initially rejected by American publishers who argued that the
experience described was too localised, and that in any case the
market was swamped with 'too many books about Africa'.

The finest passages in *Down Second Avenue* occur early, either
because this portion of the author's life is the most memorable or
because, as usually happens, early chapters get more attention and
more revision than later ones. Certainly his scenes from the slum life
of Marabastad have a poignancy and a poetic quality found more
often in forms other than autobiography. The heart-rending cries of
a mother whose child has died after a police raid rise like words

from the purest of tragic poets. As the woman's mind seeks refuge in hysteria, a torrent of sorrow, disbelief and shattered hopes floods forth (60):

> 'He's not dead, no, not my son', she wailed, her hands over her face. 'He must be well and strong again. And when he's big he will go to school. And learn how to write his name and letters to me. But how can I read his letters? I must work very hard and add another ten shillings to that money to buy him a jersey.'

It is a brief paragraph, like much else in this book a mere fragment from the mosaic of remembered life. Its starkly tragic and lyrical qualities make it a more eloquent commentary on the nature of life in the Republic than a shelf of learned tomes, government reports, and sociological treatises. Poverty and sickness, unemployment, racial fear and stratification, a stoic posture before looming despair, the consolation of fellow victims – all are there in this random passage from *Down Second Avenue*.

Exchanges overheard on wintry mornings in Marabastad tell a similar story of pain and death (58–9):

> 'I'm all right, but this blasted cold...'
> 'We're not well, all the children have whooping-cough...'
> 'A drum of boiling water tumbled over two children near the fire, they died as soon as they got to hospital...'
> 'That's a common winter story...'
> 'A family of three were found stiff and cold yesterday morning, they had a live brazier in the house all through the night...Dead as my father who lies at Bantule cemetery...'

Apart from producing the raw feel of life for non-whites, these fragments tell us much about the man who recorded them, particularly about his humanity. They also reflect the essentially powerless position in which non-whites find themselves. These elements come together when Mphahlele, writing in Denver, Colorado in 1970, says (xxxvi):

> And I am now trying to hold on to this basic humanism. This impels me to want to share what I have with others, to tune in always to people, physically dead or alive, rather than to things...

*Alex La Guma*

Two points can be made without hesitation about Alex La Guma. One is that recognition of his work has been disappointingly slow. The other is that, despite occasional assertions that the man is simply a propagandist, his writing in its fibre and tissue announces an artist committed to the acquisition and development of that whole range of skills associated with the higher forms of literary craftsmanship. La Guma has suffered too long from the misleading logic of the view that because South African conditions are inimical to the growth of good writing, none has in fact appeared; whereas his special artistic qualities, such as his power of transcending stereotype to grasp the rich variety of human character and experience, have produced a body of work broader than the cramping fences of political theory can contain and larger than anything one might remotely consider parochial. At his best, which means in his short stories, La Guma not only ranks with the finest in Africa; he can hold his head high among the finest writers in English anywhere.

La Guma's sensibility and point of view have been largely shaped by an urban environment. Though Coloured locations are generally more salubrious than the infamous ghettoes of Orlando, Soweto and Marabastad, Cape Town's District Six, with which La Guma is most familiar, possesses those same 'swarming, cacophonous, strutting, brawling, vibrating' qualities that Can Themba saw in the African townships. La Guma's scene unfolds from here, for its characters, poverty, oppression, speech, hopes, and despair provide, in *A Walk in the Night,* his artistic starting point. In La Guma an artist's curiosity about the lives and foibles of his fellow men combines with a deeply human care about their sufferings and affliction. La Guma resembles Ngugi in so far as his politics – frankly Marxist – seem as if they have grown out of a shocked response, an instinctive response, to human suffering and not from either library or lecture hall. The human condition is sensed, examined, and understood; then a politics is embraced to cure seen ills. The chronology is crucial here, for it explains how La Guma and Ngugi can both give us art rather than political propaganda; and neither seems to be shaping and falsifying experience to fit the stencils of a political ideology. Any assumption that La Guma's professed Marxism means not only that every word he writes is preaching politics but that he is bound hand and foot by a limited and tightly prescribed catechism of attitudes, postures, and

233

explanations for every human situation – in other words that he is
debarred from a free open response to life – leads to the kind of
unfortunate criticism that a scholar like Anthony Chennells offers in
the Rhodesian journal *Mambo* (November 1974). To begin with there
is notorious disagreement about the essence of Marxism itself; then
La Guma's brand of it is not clear; nor do we know from a personal
statement how many of Marxism's supposed tenets he subscribes
to. There is also as much variety of colour and approach among
Marxist writers as there is among Catholic. Hence, though La Guma's
whole effort seems to be towards effecting an improvement in conditions of life in South Africa, and though he would decry with a
withering scorn an empty aestheticism, his basic make-up as man
and artist with deep aesthetic impulses ensures that the claims of art
are always before him, always being assiduously courted, and that
while we are being deliberately taken as close as possible to the sight,
smell, and sound of reality, the thin border between art and propaganda is rarely crossed. Hence the common feeling in La Guma's
writing that behind the particular group of figures he draws for us
there stands, to use Graham Hough's words, 'the larger, not contra-
dictory presence of humanity itself, the community of all man, general
nature'. La Guma addresses his appeal to the collective conscience of
the world by way of the particular group his experience has qualified
him to speak for. And his awareness of a political bias appears itself
to work to his artistic advantage, enabling him to see clearly where the
art-politics division lies and hence ensure that neither his aesthetic nor
intellectual integrity is sacrificed.

Although Richard Rive's *Quartet* (1963) contains such early pieces
as 'Out of Darkness' (a prelude to *The Stone Country*), 'Slipper Satin',
and 'A Glass of Wine', *A Walk in the Night and Other Stories* (1967) is
the most useful volume to illustrate La Guma's early skill in tight
structures, characterisation, and verbal conjuring.[8] This volume also
charts a definite growth in the author's craft – his sensitivity to landscape as both backcloth and moral reflector, his sharpness of eye and
ear, his knack of capturing tone and phrase for his dialogue, his
determination to harness every syllable to the chariot of artistic purpose. Most particularly, *A Walk in the Night* demonstrates La Guma's
ability to choose a core idea or situation and work it out in the tightest,
most organic way. There is a further point. This volume seems to bear
out Mphahlele's claim that South African conditions are more condu-
cive to the short story than they are to the novel – for the best pieces

here are more successful than the novels which follow later, and the title piece itself, a novella, while important as a dry run for the novels, lacks the impact of short stories also collected here like 'The Gladiators' and 'A Matter of Taste'.

An early work, 'A Walk in the Night' shows the marks of a talent still flexing its muscles but not fully arrived at maturity. It begins well, but after forty-odd pages the control slackens, the hard task of showing yields to the easier one of telling, and the writing generally loses power. La Guma is a master of the short tight exercise and ventures into the long distance forms with caution and a sense of his own limitations. Michael Adonis loses his job for going to the lavatory. Unemployment, unfairly inflicted by his white boss, becomes a catalyst for social and moral disaster. Adonis falls in with thugs, presumably also victims of the system, and rapidly loses his self-respect. He goes home one night depressed and climbs to his room in a dilapidated tenement block, whose very squalor is meant to mirror the social and human decay which is South Africa (23):

> The staircase was worn and blackened, the old oak banister loose and scarred. Naked bulbs wherever the light sockets were in working order cast a pallid glare over parts of the interior, lighting up the big patches of damp and mildew, and the maps of denuded sections on the walls. Somewhere upstairs a radio was playing Latin-American music, bongos and maracas throbbing softly through the smells of ancient cooking, urine, damp-rot and stale tobacco. A baby wailed with the tortured sound of gripe and malnutrition and a man's voice rose in hysterical laughter. Footsteps thudded and water rushed down a pipe in a muted roar.

This is a typical piece of La Guma's writing in both purpose and fullness of detail. The rot, neglect, filth, cultural bastardy, smells, hysteria, and infant pain (foreshadowing Armah's method in *The Beautyful Ones*?) are recorded to make larger points of a political nature. The essence of the system, La Guma is saying, and he uses the technique repeatedly, can be sensed in the minutest details of the environment, the physical state of buildings, the gurgling even of drains. That the baby's crying can be identified as the authentic sound of malnutrition is hard to accept and strikes a false note, as if La Guma's iron control momentarily deserts him. But apart from this blemish, which typifies a weakness too common in this piece, the prose is evocative, strong, and vivid.

Ironically, and this too makes a point about the system, an old English actor lives in the same building and asks Michael to accompany him to his room. He is Uncle Doughty, a human wreck with the 'expression of a decrepit bloodhound'. His head is 'almost bald, and wisps of dirty grey hair clung to the bony, pinkish skull like scrub clining to eroded rock'. Once he 'used to be something', but as he puts it, 'Here I am and nobody to look after an old man.' Michael, full of his own troubles, calls Doughty an 'old white bastard', and won't accept his claim that they are both the system's victims, 'just ghosts, doomed to walk the night', as he puts it. In a rage, and shouting, 'Can't a boy have a bloody piss without getting kicked in the backside by a lot of effing law?' Michael hits out at Doughty and kills him. Willieboy, a friend of Michael, is seen in the vicinity and pursued as the murderer. He is cornered and shot by the police, and after suffering appalling neglect at the hands of a Constable Raalt, who leaves him bleeding in the back of a police van, dies for Michael's crime.

There is much effective inner dialogue in the story, especially in those passages where Michael reflects on the killing. Here he wonders if he should surrender and confess, but decides against it (43):

> You know what the law will do to you. They don't have any shit from us brown people. They'll hang you, as true as God. Christ, we all got hanged long ago. What's the law for? To kick us poor brown bastards around. You think they're going to listen to your story; Jesus, and he was white man, too. Well, what's he want to come and live here among us brown for? To hell with him. Well. I didn't mos mean to finish him. Awright, man, he's dead and you're alive. Stay alive. Ja, stay alive and get kicked under the arse until you're finished, too. Like they did with your job. To hell with them. The whole effing lot of them.

The inner turmoil of Mikey's mind is skilfully rendered as fear, anger, and remorse swirl together in the cause of exculpation. We are swept off in the current too, now sympathising with murdered Doughty and now with Mikey; now blaming the youth's selfishness, now forgiving because we agree that he can expect no justice from the system. We are as bewildered in our moral response as Michael himself. Clear moral choices under apartheid become as hard as everything else.

The authentic register of Michael's Cape Coloured community is also well caught, with its tough slang, its clipped, elliptical structures, its echoes of Black America rather than Britain or any part of English-speaking Africa. It is a roughly strong idiom, racy and pithy, later exploited with uninterrupted brilliance in 'The Gladiators'. Like West African pidgin, it can carry great pathos, as it does here when Mikey erupts with an exclamation that is at once subtle rationalisation and a cry ringing with the voice of an oppressed and despairing people: 'Christ, we all got hanged long ago.'

The ruminations of Constable Raalt, the cold Afrikaaner policeman who hunts down Willieboy, are also revealing. He typifies La Guma's long gallery of police portraits and represents the system officially personified. The gap between the two communities is seen through his reflections as he notes particulars at the scene of the crime (63):

> They hate us, but I don't give a bloody hell about them, anyway; and no hotnot bastard gets away with murder on my patrol; yellow shirt and kinky hair; a real hotnot and I'll get him even if I have to gather in every black bastard wearing a yellow shirt.

What emerges as an incidental detail from this flow of hatred, but which is central to La Guma's attack on apartheid, is the fact that while the law has meticulously divided the population into a variety of racial groupings, white society, represented by Raalt, sees all non-whites as simply blacks. La Guma has an acute understanding of the divisiveness at work in the Republic and repeatedly in his writing tells non-whites that they are all in the same boat together. Or as one of his characters puts it in 'The Gladiators', 'We all get kicked in the arse the same.'

Throughout the story, the question that always looms is how to survive in this hell; how to get through with dignity and a full stomach. There is no imposition of simplistic solutions and each character has his own answer. Willieboy has tried hard but after an upbringing of appalling deprivation is shot like a dog and left to die in the back of a van. Foxy's group turn to crime, others to drink. Joe, in this regard, is of particular interest. The son of a man who simply ran away, deserting his wife and children, he rejects this solution. He chooses to live close to nature, as far as this is possible in Cape Town, haunting the open spaces provided by sand, sea, and shore, braving the urban maelstrom only occasionally. He argues that running away, to the country for example, is merely to leap from frying pan to fire, because eviction and harrassment will reach there too, and the exodus begin again. The system has stripped Joe of his entire family: brothers, sisters, father, mother – all gone – scattered by poverty and unemployment. Yet he is morally superb in his refusal to accept Mikey's criminal solution. 'Like I said, we all got troubles...I got nothing. No house, no people, no place. Maybe that's troubles. Don't I say?' The penultimate scene takes us from urban insanity to the sea. South Africa's dirt and degredation are forgotten and instead, suggesting an almost Wordsworthian solution, we see Joe, stoic and romantic, walking away from the crowded streets (96):

> Somewhere, the young man, Joe, made his way towards the sea, walking alone through the starlit darkness. In the morning he would be close to the smell of the ocean and wade through the chill, comforting water, bending close to the purling green surface and see the dark undulating fronds of seaweed, writhing and swaying in the shallows, like beckoning hands. And in the rock pools he would examine the mysterious life of the sea things, the transparent beauty of starfish and anemone, and hear the relentless, consistent pounding of the creaming waves against the granite citadels of rock.

Joe is walking to the fringes of South African life, where he can survive, away from the madness and inhumanity. If men have built a chaos in human relationships, at least there is spiritual refreshment in the seas and rock pools of outdoor nature. The beauty of the passage describing a mysterious sea life that Joe wants to understand is designed to contrast with the lunatic human life that has gone before. It would be too simplistic to imagine La Guma suggesting that Joe might find an adequate alternative life here by the shore, or even that he might discover secrets applicable to human life inland. It is the lonely beauty of it all that is crucial to him, for it provides a relief from human ugliness, food for his aesthetic sense, and a milieu in which he can ponder, and bear calmly, the still sad music of the land. Those creaming waves battering against the granite citadels of rock are a figure for the positive forces of humanity struggling endlessly, as Joe's people and La Guma's are, against the craggy white citadel that seems invincible. The image speaks less of despair than of long relentless struggle: no easy victories, no quick solutions. It gets a measure of optimism from being couched in so much wild beauty and life. As far as Joe is concerned, however, it already carries a shadow of gloom cast by a previous discovery, that 'they're going to make the beaches so only white people can go there'. One is left to guess what Joe will do when that happens.

The story's final paragraph, returning us appropriately to urban

238

squalor, strikes a similar note of shadowy hope. Franky Lorenzo's wife is lying awake in the night, 'waiting for the dawn and feeling the knot of life within her'. This image of new life, of hope, is blighted by our own knowledge, for we have been shown by this time enough to feel horror at the prospect of this new human being being born into a system which will hound him from cradle to grave because he is the wrong colour.

La Guma's style, eventually even tighter than it is in *A Walk*, emphasises arresting simile and shaped phrase, though his figurative language, functional and vivid, rarely comes down to mere decoration. As Leavis once said of Bunyan, his English is plain, terse, homely, and colloquial, living close to the norms of daily speech. Michael Adonis looks at lines of workers going home after he has been dismissed (1):

> He looked right through them, refusing to see them, nursing a little growth of anger the way one caressess the beginnings of a toothache with the tip of the tongue.

Michael meets Willieboy in a cafe (4):

> They were not very close friends, but had been thrown together in the whirlpool world of poverty, petty crime and violence of which that cafe was an outpost.

Which is fine strong writing until *outpost* begins to weaken the whirlpool image. Joe is introduced in a manner that becomes a favoured mode (9):

> Joe was short and his face had an ageless quality about it under the grime, like something valuable forgotten in a junk shop. He had the soft brown eyes of a dog, and he smelled of a mixture of sweat, slept-in clothes and seaweed...
>
> Nobody knew where Joe came from, or anything about him. He just seemed to have happened, appearing in the District like a cockroach emerging through a floorboard.

The cockroach image (the harbinger of many) is sharp though unflattering; the rest is vivid and evocative. La Guma's preferred mode of physical description emphasises facial characteristics, and especially eyes – as if he accepts that these really are the betraying windows of gnomic lore. Here, describing two policemen, he writes:

> They had hard, frozen faces as if carved out of pink ice, and hard, dispassionate eyes, hard and bright as pieces of blue glass.

239

His imagination never falters in this area. Elsewhere in his writings we find: 'eyes restless as cockroaches'; 'two bright eyes, restless geckoes'; 'Little blue eyes, flat as pieces of glass'; 'they [the eyes] were hard and grey and cold as pebbles on a beach when the tide goes out'; 'eyes like smeared plus signs in the wrinkled folds of his face'; 'small, bright eyes leapt around like sparks'; 'shoe-button eyes'; 'wet, hooded, pebbly eyes'; 'eyes, pouched and watery, as if they were being pre-served in little cups of formaldehyde' (a doctor's); 'the eyes were pale and washed-out and silvery, much like imitation pearls, and cold as quicksilver'; 'the reddish eyes...peered out like predatory creatures in ambush'; 'eyes chill as new frost', 'a dry brittle face like crumpled pink tissue – paper with holes torn in it for eyes'; 'eyes alert as sparks'. Always the figures are sharp and apt; always they are both arresting yet artistically functional.

Though the city is La Guma's preferred scene, he often ventures into the countryside to show that the evils of the system pervade the whole land and all situations where the races meet. 'The Lemon Orchard', collected here, is set in a Boer farming area, a Garden of Eden blessed with the fragrance of fruit blossom and the warm caress of the sun. But in five tight pages La Guma unveils a hell-in-heaven as a black teacher who has allegedly insulted a Boer cleric is taken at night for summary punishment by a party of the *volk*. Neither teacher nor punishment is identified; but here is clearly a representative figure and his punishment will be so bad that his captors say 'he'll pack his things and go and live in the city where they're not so particular about the dignity of the volk'. These are a philistine group, despising education as much as they despise the blacks, hymning the praises of dogs as they drag a fellow human through the dark. 'We don't want any educated hottentots in our town', says one. 'Neither black Englishmen', adds another, while the leader is sure about how the law affects him. 'I will shoot whatever hotnot or kaffir I desire, and see me get into trouble over it.' Their brutality is witnessed, and registered, by nature around them (135):

> The blackness of the night crouched over the orchard and the leaves rustled with a harsh whispering that was inconsistent with the pleasant scent of the lemons. The chill in the air had in-creased...Then the moon came from behind the banks of cloud and its white light touched the leaves with wet silver, and the perfume of the lemons seemed to grow stronger, as if the juice was being crushed from them.

'Coffee for the Road', collected in Komey and Mphahlele's *Modern African Stories* (164) also has a largely rural setting. An Asian lady is driving with two tired fractious children the length of the country to meet her husband in Cape Town. Travelling all night because there is nowhere to stop (the hotels are for whites only), the woman eventually gives in to the nagging of her children and stops in a small town to get some coffee. Avoiding the foot-square hole where non-whites are served, she enters a cafe with a flask she wants filling, finding within a small, snotty-nosed white boy and a proprietress who screams, 'Coffee? My Lord Jesus Christ!...A bedamned coolie girl in here!...Coolies, Kaffirs and Hottentots outside...Don't you bloody well know?' Exhausted and at the end of her tether, the Asian lady flings her flask in the woman's face, storms out and drives off, only to be stopped several miles up the road by a riot-van, and a heavily-armed policeman who says, '*Ja*, darkie girl with brown suit and sun-glasses. You're under arrest.' The sordid arrangements at the cafe and the grossness of a Sten-gun and riot-van to intercept an unarmed mother make their own point about life for the Republic's non-whites. But their plight, and especially the hopeless, wearying frustration of it all, are reflected at every point in the landscape the car passes through and the scene that unfolds itself. Images of dust and dryness, of bare rock and inhospitable terrain, punctuate the narrative at suitable moments. This is semi-desert country sprawling away on all sides 'in reddish brown flats and depressions'. The land is scattered with 'scrub and thorn', stunted trees, parched gullies, drab farm buildings, tumbledown mud houses, occasional barbed wire, baked clay *dongas*, dust-coloured *koppies*, and shabby towns. Exactly reflecting the woman's position, and the position of all like her, at one point 'the metal vanes of a windmill pump turned wearily in the faint morning breeze, as if it had just been wakened to set reluctantly about its duty of sucking water from the miserly earth'. Elsewhere, the car passes a band of naked, dusty brown children who wave cheerfully, innocent of the system they've been born into; and further along the road, unsmiling, unwaving, and carrying the marks of knowledge that comes from experience, their adult counterparts are seen: 'Three black men trudged in single file along the roadside, looking ahead into some unknown future, wrapped in tattered, dusty blankets.' Event, scene, and moral aim blend perfectly in a story which also appears to make a 'non-Marxist' point that economic status is only one factor in the apartheid equation. The Asian lady obviously has money, good clothes, and a new car. But these can never make up for her colour.

241

Perhaps the subtlest story La Guma has written is 'A Matter of Taste', where any temptation to tell rather than show is firmly resisted. There is a shift of narrative viewpoint too, for the narrator is one of the characters, who consist of two coloured railway workers and a young white man.

The story begins with typical briskness. Setting, brief yet carrying hints of fracture and pain needed for La Guma's message, swiftly yields to event and whenever necessary filters back as the story proceeds (125):

> The sun hung well towards the west now so that the thin clouds above the ragged horizon were rimmed with bright yellow like the split yolk of an egg. Chinaboy stood up from having blown the fire round the tin and said, 'She ought to boil now.'

The description of Chinaboy is equally concise. He is small, with 'grey-flecked kinky hair, and a wide, quiet, heavy face'. There is a world of suggestion here: a hint of a man worn out, resigned, yet surviving somehow. The next comment amplifies this, for the narrator, who though a workmate must distance himself from Chinaboy, says that it was 'as if he had grown accustomed to doing things slowly and carefully and correctly'. The coloured man's South Africa and its tangle of socio-political tripwires rises briefly with this remark. We see Chinaboy being conditioned by the harassment of a thousand police-pass situations, throwing the reins on passion and tongue, and with exaggerated care producing the documents which enable him to survive. To complete the picture, and suggest more about the life he has experienced, the narrator says that despite the patience inherent in every movement, 'his eyes were dark oriental ovals, restless as a pair of cockroaches'. Again, the cockroach image, suggesting in Chinaboy's case not only perpetual alertness and readiness for flight but also the squalor of his situation. That single image is enough to evoke the world Chinaboy lives in and the feel of it for men like himself. La Guma's artistry reveals itself through minute detail of this sort, the merest brushstroke that triggers a response to a whole social system; a response provoked by the author but swiftly expanded by the attentive intelligence of the reader.

Into this rural scene, with its touch of seediness (showing how the urban social disease spreads into the countryside too) steps a young white man. He joins the two workers for coffee, chats, shares cigarettes, and is helped onto a passing goods train. This is the basic plot. He appears as if from nowhere. 'The portjackson bush and wattle cracked and rustled behind me', says the narrator, and then, with another deft touch, 'the long shadow of a man fell across the small clearing'. There is nothing forced here, this is proper detail for late afternoon; yet how suggestively sinister is that 'long shadow' which the white man casts. He is thin, fair, and scruffy, wearing jeans and a leather jacket. Unemployed, he is a sort of footloose transient, dreamy about far-off horizons, but right now hungry and thirsty. He invites himself to a frugal supper, consisting only of coffee served in condensed milk tins. The main dialogue is so brief and rich that its deserves quoting in full (127):

> The boy took his cup carefully and blew at the steam. Chinaboy sipped noisily and said, 'Should've had some bake bread. Nothing like a piece of bake bread with cawfee.'
> 'Hot dogs', the white boy said.
> 'Huh.'
> 'Hot dogs. Hot dogs go with coffee.'
> 'Ooh ja. I heard', Chinaboy grinned. Then he asked: 'You going somewhere, Whitey?'
> 'Cape Town. Maybe get a job on a ship an' make the States.'
> 'Lots of people want to reach the States', I said.
> Whitey drank some coffee and said: 'Yes, I heard there's plenty of money and plenty to eat.'
> 'Talking about eating', Chinaboy said: 'I see a picture in a book, one time. 'Merican book. This picture was about food over there. A whole mess of fried chicken, mealies – what they call corn – with mushrooms an' gravy, chips and new green peas. All done up in colours, too.'
> 'Pass me the roast lamb', I said sarcastically...
> Chinaboy said, whimsically: 'I'd like to sit down in a smart caffy one day and eat my way right out of a load of turkey, roast potatoes, beet-salad and angel's food trifle. With port and cigars at the end.'
> 'Hell', said Whitey, 'it's all a matter of taste. Some people like chicken and others eat sheep's heads and beans!'
> 'A matter of taste', Chinaboy scowled. 'Bull, it's a matter of money, pal.'

For sheer pregnant writing, this exchange would be hard to equal. The truths La Guma builds his story on are revealed by every nuance, hint,

243

and ironic statement the author can harness. The basic situation itself
– a white man seeking, and receiving, hospitality from coloured
workers – provokes us to reverse the scene and imagine a non-white
'beggar' disturbing the rich repast of a couple of white men. It is a
powerful suggestion, the more so for being unstated. There is also
Whitey's real status. Like some modern western undergraduate,
outwardly he shares the same economic level as the poor – hence his
poor clothing, dirt, and so forth. Indeed, he is theoretically worse off
than his hosts, for unlike them he is unemployed. A feeling of shared
poverty enables Whitey to identify with these workers and we begin
to see him as perhaps a white liberal opposing the system. But the story
as a whole, and this sequence in particular, is designed to separate
realities from appearances in South African life; to show, for example,
that Whitey here is not at all in the same position as Chinaboy and
the narrator. His comments on food immediately reveal that he comes
from no economic category these workers have known. For him hot
dogs go with coffee. But Chinaboy's view ('Nothing like a piece of
bake bread with cawfee') puts hot dogs in the realms of *haute cuisine*.
Where Whitey's conversation reveals that he is used to good food and
dining out, Chinaboy dreams of just once, in a lifetime, visiting a smart
café and eating in style. The truth breaks through when Whitey, in
a telling piece of insensitivity, asserts that with food 'it's all a matter
of taste'. This one word 'taste' gives the lie to Whitey's real social and
economic background and provides the key to La Guma's central
point. For taste, at one level, implies a range of options enjoyed so
often that a sense of cultivated preference has developed. The word
is infuriatingly provocative to Chinaboy because it is part of the
vocabulary of gustation, of eating, of food, and part of the vocabulary
of the fortunate, the full-bellied, the relatively leisured, the
comfortable.

It is a word associated, as Chinaboy knows at once, and as La Guma
wants us to realise, with money, with a certain kind of economic
distribution. In its narrow gustatory sense it also has an obscene
mocking quality among hungry men with only coffee for their meal
dreaming the full-bellied dreams of the poor. While mocking the status
of these non-whites who cannot afford the luxury of taste in its broader
sense (notice Chinaboy's deft Marxist point that it is all a matter of
money) it leaves Whitey looking like a man who has, for the moment,
exercising his taste, *chosen* poverty, unemployment, rags, and hunger.
The feeling is strong that the good life is still there for the asking, at

the end of a telephone wire in his parents' villa or through the good offices of a nearby branch of his bank. The nice irony of 'talking about eating' (Chinaboy's phrase) cannot for Whitey carry the pains of a permanent situation.

Whitey's basic status is further confirmed by his plans. He is going to Cape Town and 'Maybe get a job on a ship an' make the States.' These are again the tones of a man casually reviewing his options. He will take ship and go to America, *if* at the time he feels like it, if it still takes his fancy when he reaches Cape Town. He is in no hurry; other possibilities might present themselves. These are not the tones of a man desperate to escape poverty, but those of a man bored with affluence seeking a change, somehow, somewhere. The gap between Whitey's status and the two workers' is gradually opened up as the yawning chasm that it really is. Chinaboy and the narrator suffer hunger as an unavoidable way of life. They have no choice in the matter and the system guarantees that they will be denied the money that makes choice and 'taste' possible. Unlike their guest, they are in no position to consider seriously the idea of going to the States. They are trapped while Whitey is free as the wind. This is the centrepoint to which all the banter about taste has been leading, for through the whole scene and its exchanges rings the sense of that much-abused word 'freedom'. It is never mentioned, and La Guma knows that, had it been so, art might have yielded to propaganda. But the idea is there, strong and insistent. In South African society Whitey, for all his superficial poverty, is free, and his hosts are not. When he is helped onto a passing train, even the line helps to make the point. It is a symbol of escape, of progress, of movement to a better situation, open to whites but not to those whose sweat built it.

A racial encounter by a railway line, over a poor man's supper of coffee and cigarettes, an ironic conversation about food, and a nearby disused station house resembling a 'huge desecrated tomb' – these are the simple elements in a story that displays high art, a short story from the hands of a master.

'The Gladiators' is conceived throughout in the idiom of the Cape Coloured, and the choice of a boxing commentator as *persona* allows La Guma to write the whole piece in a racy, colloquial style. This is basically a comic piece with tragic racial overtones; and it is also another example of how, by judicious selection of scene and incident, La Guma can draw vivid miniatures that seem to encompass the entire South African scene. The boxing arena is an apt figure, with its predominantly black crowd, the best ringside seats occupied by whites, and the combatants seeking mutual destruction a Coloured boxer, Kenny, and a Black one, Panther. The divide and rule game could hardly be better illustrated.

The story, which has echoes of Hemingway's 'The Undefeated', begins with Kenny complaining bitterly that under South Africa's boxing laws he cannot fight Whites but only Coloureds and Blacks. Kenny is 'almost white', and rejoices in his contempt for anyone who is undisputably black. The narrator, an active character as in 'A Matter of Taste' and whose viewpoint expresses the tragi-comic nature of the piece, describes Kenny as follows (114):

> He's a good juba awright. Build like a bear if you ever see one, with sloping shoulders and a big chest, and arms and thighs like polish teak. Not exactly like teak, because he's lighter just miss being white which was what make him so full of crap. He was sorry he wasn't white and glad he wasn't black. He got a nice face, too, except for the nose that's a little flat from being hit on it a lot, almost like a black boy's nose, but not exactly.

Kenny's remarks are a model of confident contempt:

> 'I feel first class...I'll muck that black bastard.'

> 'But what the hell I got to fight black boys and coloured all the time?'

> 'You see me floor that blerry tsotsi.'

> 'That black piece of crap...The hell with him.'

The narrator is an older and wiser man with a vision that sees the total context of the incident with its broad racial and human implications. He understands – his tone suggests it – the forces which make men like Kenny despise their fellow victims of white injustice, and though he clearly censures, he has some sympathy too. We hear a strain of knowing resignation, of a man who well understands but feels a sense of impotence. He captures the essence of the situation when, replying to Kenny's 'Muck that own kind. That boy ain't our kind', he says, 'Awright...But we all get kicked in the arse the same.' A wealth of compressed truth lies in this crude statement, and this basic point, that all non-whites share the same plight, is repeated later when the narrator comments: 'I thought, Bastards, paying cash to see two other black boys knock themselves to hell.'

246

For the rest, the narrator is a skilful commentator in the best radio fashion. His performance has an *allegro* tempo, sharply visual detail, and crisp analogies that give it spice and bounce. Syntactic links disappear, punctuation is flung away, as the commentary on the fight sweeps onward (118–19):

> Well, the Panther just let Kenny come and even drop his guard. Kenny's left come in, but the Panther just shift his head and let the glove go past and then he hit Kenny you can hear it outside.
>
> That surprise Kenny and you can see it on his face and the Panther hit him again, and man, this time you can hear it down by the railway station, and then the blerry Panther dance away, like this, bobbing and dancing and waiting for Kenny to come after him and Kenny the blerry fool, go after him and the Panther hit him one two three and there's big red patches on all two sides of him, under his ribs, and he look plenty shaken...

La Guma's approach to writing novels has been slow and circumspect. Having mastered the art of creating short stories of power and tightness, prose pieces with the unity and care of poems, the temptation to write longer fiction was not yielded to easily. 'A Walk in the Night' was a *novella*, and a stepping stone to longer fiction, preceding the three novels for which La Guma is known: *And a Threefold Cord* (1964), *The Stone Country* (1967), and *In the Fog of the Seasons' End* (1972).

The progression has been such that in a remarkable way each new work seems to contain what has gone before. The world of the novels is the world of the short stories and vice versa. Indeed, meeting the novels' paucity of character and event, their restricted canvas, simplicity of plot, and thematic unity, one feels that La Guma is still trying to write magnified short stories. There is then a sense of an *oeuvre* about La Guma's output where each part reflects the whole and the whole reflects each part. Even basic material reappears from earlier work, refashioned and refurbished. Favoured images of eye, cockroach, and cigarette butt recur. Choker and his story 'Blankets' return in *The Stone Country*, a novel set entirely in a Cape Town jail. George Adams, imprisoned in *The Stone Country* for distributing anti-government literature, reappears slightly modified as Beukes in *The Fog of the Seasons' End*. And so on.

Yet it is hard to maintain in a novel the prose density achieved in a short story. The form offers a bigger canvas, room for more people and event, variety of action, growth and response. If the short story invites the artist to give the merest glimpse of a situation, the novel hints at the larger possibilities of drawing whole societies and epochs. As La Guma slowly yields to the siren voices of the larger form, an inevitable dilution occurs, a decline in intensity, a dissipation of poetic power in the prose, a pulling away of the mirror to catch a broader scene.

But a novel like *And a Threefold Cord* shows how reluctant La Guma is to surrender the strengths of the shorter form, for this is a work of fine structural unity, with one weather, one scene, one family, and one tone.[9] And it has one central message of solidarity sounded all the way from the biblical epigraph (Ecclesiastes 4.9–12) from which the title comes:

> Two are better than one; because they have a good reward for their labour. For if they fall, the one will lift up his fellow: but woe to him that is alone when he falleth; for he hath not another to help him up. Again, if two lie together, then they have heat, but how can one be warm alone? And if one prevail against him, two shall withstand him; and a threefold cord is not quickly broken.

In the cold rain-and-wind-swept slum where Charlie Pauls and his family live, this message of common cause and mutual succour under oppression is repeated often amidst the brutality, mutual exploitation, theft, murder, illicit drink and dagga of this unromanticised community. Here are people who are constantly puzzled over their plight because, unlike the reader and their creator, they cannot see why conditions are like this; they cannot see the outlines of the system and its detailed machinations.

The Pauls family live on the edge of Cape Town, without electricity, inside taps, or adequate drainage, constantly fighting the misery of winter, splashing through mud and darkness on their way to and from work – when they have it – fighting to repair roofs that will always leak, and always, always, trying to keep warm. There is no adventure or suspense in this book; its vitality derives largely from people struggling against fearful odds to preserve their dignity and achieve some kind of articulation of their problem. There are fights (as a symptom of divisiveness), police raids, fires, deaths, and everywhere squalor. The refuse pit mirrors the conditions of the whole suburb (152):

> The rubbish dump along the edge of the settlement is a favourite playground of the children. They can climb dunes of soggy paper

and rags, and clamber over the jungle-gyms of rusting iron, see-saw on lengths of decaying and slippery flotsam, breathing the air of disease dotted with flies like currents in a pudding.

There is no barrier between this and the residential area proper (42):

> Charlie walked around the house, his weight sinking into the mud, and he left behind him a soggy trail, quickly filled by brown water, around the wet, leaning, tin-and-lath side of the house, to where it faced the straggling, swampy lane between the ragged rows of tatterdemalian shacks...

And the squalor flows over the inhabitants of this appalling landscape (46):

> There were five of them, a motley collection of scarecrows, dummies stuffed with the straw of poverty, clad in the unmatching tatters of jackets, trousers and headgear, two of them barefooted, their hard, muddy feet seeking warmth in the doughy soil, their faces ageless, burnt-out and dark as charred wood.

There is an attempt at racial rapprochement, when Charlie Pauls tries to befriend the failed and lonely garage owner Mostert, left behind by the wave of affluence that has carried his fellow whites out into the smart new suburbs. Mostert is a sad case, a failure in white terms, deserted by his wife for a used-car salesman, an outcast like Doughty in *A Walk*, living on the fringe of the township, stupidly clinging to his inherited myths of supremacy – yet vaguely, haltingly, being drawn by the kindness of the slum-dwellers. A drunkard without ambition, living less vitally than his neighbours, he cuts a pitiful figure against the prevailing grey of the book. He is as much a victim of the system as his non-white neighbours. In a typical vignette that La Guma likes to draw, Mostert is seen through a simile that white society throughout Southern Africa must feel is uncomfortably apt (164):

> He peered out towards the world, like an entombed miner through a gap in a rockfall, surrounded by the dusty piles of advertising literature, the spike of dog-eared accounts, and the smudged calendar covered with long-forgotten phone numbers.

Mostert draws close to making real contact with the township, but fails because, ironically, a police raid interrupts his one firm attempt to accept an invitation.

Mostert survives, but he shows less stomach than the poor around him for the fight to better his position. We pity him but find him rather small and pathetic, whereas we pity but admire the inhabitants of the township. There is, for example, a marked contrast between the image of Mostert and that of, say, Charlie, or Ma Pauls or Charlie's widowed friend, Freda. In one memorable picture we see Ma Pauls sitting in her rocking chair in the midst of squalor and minimal expectations asserting her humanity and dignity by singing to herself, reaching out mentally to others, embracing the problems of relatives, friends, and children. She is the essence of humanity battling for her rights. Near her, on a bed where her husband recently coughed out his life, lies Freda, Charlie's girl-friend, who has just lost all her children in a fire (167):

> Ma Pauls sat in her chair in the bedroom and rocked slowly backwards and forward, her body hunched and her face withered with sadness. She sang in her old mind, and thought back on Dad Pauls, on young Ronald, on Freda's children. Her hands, corded and dry, like skeins of brown wool, were clasped in her lap, as she rocked.

Charlie Paul's movement towards an act of private rebellion against the system represents the instinctive solution that rises in the minds of the poor. When he answers back to a policeman and then knocks him sprawling in the mud, we feel he has struck a blow at the whole regime and asked it to taste the conditions it inflicts on others. But violence, whether instinctive or premeditated, is a less canvassed solution than the solidarity that is preached throughout. The refrain rings out time and again. 'We all got to stand by each other', says Ma Pauls. Charlie, speaking to his religious and jobless Uncle Ben, repeats the thoughts of a man he had once worked with: 'this burg say, if the poor people all got together and took everything in the whole blerry world, there wouldn't be poor no more...Further this rooker say if all the stuff in the world was shared out among everybody, all would have enough to live nice. He reckoned people got to stick together to get this stuff.' And it is Charlie who gives the message its final airing at the end of the novel. He is comforting the mourning Freda, promising her marriage, and reflecting that her own catastrophe, like his delinquent brother Ronny's, has been caused by unnecessary solitude. His source of intelligence is the same slim burg he once worked with up-country (168):

> He said something one time, about people most of the time takes trouble hardest when they alone. I don't know how it fit in here,

hey, I don't understand it real right, you see. But this burg had a lot of good things in his head, I reckon...Like he say, people can't stand up to the world alone, they got to be together ...Maybe it was like that with Ronny-boy.

Thematic and structural unity are preserved to the end. At the beginning it was grey and raining. And so it is at the close when Charlie, looking out into the dismal surroundings, sees a brief symbol of hope, a bird darting from among the roofs of the shanties and heading for the sky. The upward movement of the bird gives a touch of renewed hope, a poetic embleming of a people's struggle against the blows falling on them without cease. Whether it is a swallow heralding summer, or a dove announcing peace, La Guma is allowing himself a brief, and rare, gesture of hope.

*The Stone Country* (1967), dedicated to 'the daily average of 70,351 prisoners in South African gaols in 1964', (the 1973 figure had risen to 95,000 or five times the U.K. average) is epigraphed with the words of Eugene Debs:

> While there is a lower class, I am in it.
> While there is a criminal element, I am of it.
> While there is a soul in jail, I am not free.[10]

It shares much the same characteristics as its predecessor: a limited, though slightly extended, range of character and event (there is more 'story'), focus on one locale, and a single shaping principle – in this case not the need for solidarity but simply the suggestion that for non-whites South Africa is a prison that brutalises its citizens and maintains itself by an obsessive punitiveness. *A Walk in the Night* showed us humanity on the run; *And a threefold Cord* gave us humanity grovelling in the mud; *The Stone Country* shows us humanity behind bars.

George Adams, the central figure, remanded for a month for distributing anti-government literature, is our spokesman within the prison and represents ordinary guiltless, reflective humanity. A political case, he is different from his fellow prisoners, separate in kind and never completely drawn in, though as a subtle hint of long-term inevitables he is seen gradually absorbing the register of his companions, their criminal jargon and tough tone.

La Guma puts slightly more portraits into this novel. While the focus is heavily on Adams, we also get reasonable pictures of Butcherboy, the depraved monster who rules the cells; Yusef the Turk, the slim

251

spiv with a shrewd brain and a genius in self-defence; Casbah Kid, the pathetic youth in for murder, doomed to hang and follow both parents in a violent death – with his 'wet, hooded, pebbly eyes', the hopeless product of a hopeless background; Gus and Morgan, the would-be escapees. Yet structurally, while it has a familiar tightness, the book almost falls apart because La Guma exhausts one line of event too early and must spin out the text with something else. Hence, the friction between Butcherboy and his victims generates suspense as it builds towards a flashpoint, but when the inevitable confrontation occurs and the monster is floored by the Turk and covertly stabbed by the Kid, the story loses momentum, and La Guma is forced to bring in fresh personnel and have them add some excitement with a plot for a jailbreak. One result is that the book's balance is disturbed and Adams' shaping consciousness briefly moved from the centre.

The prose is energetic and spare, the imagery sharp and apt. It is noticeable too, both here and in the previous novel, that La Guma has learnt not to over-decorate his prose as he did in *A Walk in the Night*. Typical is his description of Adams' cell (80):

> With over forty prisoners locked up in the middle of summer, the smell of sweat was heavy and cloying as the smell of death. The heat seemed packed in between the bodies of the men, like layers of cotton wool; like a thick sauce which moistened a human salad of accused petty thieves, gangsters, rapists, burglars, thugs, brawlers, dope peddlars, few of them strangers to the cells, many already depraved, and several old and abandoned, sucking hopelessly at the bitter disintegrating butt-end of life.

Yet he can still shape with skill an extended metaphor such as the following in which prison and Republic are seen as one (81):

> This was the country behind the coastline of laws and regulations and labyrinthine legislation; a jungle of stone and iron, inhabited by jackals and hyenas, snarling wolves and trembling sheep, entrapped lions fighting off shambling monsters with stunted brains and bodies armoured with the hide of ignorance and brutality, trampling underfoot those who tried to claw their way from the clutch of the swamp.

Though the theme of solidarity is not centrally present, Adams is appalled, like the narrator of 'The Gladiators', at the divisiveness which the regime cultivates. 'What a waste', he says; 'here they got us fighting each other like dogs.' But there is little he can achieve in the cells and his only success lies in establishing humane contact with the hapless Casbah Kid, making his last days on earth a little less bleak. He can do nothing about the divisiveness, nothing about the preferential conditions given to white prisoners, and nothing about his own prospects of a long sentence once his own case comes up for a hearing.

The general state of the prisoners and their relationship with the white regime is carried, though rather too obviously, in an incident involving the prison cat. The cat is sleek, which makes its own point; and in the exercise yard one day it chases a mouse while a group of prisoners look on. Badly mauled, the mouse escapes up a drain pipe to lick its wounds; and Adams later reflects on it all (127):

> You were on the side of the mouse, of all the mice, George Adams thought. The little men who get kicked in the backside all the time. You got punched and beaten like that mouse, and you had to duck and dodge to avoid the claws and fangs...

*In the Fog of the Seasons' End* (1972), dedicated to men who died in 1967 in the early stages of Rhodesia's guerilla war, is a less tightly woven piece than any of its predecessors and reflects the steady dilution seen after the short stories.[11] First, the scene shifts in a way not found earlier. We are taken out and about round Cape Town, with the principal character, Beukes, establishing contacts and fleeing before the law. Secondly, Beukes's clandestine house-calls involve a larger group of figures than usual – though in the nature of things they are not all fully drawn and some of them, Beatie Adams for example, quickly disappear altogether, as though forgotten, a quite new development. There is too, for the first time, an unevenness of tone in the narrative – witness the excellent yet awkward change of gear into the ironic tones of a sequence on the pass laws and a recreation of Sharpeville that is powerful yet too digressive. The prose is slacker, the rich poetic quality of earlier writing giving way to a more discursive mode, energised only occasionally by figurative touches as if, perhaps, the artist feels guilty at wallowing in verbal aesthetics when the cause is so urgent. The trouble lies possibly in La Guma's setting out with a clutch of aims. Ignoring his established practice of building a book around one central idea, he sets forth to write a piece which is part police chase (humanity is again on the run), part documentary, part an exploration of a developing politics, and part a contrast between

South Africa's image to the world and the reality behind it. The result is a book that succeeds in sections, but not entirely as an organic whole: Beukes' career and flight from the law are what hold it together.

La Guma has also become impatient with the subtleties of high art and must spell everything out. Hence we get set speeches from both sides of the struggle in a manner quite alien to the delicate suggestiveness of his best short stories. Elias, the tortured prisoner in the Prologue, addresses his police interrogators in a speech suggesting that the long racial conflict is now coming swiftly to the boil (6):

> 'You are going to torture me, maybe kill me. But that is the only way you and your people can rule us. You shoot and kill and torture because you cannot rule in any other way a people who reject you. You are reaching the end of the road and going downhill towards a great darkness...'

Beukes is like a disguised George Adams, out of jail and again distributing anti-government pamphlets. A quiet, determined man, undistinguished in physique or looks (we don't see him very clearly), he is a moderate in his thinking, but like Adams a man who, from his own rough estimate, has decided that enough is enough. Unheroic, unselfish, never deeply scornful of those less committed than himself, neither particularly eloquent nor brave, he goes the rounds, getting help where he can, raising morale, showing gratitude and a dim confidence that victory will one day come. Some of his contacts live with a more or less passive acceptance of injustice around them; but there is no arrogant scorn of them. Dancing Tommy is an example, prepared to help activists like Beukes, but unwilling to join him in the firing line. Faced with the horrors of life, Tommy, like Kibera's Cobbler and La Guma's own Joe, builds his own little world in which he can survive without looking too closely at the misery around him (30–1):

> He was gay, he was forever happy, nothing bothered him: he lived in a world of sugary saxophones and sighing strings. The other world was coincidental...Give him a dance band, a light-footed woman, a smooth floor, and he was happy.

But though Beukes can mentally describe him as a 'useless bastard', he sympathises with his position, and is grateful for his help. He almost appreciates Tommy's view that a man must be slightly crazy to be 'worried about governments and speeches instead of enjoying life'.

254

One of the most memorable scenes from this novel occurs when Beukes, wounded and fleeing from the police, finds himself outside the grounds of a smart villa while a party proceeds on the lawn within. Like some eavesdropping figure from Hardy, Beukes lies in the dark listening to the banter and clink of glasses. It is a piece of rich symbolism as the whites pursue their hedonism within the fort and the black majority lie bleeding and hunted without. On the vast lawns stand two marquees. Coloured lights are on, the swimming pool splashes with life, skewered mutton chops splutter and sizzle in the barbecue pit, and 'there's gallons of champagne'. Beukes overhears snatches of conversation blowing off this scene and his blood and pain mix curiously with it all as South Africa's two lifestyles are brought close together (149):

> Beukes was carefully drawing off his coat with his good hand. The left sleeve was black with blood.
> 'It's that Davey', a girl's voice complained. 'Can't keep his awful hands to himself'.
> 'Don't blame him', a man laughed. 'Come on, forget it and let's go and get another drink. There's gallons of champagne.'
> 'Who wants champagne?' Just because his father's got lots of cash to buy the stuff doesn't mean he can do what he likes. I'm particular who handles me'.

While this is far from La Guma's best effort at capturing the flavour and rhythm of real conversation, the power of the basic situation and its statement of the wrongness of South African life are undeniable. The Rhodesian scholar Anthony Chennells, however, objects to it in the pages of the literary review *Mambo* (Nov. 1974). Chennells accepts the scene's broad symbolic purpose and the telling point about white society's use of money as a measure of dignity. Other details, however, he finds objectionable:

> Privilege especially in South Africa is more complex than having lots of money and drinking champagne. Why the scene is damaging to the book is not because it is being nasty about whites but because this is the only real indication we have in the book of what it is that the revolutionaries are revolting against, and as such it leaves us confused. Is La Guma's objection that whites have champagne and blacks live in slums? Or is it against a system that has degraded black and white alike? Surely as a Marxist La

> Guma must believe the latter and yet he shows no compassion for the whites whom privilege has made brutal or superficial. They are simply seen as evil or culpably indifferent.

Privilege in South Africa is indeed more complex than having money and drinking champagne; but as Chennells himself admits, this is a symbolic scene, and it is unfair to allow this at one moment and then object to it the next. And of course the power and comfort which privilege involves is either implied or spelt out in many parts of the book: it does not require a very astute reader to invert every inconvenience and pang suffered by the non-white community and see its white equivalent. If Elias is beaten unconscious and urinated on in the police cells, we are meant to assume white privilege would never incur this. If Elias as a youth is humiliated by the bureaucracy and made to drop his trousers to reveal his adulthood, we can assume that white privilege never suffers this way. If the schoolmaster Flotman has to teach that the Boer War was a holy crusade and that nobody existed in the land before Van Riebeeck arrived, then we must presume privilege has a freer pedagogic range. When the highly intelligent Isaac works as a dogsbody for overpaid white women with scarcely half his ability, then we can see what white privilege consists in. The charge that the party scene gives the only real indication of what Beukes and his friends are revolting against cannot be substantiated, and the suggestion that 'it leaves us confused' is scarcely credible. Chennells knows well enough what Beukes is revolting against, and there are scores of examples outside the party scene. The brutality of a police state, where the blows fall always in one direction; the eviction of old ladies and dumping them on the street; separate days at the museum; summary dismissal from work to make way for white employees; the pathetic life of Beatie Adams and all like her spending their time bringing up the children of too-busy whites; the Sharpeville recreation in which dozens of unarmed innocents are gunned down; Old Tsatsu 'dead on a heap of rubble by the road, a collapsed dummy, something unimportant left aside'; a legal system which 'defends injustice, prosecutes and persecutes those who fight injustice'; Elias' mother fobbed off with forty pounds compensation for her husband's death when white miners' widows get fifteen pounds a month for the rest of their lives – the list is long. La Guma's whole literary effort here and everywhere is designed to leave his readers in no doubt about what his people are revolting against. Nor is it useful to phrase the questions in an either–or mode: 'Is La Guma's objection that whites have champagne and blacks live in slums? Or is it against a system that has degraded black and white alike?' La Guma is objecting to both the economic injustice implied in the first question and the moral damage implied in the second. And as for the assertion that La Guma shows 'no compassion for the whites' affected by the system, what of the sympathetic understanding of the brutal Raalts' inner problems in *A Walk in the Night*? What of the plight of poor Doughty in the same work and of Mostert in *And a Threefold Cord*? And is there no whiff of sympathy in the reflections of Isaac as he sits in his hot steamy kitchen (114–15)?

> The silly bastards, he thought, they had been stupefied into supporting a system which had to bust one day and take them all down with it; instead of permanent security and justice, they had chosen to preserve a tyranny that could only feed them temporarily on the crumbs of power and privilege. Now that the writing had started to appear on the wall, they either scrambled to shore it up with blood and bullets and the electric torture apparatus or hid their heads in the sand and pretended that nothing was happening. They would have to pay for their stupidity the hard way. Isaac felt almost sorry for these people.

Chennells' final remark in this section of his essay, that all La Guma's sympathy 'goes out to politicians whom he invests with an aura of heroism' is similarly hard to accept. Many who appear in this novel, and elsewhere, and get La Guma's sympathy are patently not politicians but humble folk with little or no political formation. The old woman sitting in the road with her belongings, with her 'ancient liquid eyes' and her 'impregnable dignity'; the old man dead by the roadside; Beatie Adams the nanny; Elias' mother; the teacher in 'The Lemon Orchard'; the Pauls family; the prisoners in *The Stone Country* – are these politicians? Even Beukes and Adams, for all their activism, are scarcely hard-bitten politicians in the normal sense. They are simply representative common men involved now because they have had enough. A profound sense of how little has been achieved and the enormity of the problem prevents La Guma's drawing political super-men, and of the activists only Elias comes even near being invested 'with an aura of heroism'.

The end of this novel shows the police torturing Elias, and Beukes, at the end of another long trek, watching a handful of men drive off

257

for overseas training in guerilla warfare. Taking La Guma's work from the short stories right through to this novel (and a weakness of Anthony Chennells' essay is that he seems to be aware of only one novel), one can see that the violent solution at the end of *In the Fog* is drifted towards, not preached from the outset. From pointing out human and economic injustice to attacking the regime by way of ugly pictures of it and suggesting that the victims of oppression ought to band together, there emerges, tiredly and hesitantly, the idea of violence as the only course of action that holds out hope, the only course of action the regime will respect. This development is presented so objectively that the author seems almost to have no part of it. It appears as a tired inevitability. And who, examining current events in Southern Africa, would deny its force?

# A footnote on drama

Several broad generalisations are heard about drama in East, Central, and Southern Africa. One is that as yet it lacks the quantity and vitality of its counterpart in West Africa. Another is that, while along with verse and prose it has developed later than its West African equivalent (untrue of South Africa of course), it appears to lag behind prose and verse even in its own area of the continent. At the moment there is more prose and verse in print than there is drama; and no dramatist in East, Central, and Southern Africa is as well known as either Ngugi or Okot p'Bitek.

Those who have argued that drama has richer prospects in Africa than any other literary form – because of its communal nature, its flexibility, its ability to live without texts, its accommodation of the popular arts of song, drumming, and dance, its links with traditional religion, and its easy movement into film with its multi-translation dubbing techniques – might find the apparently weak state of drama outside West Africa a rather cooling fact. Where on this side of the continent, they might ask, are the Soyinkas, Clarks, Henshaws, Ogunmolas, Addos, De Graafts, Ousmanes, Johnsons, Aidoos, Sutherlands, Oforis, Ogundes, Rotimis, and Ladipos? Are they beginning to appear? If so where, and if not, why not? And why the delay?

A crude answer must be that appearances mask the reality. There are already in East, Central, and Southern Africa, more dramatists than are yet internationally known, more plays than those yet published, and more grass-roots experiment than reaches the West End. There is, for instance, in some quarters a strong and growing use of radio and TV rather than the printed book as a means of disseminating dramatic material. Yet the broad impression is correct: there is not yet that solid, flamboyant dramatic presence here that one has come to admire in West Africa; and reasons for a slower development might

259

be social, historic, political, or all three. Formal, institutionalised drama seems to flourish best in firmly settled societies, among people rooted in one locale, be it urban or rural. Hence in the densely populated, long-settled areas of West Africa, rich in their multitudes of cults and fraternities, the growth of a modern kind of drama has been a natural development. Elsewhere, however, outside South Africa, there has been far less urbanisation and a distinctly less historically settled pattern of habitation. Huge areas are still inhabited by nomadic pastoralists like the Maasai and Samburu; and other stretches are peopled by those who in the recent past practised a shifting cultivation. Furthermore, what towns have developed have often been European settlements. There are very few genuinely African towns here resembling Ife, Abeokuta, Ibadan, Accra, Onitsha, or Kumasi, and a town like Malawi's Nkhota Nkhota is a rare exception. While it is true that scholarship is slowly revealing that West Africa has no monopoly on those fertile seedbeds of drama such as ritual and mime, charade and dance, it is also true that mask and masquerade are simply not everyday facts of life in the streets of Blantyre, Salisbury, or Lusaka. The ancient mask tradition of the Nyau society in Malawi and Zambia has been contained largely within a village milieu. Nor has there been an equivalent of the West African Concert Party tradition associated with Ishmael Johnson which James Gibbs has pointed out as a crucial link between purely traditional modes and the modern scene.

As with other literary forms, the drama growth now evident stems from a blend of forces: political independence; a burgeoning of new schools, colleges, and Universities; the desire to repatriate the syllabus; increasing economic prosperity; the spread of radio, television, and the printed word; the desire to encourage popular and effective modes of crystallising distinctly national identities, and finally the catalytic example of West Africa.

Uganda, doubtless because of the mature presence of Makerere, was a pace-setter in East Africa. Also it is curious that while the historic Kampala Conference of 1964 (where East met West) caused a sudden flowering of prose and verse, in the same year David Cook and Betty Baker began planning Makerere's highly successful Free Travelling Theatre. By 1965 this University group was already performing in four languages (English, Luganda, Swahili, and Runyoro-Rutoro) had 42 productions to its credit, and had reached with a mixed fare of sketches and short plays no less than 17,000 people. Such an immediate

willingness to move beyond English into the vernaculars is of a piece
with David Cook's openness to the whole question of theatre growth
and its cultivation. In a foreword to his collection of East African Plays
he notes how old patterns are changing as traditional village material
resurfaces, slightly metamorphosed, in the clubs and halls of the towns:

> Though in many places, with the spread of urbanisation, the
> traditional dance-forms signifying birth, initiation, war, worship
> and death have lost their earlier key position in the life of village
> societies, yet dance-halls and night-clubs still allow town-dwellers
> to express their happiness, or overcome their worry and the
> effects of their labours in the city, through the medium of move-
> ment...And likewise the epic art of the narrator has survived
> by adapting itself to new conditions. The story-teller has become
> more of an actor than he used to be, and he now often enlists
> the help of his wife and friends to act out the tale he is telling;
> while he himself emphasises the main thread of the narrative,
> his small supporting company embellishes the events with song
> and music and further words. So a link is formed between the
> arts of traditional dance and narration, and that of formal drama:
> and as different modes intermingle, new patterns emerge.[1]

On the worrying question of language – more crucial in drama than
in any literary form – Cook agrees that 'the majority of people can
interpret emotion more fully and freely in their mother tongue' than
in a second language; but he asserts that his experience shows that
language is not an insuperable hurdle, and that 'in lands with widely
divergent vernaculars, drama which is to be more than local in its cast
or audience must make bold, arbitrary decisions about the language
employed'. On the broad question of dramatic form, he reports that
most of the young dramatists he has worked with argue that 'Africa
wants, needs, and can absorb every possible kind of play-acting.'

Judging from the plays produced and performed by the Free
Travelling Theatre, Cook aimed at both local-rootedness and experiment. Hence, pieces like *The Famine* and *The Mirror* are straight
translations from two vernaculars, Luganda and Runyoro-Rutoro, one
play being centred on a man's illicit killing and hiding of a rat in the
midst of famine, the other describing the shock of a woman who first
looks in a mirror and believes her husband has taken another wife.
Similarly, Tom Omara's *The Exodus* is a dramatisation of the great Luo
migration epic that would appeal to Nilotes throughout East Africa.

261

Though a rather thin rendering of the epic, necessitating drastic telescoping and clothed in verse which neither obtrudes nor really recommends itself, Omara's play is an important pioneering attempt in these parts to weave the stuff of local tradition into a scripted modern play. Cook was also happy to see Erisa Kivonde take Synge's *The Shadow of the Glen* and transplant it 'lock, stock, and barrel into Uganda', so that it appeared to have grown there. So successful was the transplant that when the play crossed the border into Kenya it became a cherished acquisition of University College, Nairobi, and was performed with ritual regularity for many years. But the impulse towards experiment is best seen in Robert Serumaga, who now dominates not just Uganda but the East African scene as a whole, in much the way that Soyinka has come to dominate West Africa. When Serumaga's *A Play* appeared in 1968, the signs of a strongly individual talent were unmistakable. The nightmare of a guilty man on the anniversary of his wife's death, *A Play*, superficially, seemed highly derivative, with echoes of Brecht, Beckett, Soyinka, and even Okigbo ghosting forth. Lines such as 'this is a death cell not a theatre', and 'we must pass the time, somehow, before we die tomorrow', or 'We are all just different kinds of germs. Different kinds of death', strike the authentic note of absurdist theatre not the note of *The Exodus* or any other kind of traditional piece. Yet despite derivative elements and occasional linguistic ineptness when a wrong register is used (see, for example, the Old Man's 'undeniable cardiac contortions'), elemental forces are at work and there is a sense of familiar viewpoints being expressed with originality and force. Serumaga's work now is far more maturely independent. As actor, producer, playwright, director of Theatre Limited and the Abafumi Company, he delights in unchained experimentation. *Majangwa* (1971) explores the life of an entertainer and his wife. Having failed to impress audiences with the traditional arts of dancing and drumming, these two turn to obscenity as a desperate throw for success – rather as British cinemas in decline turned to pornography and wrestling. James Gibbs describes these obscenities as 'startling salaciousness' carrying the disturbing suggestion that 'they constitute a symbol for the plight of the creative artist in a sick society'. *Renga Moi*, Serumaga's most recent piece using music, ritual, dance, and four Ugandan vernaculars, is now among the repertoire of a company that has played to enthusiastic houses as far apart as Manila and Chicago. *Renga Moi* was particularly welcomed at the Belgrade International Festival, and a lengthy review in the newspaper *Politika* included the following comment: 'a peculiar mixture of originality, the ancient and exotic, traditional and experimental, national and international'. The *Guardian* critic for 3 May 1975, reviewing a performance of *Renga Moi* at the Aldwych Theatre, London, found it a difficult piece to understand, though undeniably impressive:

> A strange, stylised ritual-drama...I cannot pretend to have followed the story with any great ease: but Serumaga clearly has a sense of theatre, uses light, sound and movement with skill and is at least attempting to explore indigenous African culture rather than (like the South African company with *Umabatha*) exploit a universal myth. To a western spectator, however, the impression made by *Renga Moi* is of highly sophisticated technique applied to somewhat inaccessible material...I remain puzzled as to why so much African drama seems mythic and folk orientated while the African novel has achieved a concrete contemporaneity.

Apart from revealing a curious insensitivity to drama's nature and origins and the nuances of its present growth in Africa, this critic nevertheless shares with many others a puzzlement over Serumaga's aims. The dramatist himself has tried to help with his own explanation:

> We believe in the body as the supreme instrument of theatre and then the voice, and when I say voice I simply mean sound. Even words to us are sounds first and meaning second. Then we believe that in as much as words are communication through sound, that silence is even more important than words, and in many cases we consider this a breach of silence...

One can see, perhaps, that this approach might also be Serumaga's answer to the formidable problem of second language styles for African drama so deeply pursued by J. P. Clark and students of his work such as Fr Patrick O'Malley. Serumaga is boldly saying that language does not matter at all, and away with all those vexing problems of linguistic register and cultural transference. Four vernaculars are fine, and silence even better. Yet this is probably as much personal weakness as preferred philosophy. The texts of Serumaga's plays often suggest a slight discomfort with English and his strengths are more technically theatrical than linguistic. *The Elephants* (1972) is a useful example of a play with a measure of psychological power, but which, stylistically, is rather vapid. Except in isolated cases, and despite Serumaga's claim in the introduction that 'every word matters', there is neither rhythmic energy nor pungency of statement. Though stylistically it is a more even performance than *A Play*, the intensity of the author's account of city alienation is reduced by the nagging feeling that the rural world alternative is available only yards away beyond the city gate. But *The Elephants'* warm reception in Nairobi and elsewhere suggests how skilfully Serumaga has exploited those areas of his craft where he knows his strengths lie.

If less well-known than Serumaga, the young Ugandan John Ruganda is an equally serious dramatist, cultivating an assuredness in each area of the conventional playwright's craft, building his plays around acutely modern problems, and, like Nigeria's J. P. Clark, is much exercised by the question of choosing a suitable medium for English-language drama. He works hard at fashioning a strong pungent prose and dramatic poetry is an option occasionally used and always felt to be in the background. In his Beckettian play *Covenant with Death*, in which two characters alienated by an intolerant rural society forlornly try to travel back to their past, Matama, who failed under the traditional code because she was infertile says: 'as long as ghosts whisper in dark corners, and ancestors guard the secret chambers, if there are groaning rocks, and sobbing trees, and weeping rivers – you can't forget the past'. This is poetic prose in much the same mould as her companion Motomoto's way of alluding to his own impotency: 'I had a garden to cultivate. I had a hoe, I had everything.' The temptation to use formal dramatic poetry is signalled by Odiambo, a young Sociology student in *Black Mamba* (1973), who responds to another figure's mystification at his metaphoric style with the words, 'Never mind, old chap, I was trying to see whether I could talk in blank verse.' It is as if Ruganda has studied closely Clark's verse experiment and decided, by choosing poetic prose as his main medium, that he wants verse's idiom but not its restrictions.

A product of Makerere's Honours School of English, Ruganda shows the influence of a wide range of dramatists, both European and African. Echoes in *Covenant with Death* suggest Beckett and Brecht. A houseboy in *Black Mamba* resembles Jonson's Mosca and Soyinka's Samson. Behind the style there is the shaping influence of Clark and possibly p'Bitek. But Ruganda is as acutely aware of these as he is of his own artistic ambition, which is to produce a body of drama at once technically assured, linguistically rich, and morally relevant in thrust.

264

The issues are carefully chosen and handled with skill. *The Burdens* (1972), describing the return to squalor of a once-rich minister, 'tries to diagnose the symptoms and damage of this modern cancer – empty-headed ambition'. Its account of the minutiae of modern poverty is carried over into *Black Mamba,* where the central issue is prostitution as one immoral solution for the poor man. The conflict between old and new, the growth of class conflict, protest over land seizure by the new élite – these are all explored by a writer who has in one special area perhaps more skill than any of his colleagues; for no one can capture so surely as Ruganda the delicate psychological interplay between dramatic characters. Their fears, hesitations, the freight of real human communication, are handled here better than in almost any African dramatist on this side of the continent.

In Kenya, though there have long existed schools' drama festivals, the National Theatre in Nairobi was designed primarily for the needs of a European audience. The finest dramatic activity in the country was for many years Nairobi's Donovan Maule Theatre, which combined the qualities of international professionalism with supreme indifference to the African culture around it. Here was an unrivalled example of Restoration Theatre in the tropics, whose overshadowing influence together with that of a scattering of amateur groups made the start of a local modern tradition very difficult.

Early developments at the University were under the guidance first of T. P. Gorman then later of the Ghanaian dramatist Joe de Graaft. More crucially, however, adjacent to the University, in a corner of the National Theatre building, Seth Adagala, fresh from drama studies in America, set up the National Theatre School, officially opened amid mild euphoria by Mr Tom Mboya in 1968. Adagala's move into the National Theatre building might be seen symbolically as the beginning of the Africanisation of Kenya's drama scene. The school and its group are now securely established and often move beyond their city centre confines into the suburbs and villages. Another group is the Tausi Drama Club whose ranks include David Mulwa, a playwright and first-rate actor recently returned from drama studies at the University of California, Los Angeles.

Ngugi wa Thiong'o wrote his rather thin piece, *The Black Hermit,* while at Makerere in the early sixties. A second play, *This Time Tomorrow,* is a tight piece of social protest provoked by the same

265

slum-clearing exercise in Nairobi that Jared Angira attacked in his preface to *Juices*. Though short, the play repays careful study, and memorable lines include: 'You have fought with drunks, wrestled with wolves and hyenas in this Uhuru market' and 'I've been doing fine ... That is, I have not starved.' There is a deftly satiric manipulation of language as Ngugi explores the contrast between the eloquent polished style of an élite bureaucracy and the rough simplicity of a suffering people. A moment of fine poignancy occurs when the ill-favoured Wayiro recollects how just one man, once, touched her. 'I could not believe it', she says. 'I ran to a glass window in the city, and looked at my reflection.' The play ends, like La Guma's *And a Threefold Cord*, with a plea for class solidarity. 'If only we could stand together', lament the representatives of the poor.

Though initially deep-dyed in Ngugi's influence, Kenneth Watene's work shows a strong promise of growth. Exploring with even greater emphasis than Ngugi the fratricidal nature of the Mau Mau struggle, his first three plays, *My Son for my Freedom*, *The Pot*, and *The Haunting Past* are in verse and also use mime and dance, sometimes to very fine effect.[2] His verse, though from the start it has attempted to reflect inner movements of soul rather than the external landscape, possesses a laboured quality which is slowly diminishing as Watene comes under healthy influences. For if the example of Ngugi is responsible for much of the plays' thematic drift – their attack on Gikuyu loyalists, the picture of Christian converts materially richer than their fellows, the lauding of traditional Gikuyu morality, and the idea of the whites stealing land 'behind your back while you prayed' – the influence of Okot p'Bitek can be felt in the verse which has a simplicity and movement (though not yet a smoothness) reminiscent of the Song School. Here a character faces up to the past (78):

> I am he that will wrench himself free,
> Pull himself out of your esteemed drab life
> And flee into the floodlights of a new world.
> My spirit will not receive the summons
> From this image of adoration, the past.

Apart from the unhappy internal rhyme in the first declaration and a certain stiffness, one can see the attempt to work with alliteration and the effort to select apt figures for the material. There is a hint too of a characteristic in Watene which is peculiarly his own, for he writes quite naturally in a religious idiom. His plays show not simply the trite struggle between traditional spirituality and modern materialism, but strife between an old spirituality and a new one. Significantly, in *The Haunting Past* the hero is tempted by tradition on a mound in an echo of Christ's temptation by the Devil (77):

> Get behind me and shame be on you
> Despair then, miserable memory!
> I belong to the future, not to you!

As yet, Watene's ability to write dramatic verse is hampered by inexperience and possible narrowness of vocabulary. But the will to improve is there and throughout his texts there is evidence of hard effort expended on the verse. If these two lines do not quite succeed:

> The definite death that will ultimately
> Creep into your collapsing blood tubes

the following are on the verge of being very strong indeed (79):

> He visited me last night, the dotard
> And eased his jointless skeleton
> Against the verge of my dreams.

Watene's play *Dedan Kimathi* (1974), which examines the life of the Mau Mau leader of that name during the closing moments of the struggle in the Aberdare forests with the Gikuyu nation split and the movement itself very divided, shows again how Kenya's writers simply will not idealise their heroes. Kimathi is portrayed as suspicious and autocratic, a killer of his best friend, Nyati, who, because he is so humane, morally dwarfs his leader. Though little dramatic tension is generated, this is a play for the present, carrying within it Kimathi's blueprint for the new Kenya and reminding the living that the dead did not fight to usher in an era of greed and brotherly injustice. With appropriate modifications, Kimathi's relationship with Nyati echoes the Brutus-and-Caesar friendship, and Shakespeare's text has a knack of constantly getting in Watene's way. Among a scattering of imitated lines, one finds these:

> For his nobility I loved him,
> For his humanity I esteemed him,
> For his love I revered him
> But his spirit longed to be free
> From the hot pursuit of victory,
> Therefore I killed him.

Impressive is his use of mime and ballet. The start of *The Haunting Past* resembles Clark's *Ozidi* in its fusion of dance, mime, and ritual, providing an excellent lead-in to verse drama. The physical heightening and formality that are dance and religious movement yields to a parallel verbal heightening which is dramatic verse.

Theatre in independent Tanzania discovered that it had a President who could translate Shakespeare into Swahili and a University College with the only Department of Theatre Arts in East Africa. It also felt the convenient shaping effect of a national philosophy in Nyerere's African Socialism, as a result becoming quickly an art form expressing the local and national aspirations of a nation. Theatre as an instrument of education, of shaping political awareness, of furthering the physical process of development, of feeding national pride – this seems to be the kind of drama Tanzania has opted for. The playwright Bob Leshoai, a South African recently in charge of the University's Theatre Arts Department, succeeding Herbert Shore, summarised this view in *New Theatre Magazine* (Vol. XII, No. 2):

> The theatre of a nation, generally, expresses the ideals for which that nation will pay the price of death. If the theatre fails to do this then it has no significance and relevance...the theatre, I believe, must serve the nation; and this is what the various attempts depict in the growth of a Tanzanian national theatre. The attempts are carried out at the university, in the schools and by private adult and youth groups throughout the country...A careful look at the theatre of Tanzania – its drama, music, dance and even its art – will clearly show that it expresses the socialist ideals in which Tanzania believes, as enshrined in the Arusha Declaration of 1966...The Tanzanians have come to accept the fact that their theatre must be both entertaining and instructive with emphasis on its value as an educational medium.

The dangers in this lofty approach have been outlined by James Gibbs. If the national educational goals are too narrow or are pursued too dialectically, it is easy, he says, for the transmission to become mere propaganda:

> It is also easy for the theatre to become a subsidiary museum service, artificially preserving African traditions and customs rather than responding to the reality of the changing society.

The aspirations Leshoai describes are so worthy and high-minded that there is a danger that irreverence, humour, and indeed humanity may become an afterthought, last and least, to entertain.[3]

Meanwhile one of the most significant developments in Tanzanian theatre has been the increasing use of Swahili as a chosen medium. Playwrights like Ebrahim Hussein, Farouk Topan, and Penina Muhando are writing works which are granted that instant response characteristic of vernacular theatre and this from all sections of the population throughout East Africa. Hussein's *Kinjeketile*, based on the Maji Maji uprising against the Germans in colonial times, receives as electrifying a reception from packed audiences in Nairobi's slums as it does in the towns of Tanzania. Certainly, if Tanzanian theatre lacks the openness and plurality of approach seen in Uganda and Kenya, then it enjoys the advantage of a definite ideology and purpose; and its increasing espousal of Swahili makes it a focal point for a continuing debate on whether African drama should move away from English and firmly into the vernaculars.

Zambia and Malawi share some common approaches to modern drama. Both have vigorous annual schools' drama festivals (Malawi's much the biggest on the continent); both make good use of radio (and in Zambia's case, TV); both have active Travelling Theatres; and both have rejected the proscenium arch in favour of outdoor theatres. In Zambia Fay Chung, Andrew Horu, Michael Etherton, and more recently David Kerr, have focussed their energies on the University and its outdoor Chikwakwa theatre, and through rural workshops, vernacular school plays, and the travelling theatre have ensured that remote country areas also benefit from the national dramatic awakening. 'The idea of the Chikwakwa Theatre' says Etherton, 'was to develop, through self-help, a theatre place that would allow an expansion of the traditional performing arts into drama in which the spoken words developed the action. Or put the other way round, the theatre was meant to develop a style of drama that used the dances, songs and music of the rural areas and the urban townships, the masks and the fabulous costumes, the artefacts, the fires, and the lamps of traditional story-telling.' Like its Tanzanian counterpart, Zambia's theatre has a tradition of political awareness and comment; it has always supported the national philosophy of humanism and attacked racialism in

Rhodesia and South Africa; and there has been a steady determination among University Dramatic Society members to address their work to all levels of Zambian society. Godfrey Kasoma's plays, *The Long Arms of the Law* and *The Fools Marry*, deal specifically with life in the townships, and his *Black Mamba* trilogy recounts the rise of Dr Kaunda and his UNIP party during colonial days. Kasoma is the sort of brilliant all-rounder (actor, producer, writer, and politician) one normally associates with the flamboyant theatre groups of West Africa. Both he and Masauto Phiri, the author of *Nightfall*, a play on Ngoni history and a dance drama, *Kuta*, work hard at bringing drama to the people. An open air theatre like Chikwakwa allows the large epic type of play pioneered by Clark's *Ozidi* to be amply accommodated. Fwanyanga Mulikita's *Shaka Zulu*, a clear, sweeping chronicle play, and Andrea Masiye's *Kazembe and the Portuguese* are typical local examples. An old struggle against the expatriate-dominated Theatre Association of Zambia seems now to have been won, and Zambian theatre has a genuinely local and experimental posture, exploring, in addition to radio, TV, and the schools, any path likely to lead to the rise of a truly national and popular drama.

In Malawi, after growing at random in the schools, modern drama, as in Uganda, Kenya, Tanzania, and Zambia, has found a focus in the University. The early work of Trevor Whittock, John Linstrum, and David Kerr has been consolidated and extended by James Gibbs and Mupa Shumba. The arrival of James Gibbs and his Ghanaian playwright wife Patience Addo brought to Malawi formidable expertise and theatre scholarship. A leading authority on Soyinka, and with experience in Ghana and the Sudan, Gibbs' professionalism and openness have achieved swift results. Joined soon after his arrival by Mupa Shumba, fresh from postgraduate studies in West African drama (and the man who, with John Linstrum, had founded the Travelling Theatre in 1969), he quickly fashioned instruments to foster and tap local talent. Theatre workshops, courses in practical drama, a remodelled Travelling Theatre, use of the new Malawian Writers Series, construction of an open air theatre under the shadow of Zomba Plateau – to these must be added an insistence on pace and punctuality in all productions, care over detail, and, what is often neglected elsewhere, the urgency of critical reflection at every step. Gibbs and Shumba have a flair for flysheet reviews and each performance brings a paper storm as students, teachers, and members of the public rush into print and do battle with banner and manifesto. Willing to keep a mind open to influences from all parts of the continent and beyond, and reluctant to impose one chosen doctrine, Gibbs and Shumba have encouraged a wide-ranging approach. Anything with dramatic potential becomes material for their actors, whether poems by Soyinka and Okot p'Bitek, moral tales from Chaucer and Hans Andersen, or local myths and legends. But while the standard Western repertoire gets adequate coverage, the broad push has been towards plays written, produced, and acted by Malawians.

James Ngombe's *The Banana Tree* and *Beauty of the Dawn*, Joe Mosiwa's *Who Will Marry Our Daughter?*, Innocent Banda's *The Lean Years, Lord Have Mercy, Cracks* and *The First Rehearsal*, Chris Kamlongera's *Love Potion* and *Graveyards*, and Bayani Ngulube's *Phuma-Uhambe* all use local material and local approaches, but usually in a fresh imaginative way. Ngulube's play questions 'the values of the Ngoni/Tumbuka tradition of banishment'. Mosiwa's, built on a theme of social ambition, uses to superb effect a Narrator–Chorus device and visits to Cloud, Sun, and Wind. Instead of a stale exercise in the struggle between tradition and modernity, Mosiwa offers a complex fight in which a kind of modernity wins out on completely traditional terms. The most ambitious play to date, Steve Chimombo's *The Rainmaker*, uses both the material of Malawi's ancient M'bona legends and also the M'bona cult's surviving mask convention. The appearance of the play in March 1975 (itself a remarkable testimony to Chimombo's talent) came only three months after a Conference on Drama in Malawi during which Fr Matthew Schoffeleers, an eminent authority on Malawian traditions, described the Nyau cult and its proto-dramatic characterists, and urged that it be used as the basis for a distinctively modern Malawian theatre. Arising roughly in the thirteenth or fourteenth centuries from hunting rituals, though significantly changed during the nineteenth-century struggles between the Chewa and Ngoni, Nyau performances still last for several days and have a definite cyclical pattern. They have absorbed some Christian influences (Maria and Simone for example) and work with both tragic and comic modes. Nyau, Schoffeleers argues, 'is a genuine form of theatre and since most genuinely creative work is rooted in the culture and the past we have a duty to take up Nyau where it [is] uncorrupted and develop it from there'. Chimombo's *Rainmaker* was an immediate response to Schoffeleer's call. This is a deep, echoing play, its re-

271

sonances sometimes elusive, but its overall impact heavy and menacing. The quality of much of its writing can be gauged from these comments from the Matsano, the spirits of the past who act as a chorus:

> Fractured elongations of circles
> ride the ripples of the pool
> and multiply in the crest
> only to die on the mossy banks
> of oblivion.
> Atomised reflections reveal phantoms
> smuggling skullfuls of teeth
> crawling to gnaw
> at the python's mind[4]

In the meantime, the Malawian approach remains open. Apart from a commitment to African modes, there is as yet no fixed direction, and no central ideology such as there is in Tanzania and Zambia. Questions remain to be debated: which way are the winds of theatrical change blowing? What plays, in what language, should Malawian theatre be encouraging? The question of vernacular drama draws attention here as elsewhere. After an evening of drama at the open air theatre given by the Zomba Community Centre Drama Group, in which a Chichewa play was easily the best piece and drew electrifying applause, Ken Lipenga in a review felt obliged to make the following comments:

> And talking about language, it so happened that the Chichewa play crushed the two English plays (*Mr Death* and *She is Too Polite*) into oblivion that evening...the fact that it was in Chichewa was the most important factor: it was the language best suited to the theme, the setting, the characters, and, believe it or not, the audience...so let us go, you and I, now the Dawn is here, let us sit ourselves beneath the mango tree, and with our pencils, teach Messrs Sophocles, Shakespeare, and the rest, teach them the rudiments of Chichewa, and take them to the people.[5]

Almost in answer to Lipenga's call, *Opera Extravaganza* appeared early in 1976. The creation of Peter Chiwona, a lecturer in Education, and Fr Joseph Chakanza, a student of Sociology, this piece compensated for the thinness of its plot (courtship, betrothal, marriage, and village peace-making) with a breathtaking swirl of dancing, drumming, and singing, A huge cast swept on and off the stage, singing songs instinct with local humour and allusion, and accompanied by a large band.

Conceived almost entirely in Chichewa, and carelessly mixing buf-
foonery with serious social comment, its reception was so rapturous
that it drew from more orthodox drama circles an immediate warning
that this was not the way for Malawian drama to develop. Neither as
tightly woven nor as poetically rich as the best-known Yoruba folk
operas, *Opera Extravaganza* clearly represents the blue-print of a form
with an exciting future. Like Okot p'Bitek and his *Song of Lawino*,
Chiwona and Chakanza will swiftly find a dozen imitations of their
opera.

In the meantime, government approval of the University's efforts
has been seen in the interest of the Ministry of Youth and Culture,
which is talking about the creation of a National Theatre. But this
must gestate slowly, for as James Gibbs has written: 'The origin of
a national theatre is not in bricks and mortar, but in theme, thought,
experiment, research, and discussion.'

# Notes

Chapter One: Language problems

1  'Languages and Education in Africa' in John Spencer (ed.), *Language in Africa*, London, CUP, 1963, 43.
2  See W. H. Whiteley, *Swahili: The Rise of a National Language*, London, Methuen, 1969.
3  *Africa Report*, June, 1967.
4  Julius Nyerere, *Uhuru na Ujamaa*, London, OUP, 1968, 2.
5  'The Future of Vernacular Literature in Uganda' in *East Africa's Cultural Heritage*, Nairobi, EAPH, 1966, 100.
6  W. H. Whiteley, *A Selection of African Prose*, London, OUP, 1964.
7  'The Future of Vernacular Literature', in *East Africa's Cultural Heritage*, Nairobi, EAPH, 1966, 70.
8  Report submitted to the Schools of Arts and Social Sciences, 1974.
9  Ulli Beier (ed.), *African Poetry*, London, CUP, 1966, 18.
10  *Ibid.* 19.
11  Francis Berry, *Poets' Grammar*, London, RKP, 1958.
12  Beier, *African Poetry*, 23.
13  Collected by Onyango Ogutu. See also Ogutu and Roscoe (eds), *Keep My Words: Luo Oral Literature*, Nairobi, EAPH, 1974.
14  I. Schapera, *Praise Poems of Tswana Chiefs*, London, OUP, 1965.
15  H. F. Morris, *The Heroic Recitations of the Bahima of Ankole*, London, OUP, 1964.
16  Beier, *African Poetry*, 63.
17  *Ibid.*, 66.
18  J. Mbiti, *African Religions and Philosophy*, New York, Praeger, 1969.
19  'Future of the Vernacular Literature', *East Africa's Cultural Heritage*, Nairobi, EAPH, 1966, 76.
20  Beier, *African Poetry*, 26.
21  Material provided by Mr Nelson Mlomba, Zomba, Malawi.
22  Beier and Gbadamosi (eds.), *Not Even God is Ripe Enough*, London, Heinemann, 1968.
23  A. Damico, 'An "Ideal Type" in Reference to Mythology – Land Tenure on a Cross-Cultural Basis', *Pan-African Journal*, Vol. v, No. 2, 1972.

274

24  For a more detailed survey, see Ogutu and Roscoe, *Keep My Words: Luo Oral Literature*, Nairobi, EAPH, 1974.
25  Paul Zeleza, *Night of Darkness and Other Stories*, Limbe, Montfort Press, 1976.
26  Grace Ogot, *Land Without Thunder*, Nairobi, EAPH, 1968, 99.
27  *Ibid.*, 148.

### Chapter Two: Developments in verse

1  'Poetry and the Microphone' in Orwell and Angus, *The Collected Essays, Journalism and Letters of George Orwell*, London, Secker and Warburg, 1968, 332.
2  George Steiner, *In Bluebeard's Castle*, London, Faber, 1971.
3  Francis Berry, *Poets' Grammar*.
4  'A Sense of Shame', *Busara*, Vol. II, No. 2, 1969.
5  Per Wastberg (ed.), *The Writer in Modern Africa*, Stockholm, Almqvist and Wiksell, 1968.
6  Taban Lo Liyong, *The Last Word*, Nairobi, EAPH, 1969.
7  Ngugi wa Thiong'o, *Homecoming*, London, Heinemann, 1972, 75.
8  G. D. Killam, *African Writers on African Writing*, London, Heinemann, 1973, 127.
9  *Busura*, Vol. 3, No. 2, 1970.
10  Okot p'Bitek, *Song of Lawino and Song of Ocol*, Nairobi, EAPH, 1972.
11  *Ibid.*, 210.
12  Okot p'Bitek, *Two Songs*, Nairobi, EAPH, 1971.
13  G. D. Killam, *African Writers on African Writing*, 127.
14  Okello Oculi, *Orphan*, Nairobi, EAPH, 1968.
15  Killam, *African Writers on African Writing*, 129.
16  Joseph Buruga, *The Abandoned Hut*, Nairobi, EAPH, 1969.
17  Personal papers. But see also the Appendix to Ngugi wa Thiongo's *Homecoming*.
18  'A Postscript on Eight Poems', *Busara*, Vol. I. No. 1, 1968.
19  Jared Angira, *Juices*, Nairobi, EAPH, 1970.
20  Jared Angira, *Silent Voices*, London, Heinemann, 1972.
21  Interview in *Focus*, 1974.
22  Jared Angira, *Soft Corals*, London, Heinemann, 1973.
23  R. C. Ntiru, *Tensions*, Nairobi, EAPH, 1971.
24  Taban Lo Liyong, *Frantz Fanon's Uneven Ribs*, London, Heinemann, 1971.
25  Taban Lo Liyong, *Another Nigger Dead*, London, Heinemann, 1972.
26  Chris Wanjala, 'The Tabanic Genre' in Wanjala (ed.), *Standpoints on African Literature*, Nairobi, EALB, 1972.

### Chapter Three: Aspects of South African verse

1  Ezekiel Mphahlele, *South African Writing Today*, London, Penguin, 1967.
2  Oswald Mtshali, *Sounds From a Cowhide Drum*, London, OUP, 1971.

*Notes*

3  Can Themba, *The Will to Die*, London, Heinemann, 1972.
4  Arthur Nortje, *Dead Roots*, London, Heinemann, 52.
5  Mazisi Kunene, *Zulu Poems*, London, Deutsch, 1970.
6  Cope and Krige (eds), *The Penguin Book of South African Verse*, London, 1968.
7  Dennis Brutus, *A Simple Lust*, London, Heinemann, 1973.

### Chapter Four: Prose

1  Ngugi, *Homecoming*, London, Heinemann, 1972.
2  Ngugi, *The River Between*, London, Heinemann, 1965.
3  *Ibid.*
4  Orwell, 'Why I Write' in Orwell and Angus, *The Collected Essays, Journalism and Letters of George Orwell*, London, Secker and Warburg, 1968, Vol. 1.
5  Ngugi, *Weep Not, Child*, London, Heinemann, 1964.
6  Ngugi, *A Grain of Wheat*, London, Heinemann, 1967.
7  Orwell, *Keep The Aspidistra Flying*, London, Gollancz, 1937.
8  Kibera and Kahiga, *Potent Ash*, Nairobi, EAPH, 1968.
9  Kibera, *Voices in the Dark*, Nairobi, EAPH, 1970.
10 Palangyo, *Dying in the Sun*, London, Heinemann, 1969.

### Chapter Five: Central and Southern African verse

1  Kayira, *The Looming Shadow*, London, Longmans, 1968.
2  B. Dobrée, 'The Comic Spirit' in Barnet, Berman and Burto (eds), *Eight Great Comedies*, New York, The New American Library, 1958.
3  Kayira, *Jingala*, London, Longmans, 1969.
4  Kayira, *The Civil Servant*, London, Longmans, 1972.
5  Essay in Killam, *African Writers on African Writing*, 110.
6  Ezekiel Mphahlele, *Down Second Avenue*, London, Faber, 1959.
7  Mphahlele, *In Corner B*, Nairobi, EAPH, 1967.
8  Alex La Guma, *A Walk in the Night*, London, Heinemann, 1967.
9  La Guma, *And A Threefold Cord*, Berlin, Seven Seas, 1964.
10 La Guma, *The Stone Country*, London, Heinemann, 1974.
11 La Guma, *In the Fog of the Seasons' End*, London, Heinemann, 1972.

### A footnote on drama

1  Cook and Lee (eds), *Short East African Plays in English*, London, Heinemann, 1968.
2  Watene, *The Haunting Past*, Nairobi, EAPH, 1972.
3  James Gibbs, *Drama Newsheet*, University of Malawi, 1975.
4  Steve Chimombo, *The Rainmaker*, Limbe, Montfort Press (forthcoming). Notice the re-use of material from his poem 'Chaosis'.
5  Ken Lipenga, 'Anansi's View', cyclostyled review, Chancellor College, University of Malawi.

# Index

# Index

# Index